Student Advisories

in Grades 5-12:

A Facilitator's Guide

~~~~~~~~~~~~~~~~~~~~~~~~~~~~~~~~~~~~~~

Student Advisories in Grades 5-12: A Facilitator's Guide

Susan MacLaury

Christopher-Gordon Publishers, Inc.
Norwood, Massachusetts

Copyright Acknowledgments

Introduction

Paraphrased material from *Your Adolescent: Emotional, Behavioral and Cognitive
Development from Early Adolescence through the Teen Years,* by David Pruitt, MD
and the American Academy of Child and Adolescent Psychiatry, © 1999 by
HarperCollins Publishers, Inc., New York, NY. Used with permission.

Chapter 1

Excerpt from *Belonging: Self and Social Discovery for Children and Adolescents,* by
J. Devencenzi and S. Pendergast, © 1999 by Jalmar Press, Carson, CA. Used with
permission from Jalmar Press.

Chapter 2

"Table 1: A Typology of Advisory Emphases" from *Advisory: Definitions; Descrip-
tions; Decisions; Directions,*" by J.P. Galassi, S. A. Gulledge, and N. D. Cox, ©1998,
NMSA Westerville, OH. Reprinted with permission of the National Middle School
Association.

"Advisory: Advocacy for every student" by R.M. Burkhardt from *Middle School
Journal* (Vol. 30 #3, pp. 51–54). © 1999 by NMSA, Westerville, OH. Used with
permission from National Middle School Association. These materials originally
appeared in the January 1999 issue of *Middle School Journal*.

Chapter 3

Excerpt adapted from *Talk with Teens About Feelings, Family, Relationships, and the
Future: 50 Guided Discussions for School and Counseling Groups* by Jean Sunde Peterson
© 1995 by Free Spirit Publishing Unc., Minneapolis, MN. Used with permission from
Free Spirit Publishing Inc.; 1-800-735-7323; www.freespirit.com. All rights reserved.

Adapted material entitled, "Self-Assessment from for Leaders" from *Group Techniques Second Edition* by Gerald and Marianne Corey, Patrick Callanan, and J.
Michael Russell, © 1992 by Thomas Learning, Pacific Grove, CA. Used with permission of Wadsworth, an imprint of the Wadsworth Group, a division of Thomson
Learning. Fax 800-730-2215.

List entitled "The Effective Teacher Advisor" from Gilbert Hunt, *The Middle Level
Teacher's Handbook* © 1997 by Charles C. Thomas Publisher, Ltd. Courtesy of Charles
C. Thomas Publisher, Ltd., Springfield, IL. Used with permission.

The Johari Window, Figure 5.1, from *Group Processes: An Introduction to Group
Dynamics, Third Edition*, by Joseph Luft © 1984 by Mayfield Publishing Company,
Mountain View, CA. Used with permission.

Chapter 6
"Functional roles of group members" by Benne, K.D., and Sheats, P. from *Journal of Social Issues* (Volume 4 #2, pp. 41-49). © Journal of Social Issues and Blackwell Publishers, Malden, MA. Used with permission of Blackwell Publishers.

Chapter 10
Activity "The Baseball Team Exercises" from *Treasury Chest: A Teacher Advisory Source Book* by John Lounsbury, et. al. Reprinted with permission of the authors and the National Middle School Association.

Chapter 12
Excerpt from *Group Techniques*, Second Edition by G. Corey, M.S. Corey, P. Callanan, and J.J.Russell © 1992, Wadsworth, Pacific Grove, CA. Reprinted with permission of Wadsworth, an imprint of the Wadsworth Group, a division of Thomson Learning. Fax 800 730-2215.

Chapter 14
Excerpt from Designing Groupwork by Elizabeth G. Cohen, © 1994 by Teachers College Columbia University, reprinted by permission of Teachers College Press, New York, NY. All rights reserved.

Chapter 15
Teacher experiences reprinted with permission.

Author photo © by Amber Kayo. Used with permission of photographer.

Christopher-Gordon Publishers, Inc.
1502 Providence Highway, Suite 12
Norwood, MA 02062
800-934-8322

Printed in the United States of America

10 9 8 7 6 5 4 3 2 1   06 05 04 03 02

Library of Congress Catalog Card Number: 2002103387

ISBN: 1-929024-46-0

For Albie

Table of Contents

~~~~~~~~~~~~~~~~~~~~~~~~~~~~~~~~

Acknowledgements

I would like to thank several people who have helped me as I re-searched and wrote this book. First of all, my special thanks to my husband and children who gave me every encouragement, both emotionally and practically. I must also acknowledge my editor, Sue Canavan, for her belief in the importance of advisories and her efforts to ensure that this book did them justice.

Several colleagues have also guided me. Lorna Morgan believes in advisories and has helped to introduce them throughout New York City. Josephine McDowell and Alexis Colander are both exceptional administrators who model advisory skills at the school and district levels respectively. Jeff Glanz helped me to find a home for this book with Christopher-Gordon Publishers.

I would like also to express my admiration and great respect for the administrators, teachers, and staff with whom I have had the privilege of working these past 10 years and who have lent their voices to this text. I am particularly appreciative of Jon Gamarra, Richard Pashley, Rosalie Scaglione, and Karen Stevens for their personal testimonials detailed in chapter 15.

And finally, I thank the students themselves, whose need to express themselves and courage in doing so forms the heart of this work.

Preface

〰〰〰〰〰

If you are reading this, you are likely a teacher or an administrator who senses intuitively that something is missing in your middle school or high school program. You have heard about advisories. It may be that your school has implemented this program and you're seeking techniques to increase its effectiveness, or you may be trying to decide if it is an approach that will serve your students and staff. In either event, you are willing to look at the adolescents in your care more closely than their academic performance alone allows.

You are not alone in your interest. Group approaches have been integrated into American education since early in the 20th century and became more prevalent with the increased interest in affective education in the 1960s and 1970s.

I was first introduced to school-based groups in the mid-1980s while working in a parochial high school drug prevention program in which I trained religious and lay teachers to facilitate what were then called "rap groups." In 1991, I was hired by a New York City settlement house to work in a junior high school running advisories myself, and training staff to do the same. This experience allowed me to develop a district-wide program for junior and senior high schools. All told, I have worked in a similar capacity in 10 junior, middle schools, and high schools in New York City and New Jersey. My own background in social work and health education has convinced me that advisory groups can play a very important role in providing students with the chance to be supported and heard as they struggle to make decisions that may be life defining.

This book is, therefore, written for middle and high school teachers and administrators who want to play a greater role in promoting their students' emotional well-being through advisories. The type of advisory I propose, however, is not one in which every group within a grade does the same activity simultaneously, often using paper and pencil techniques. Rather, I train staff in basic facilitational skills, preparing them to run groups that are less structured than those reliant on preplanned programs.

This approach presumes that the staff member acting as an advisor is confident and competent to listen to the needs of his or her group members and is flexible enough to try to meet students where they are emotionally. Such facilitators may begin group sessions with an activity in mind, but they are willing to forgo it if student needs dictate; and they trust their advisory members to determine what they need to address at a given time.

This book contains three sections. The first section examines the needs of young adolescents and discusses how these needs must be met in school, describes interventions that support adolescent growth, defines advisories as an exemplary form, and suggests ways for successful implementation in middle and high schools.

The second section applies group theory to advisories. It focuses on the advisor and is dedicated to describing the skills he or she needs to facilitate groups. Topics such as differentiating group process from content, understanding stages of group development, recognizing membership roles, assessing one's own leadership styles, and "troubleshooting" problems as they occur are addressed. The material is at times presented conversationally, with numerous examples and anecdotes from teacher-advisors intended to help the reader imagine him or herself in a similar role. Each chapter ends with questions and activities designed to allow prospective advisors to interact with the material and assess their own approaches to match their expectations to students' capabilities.

The third section goes beyond the advisory to consider how it complements a school's existing support infrastructure by addressing the needs of the "at risk" student both within and outside of the group. It also considers what advisors gain from the experience and how the skills that both staff and students learn from their advisory translate powerfully into the classroom experience. As a college instructor of a methods course for prospective health educators, I am struck by the profound connection between advisory group facilitation and the constructivist classroom in which learning activities are geared toward children's multiple intelligences and are realized via cooperative learning. The third section also contains testimonials written by 4 middle school teachers who reflect on their experiences after running a daily, year-long advisory program.

Because this is intended as an accessible, hands-on manual for teachers and administrators working with advisories, I have kept footnotes to a minimum. Those researchers upon whose work I have drawn are acknowledged in the reference list.

I have written this book because I believe passionately that our students need and deserve to be heard. Advisories provide us with opportunities to better know them while also improving our listening and groupwork skills, which in turn make us better, more caring teachers. The truth is that we facilitate learning and growth in our classrooms everyday, whether or not we ever become advisors in the strictest sense. The techniques presented in this book are surely not new and will resonate with any who have studied group process in any of its guises. Ideally, their applicability to our everyday teaching will also be evident.

Hopefully, these skills are presented clearly and logically enough for you to become believers in the power of group process, too. We must not fear becoming involved with our students personally. This book presents techniques which are simple to use and are effective and respectful of both our feelings and those of our students. The potential benefits to all of us are considerable.

Susan MacLaury

Introduction
~~~~~~~~~~~~~

Early Adolescents and What They Need from Us

When my father was 15, a teacher told him that he wasn't college material and suggested that he transfer to a vocational school. Outraged, my grandmother instead enrolled him in a military academy where he boarded for the next two years. He graduated then attended a well-known engineering school, from which he also graduated in four years. He went on to have a successful career as a mechanical engineer, but the truth is that all his life he considered his success to be a fluke. On some level, he accepted this teacher's appraisal of him and believed that he was indeed stupid. As teachers, we can never forget the powerful affect we have on the ways in which our students perceive themselves.

What made you decide to teach adolescents? Do you recall educators who were meaningful to you growing up, who inspired you in some way? Perhaps they were excellent communicators, passionate about their subject. Possibly they saw more in you than you dared hope to imagine. Somehow, they conveyed the message that they knew who you were and believed in what you could be. They made a difference in your life and, like the rest of us, you hoped to do the same for your students. We often begin with high aspirations—carefully crafting lessons, developing unit plans, and learning how to assess students' performance. We go to staff development trainings, meet with parents, take on one new initiative after another—each designed to improve our students' performance. We take our jobs seriously.

Yet many of us become disillusioned because our methods don't achieve the results we had hoped. We cannot reach all our students. We may not even be able to reach as many as we once could. Certain students' problems seem to intensify over time and their behaviors worsen, despite our best efforts. As a consequence, our feelings about teaching may diminish as we question our effectiveness. Worse still, our expectations of our students may suffer.

> A continuing difficulty in providing developmentally respon-
> sive schools for young adolescents is widespread ignorance
> about the characteristics, needs, and interests of the age
> group. Many people, both inside and outside the profes-
> sion, are not only unenlightened about the age group, but
> hold negative stereotypes about them. (McEwin, Dickinson,
> & Jenkins, 1996, p. 157)

Disturbingly, one poll revealed that more than half the teachers surveyed didn't believe that current adolescents would significantly contribute to American society. Not surprisingly, our students know this. More than 50 % of adolescents in another study indicated that they did not believe that their teachers cared about them.

Compounding the problem is a marked decrease in contact between adolescents and adults. While adolescence is a stage rich with opportunities for educators to guide their students, it is also one of minimal contact between the two age groups. Typically, teenagers spend less than 5 % of their time with parents and 2 % of their nonschool hours with other adults. Although 25 % of this population experience symptoms of emotional distress, only about 11 % of students talk to a school counselor in any given academic year. This is possibly due in part to the fact that there is only one guidance counselor for every 600 students nationally, and counselors may thus have difficulty addressing individual students' needs. One study of high school students, for example, revealed that while 20 % had admitted to suicidal behavior in the previous year, 75 % of these students received no therapeutic intervention. These statistics represent a terrible missed opportunity.

As Kohn (1997) comments,

> Let there be no question then: educators, parents, and other
> adults are desperately needed to offer guidance, to act as
> models, to pose challenges that promote moral growth,
> and to help children understand the effects of their actions
> on other people, thereby tapping and nurturing a concern
> for others that is present in children from a very young
> age. (p. 11)

Early adolescence is a time of tremendous change. So much is happening to this group so rapidly that it is difficult for many to express their feelings. The developmental "compression" many young adolescents experience as they enter adolescence is stressful and confusing. Puberty, sexual experimentation, and mixed messages about expectable behaviors from the media often precede their actual readiness for these role changes.

It also appears that teachers may not always be aware of their students' developmental needs; or if they are, they may feel unprepared to integrate this knowledge into their instructional practice. Accordingly, one of the most important skills we can possess is the ability to understand what adolescents are experiencing, and one way which helps us do so is to remember ourselves at this age.

- What was happening in your life at the age of 13?
- What did you look like?
- What was your favorite outfit?
- How did you wear your hair?
- What music did you listen to?
- Who was your best friend?
- How did you feel about school?
- How well did you get along with your parents, brothers, and sisters?
- What activities might a perfect Saturday have included?

Such a guided recall exercise can be illuminating as we strive to understand our students and to maintain stable relationships with them, even when their mood swings and shifting perspectives make this a challenging task. Because adolescence is potentially so confusing for our students, it is particularly important for us to understand the scope of what they are experiencing physically, emotionally, socially, intellectually, and morally; to observe how they demonstrate these states behaviorally; and to know what our most helpful response might be.

Figure 1 illustrates many of the developmental changes inherent in early adolescence as described by The American Academy of Child and Adolescent Psychiatry (1999). As we can see, and we certainly recall from our own early adolescence, tremendous change is occurring.

Early adolescence begins at puberty, approximately the age of 10 for girls and 12 for boys. Within a period of 4 to 5 years, the average child grows 10 to 20 inches and gains 40–50 pounds. Compounding the impact of these physical changes is the fact that they occur differentially in various parts of the body. Hands, feet, noses, and ears tend to grow faster than the torso, other facial features, and the body's erogenous zones. Not only can these irregularities increase a youngster's self-consciousness, but they also contribute to physical awkwardness. Given this fact, any youngster can feel awkward when his or her growth doesn't equal that of peers.

The development of secondary sex characteristics in girls occurs first with the growth of breast "buds," then pubic and underarm hair, followed by increasing breast development and deposits of body fat around the hips. Menstruation soon follows, usually between the ages of 12 and 13, although it can occur significantly earlier or later depending on a girl's percentage of body fat, diet, stress, and other environmental influences.

Boys will notice genital changes first. After penile growth begins, they begin ejaculating semen; and over the next several months, their sperm count begins to increase. They, too, develop pubic, underarm, and chest hair and will also experience changes in their larynxes which affect their voices. By midadolescence, boys' musculature has increased significantly, their body fat is reduced, and their shoulders have broadened.

These hormonal changes also create significant emotional consequences for both sexes. Girls may find their moods are far more labile, in large part dictated by where they are at any given point in their menstrual cycle. For boys, the increased levels of testosterone cause them to experience greater energy levels, adrenalin rushes, and, at times, heightened aggressiveness. Both sexes may experience other bodily changes, like acne, which are also related to hormonal increases.

Many of the emotional changes experienced by adolescents are no doubt in reaction to others' expectations of them based on their physical appearance. Those who develop earlier than average may find themselves pressured to engage in sexual or other activities for which they are not emotionally ready. "Late bloomers" may perceive themselves as lagging behind their peers developmentally and can feel inferior as a result. Indeed, many youngsters, particularly girls, experience a decline in self-esteem mediated at least partially by physical changes they cannot control.

The classic image of adolescents, particularly younger ones, is that of individuals who are intensely self-conscious, sure that everyone is watching and judging them. It may be that while adolescents are initially depressed about the fact that they are "different" from others and equate this uniqueness with inadequacy, it is the personal drive to overcome this "deficit," that fuels much of youngsters' ultimate per-

Figure 1: Adolescent Development

PHYSICAL	EMOTIONAL	SOCIAL	COGNITIVE	MORAL
Females Breast growth	Females Mood lability	Females Less assertive	Both Have mastered concrete operations	Both Increase in prosocial behaviors
Changes in body fat Menstruation	Males Increased energy Heightened aggression	Relationally oriented	Learning to see cause/effect	Conformity to social norms
Males Genital changes	Both Heightened self-consciousness	Males More competitive and performance oriented	Transfer learning	Shift from egocentrism to sociocentric behaviors
Ejaculation Sperm devlopment Changes in musculature	Quest for personal identity	Both Experimentation	Learn sequentially	Development of moral purpose
Voice changes		Need for peers		
Development of pubic/body hair		Separation from parents		
Growth spurts				

Reprinted by permission of HarperCollins Publishers, Inc.

sonal accomplishments. One student may strive to succeed academically, another in sports, and yet another by being popular with peers. It is precisely this balance between an adolescent's perceived successes versus failures that determines his/her personal identity. Yet there is no question that striving for this balance is a difficult task.

Here is how one 6th grader, Emily, describes adolescence in her essay "Trapped: An excerpt from the diary of Katie Brown, a 6th-grade girl".

> Mom always uses the word "trapped" to describe my sticky situations in middle school. I never really knew what she meant, but now I think I do. It feels as though my world is a bubble that will not pop. All my problems are in it with me, and they are all attacking me at the same time. But the biggest problem of all is the middle school popularity scram. That's what I call it. It all started off with my friends and me in the beginning of the year. Everything was perfect. No worries of "Is this the correct outfit to wear tomorrow or will I be excluded from that crowd?" or "Should I wear purple or blue eye shadow?"
>
> Friends are a really big issue in middle school; that's all you seem to care about. The popular girls for this year have been decided. It seems like there is a new one every month though and it is hard to keep track. But I am not one of them and I really, really wish I was. You know those girls who always try to dress like them and to be them so the cutest, most popular guy would like them? Well that's who I am. I am starting to wear the floozy clothes with the huge shoes and tons of makeup. But I know that how I am dressing is not me. How you dress is supposed to describe who you are, right? But how I am dressing now is not describing me. It is describing one of them, Britney or Whitney, I always get them confused. They are the popular girls right now. And all us nonpopular girls are trying our very hardest to be them and to be noticed. That is all a girl wants, to be noticed and liked by others and to be able to fit in like a puzzle piece in the middle school puzzle. But it does not always work. I am not being me, by dressing the wrong way for me but the right way for my school friends. I cake myself in makeup until I look just like some makeup fanatic walking out of a Sephora store, and I don't look anything like myself. I am trapped. Forbidden to be me. Forbidden to express me and only allowed to express Britney or whoever we all look up to. I arrive home from school feeling

miserable, thinking why can't I just be me? Why can't I build up the courage to walk into school wearing "dorky" clothes and wearing no makeup whatsoever? I can't. I can't be me. I can't walk into school wearing no makeup and looking like a child walking out of Talbot's Kids.

I wear the same thing everyday. My tight jeans are getting a little small for me now, but I am not going to get new ones because what if the new ones I buy are not acceptable? And then I won't be liked, and then no one will talk to me. I wear the pink shirt that is starting to get salad stains and diet coke on it. (I have to watch my diet so I don't get fat.) I never smile a real smile that means something anymore. I smile pretending to be happy for Whitney and Will and how they go out now. I smile because my salad is good. Ridiculous things that mean nothing in the world to me. I never laugh anymore, because there is nothing funny to laugh about.

I wonder if this bubble will ever pop? I hope so but if it doesn't, answer one question please. Will I ever be me again?

Intellectually, it is ideally during early adolescence that youngsters move from the stage of concrete operations to formal operations. The majority of middle school students do not function at this level, however. While most have mastered concrete operations, they have only begun to experiment at the higher cognitive level. Only about one third of 8th graders have attained formal operations; and in fact, many individuals do not attain formal operations until later in adolescence or even young adulthood.

Without the capacity for abstract thought that is the hallmark of formal operations, adolescents often have difficulty applying what they learn from one situation to another. They also may not be able to learn sequentially which can cause academic problems, particularly in disciplines like mathematics in which each course builds on skills taught in the previous one.

Of equal significance are the problems that may exist in fully understanding cause and effect relationships, which in turn may prevent young adolescents from fully appreciating the risks inherent in their behaviors. By 9th grade, for example, nearly 1 in 4 students has had sexual intercourse, but many—perhaps the majority—do not use contraception.

Even if they intellectually understand the consequences of their actions, they may make decisions without considering their potential emotional impact. One study of girls who had lost their virginity at this age suggested that nearly three fourths were conflicted over their decision or sorry they had made it at all. It is often not until he or she has reached high school that the average adolescent has mastered these cognitive skills and can see the larger picture when asked to solve problems.

Puberty's physical changes may also affect youngsters' moral behavior. Greater size and strength alert adolescents to the fact that they can do more now both for themselves and others, and adults are likely to allow them to help in ways they wouldn't have previously. Their desire to experiment sexually may also increase their need to forge intimate relationships and to engage in the behaviors that promote them.

Moral development is assumed to progress through specific stages. Initially children are egocentric, but by mid and late adolescence they shift to more sociocentric thinking, partly as a result of shifting from concrete to formal operations, and being able to understand others' points of view. Such empathy is also thought to develop in line with cognitive growth.

By high school age, students become increasingly aware that some social practices themselves may be immoral. In such cases, many adolescents hold themselves to higher ethical standards and make the decision to act outside parameters which are socially acceptable.

Although parents play a role in their children's moral and prosocial development throughout adolescence, peer influences form the basis for youngsters' sense of morality. Adolescents whose friends value school, also value school. Those whose friends are involved in deviant behaviors, also tend to be.

Indeed, at no other time in life do individuals face a more contradictory task than during adolescence when they attempt to determine who they are individually while simultaneously belonging to a social group. Strong ties with peers, and conformity to their norms, help youngsters to negotiate the process of separation-individuation from parents and family.

The earliest stage of adolescence is marked by an increased curiosity in the outside world and the need to "hatch" from the family unit via strong peer group associations. Young adolescents often feel strongly that only their peers really understand who they are and only in their company can they comfortably be themselves. They require "supported autonomy" from parents as they begin to push away and discover who they are. In other words, their relationships with their parents are still intensely important; but adolescents have to know that they can successfully break out of their parents' orbits to create their own lives.

They begin this process by practicing "adult" behaviors with their friends: Dating, becoming sexually active, experimenting with drugs and alcohol, and generally testing parental limits. Once they feel confident that they have developed their own sense of identity they will return to a closer, yet redefined relationship with their parents. Ultimately, they will enter young adulthood on their own terms.

Friendships at this stage occur primarily in small, same-sex groups. While these youngsters are more likely to be influenced prosocially by their peers than antisocially, the greatest risk of all at this age is social rejection; and those young adolescents lacking a positive peer group may find themselves acting out simply to be accepted by others who also behave self-destructively.

As adolescence progresses, interest in the opposite sex increases and dating begins, first often as group events, then in pairs. Cliques also tend to become increasingly important as students move from middle school to high school, and there is some thought that these may represent "families of peers" that provide them with security. Membership in such social groups helps to mitigate against the loneliness that many adolescents feel.

Middle schoolers are probably the age group which is most susceptible to peer pressure, and this can put them at risk for different types of self-destructive behaviors. The percentage of youngsters who have experimented with alcohol rises from 14 % of 10-years-olds to 42 % among those who are 13. Drug use rises from0 to 11 % in that time period, and smoking quadruples from 11 % to 44 %.

The good news is that by and large children and adolescents are doing fine psychosocially. Ninety percent say they feel safe in their neighborhoods and at school. Their biggest complaints seem to be having too much homework and feeling bossed around by adults and older siblings. Four out of five name their parents as the adults they admire most. Ninety-five percent describe themselves as religious and 80 % pray. Overall, adolescents report far more positive major life events than negative.

Despite these optimistic statistics, young adolescents in particular still face social obstacles, both real and imagined. Only 3 in 10 surveyed believed that adults respect them "a lot," and this figure is slightly lower among middle school children (27 %). This perceived lack of respect can clearly have serious repercussions for the quality of relationships between students and teachers.

What Adolescents Seek From Us

As teachers and administrators, we spend more time with young adolescents than any other adults, including parents, in some cases. This provides us with a tremendous opportunity to positively impact on our students, to increase their personal assets and their emotional resiliency. To do so, we have to care about their well-being and to demonstrate this caring in ways that both nurture and expect the best from them.

Schools which concentrate on developing positive relationships both among students and between students and teachers produce academic excellence. While nearly half of middle and high school students complain of being bored most of the time, those who perceived that their teachers and peers cared about them were more likely to come to school prepared and to be engaged in the learning process.

We must pay heed to these interrelationships. At the other end of the spectrum is the researcher's dismal finding that while nearly two thirds of 6th graders feel a part of their schools, by 8th grade this figure has dropped to 46 %. This finding appears to corroborate Eccles and Midgley's (1989) contention that "the quality of teacher-student relationships deteriorates when adolescents are in particular need of adult role models". The consensus of some researchers is that while this figure may be reversed somewhat for girls if their perceptions of the school environment improve, it probably will never be for boys. We cannot afford to lose these students.

When we listen to adolescents talk about what matters the most to them in their teachers, what we learn, not surprisingly, is that they want to believe that we really are concerned about them. Phelan, Davidson, and Cao (1992) write,

> Students want teachers to recognize who they are, to listen to what they have to say, and to respect their efforts. In classrooms where personalities are allowed to show, students respond more fully, both academically and personally. . . . In fact, the number of student references to 'wanting caring teachers' is so great that we believe it speaks to the quiet desperation and loneliness of many adolescents in today's society. (p. 696)

Sometimes teachers and students differ sharply in their perceptions of whether or not the teacher does provide emotional support. In one study, for example, students felt their teachers gave more support to high achievers, whereas teachers' views were the opposite. Another potential problem is that too often teachers are perceived as caring exclusively about how well students perform academically and not appreciating the emotional distress they experience. Clearly, students who believe that they are competent and who value school are more motivated to succeed academically than are others who perceive themselves to be poorly treated by school personnel.

It also appears that student achievement depends on how well their teachers perform, and teacher ability and motivation seem to be a function of how much support they receive from their principals and how committed they are to their school and their students. As many of us in this profession can attest, it is possible to be in the classroom with dozens of students daily but still feel personally and professionally isolated. As many times as I have conducted the advisory facilitation training, which includes a weekly group experience for the teacher-advisors, teachers invariably comment that they need their own advisory group to support them as they cope with their personal issues.

According to middle school students themselves, there are several ways teachers show that they care. Some students believe that caring teachers are those who can successfully control students' behavior. Others prize teachers who treat them fairly, like everyone else. Still others treasure teachers who forgive them when they make mistakes and give them an opportunity to learn from their mistakes.

A caring teacher is also perceived as one who teaches well, meaning that he/she makes sure material is understood and makes learning fun and interesting. Finally, and perhaps most importantly, these students believe that teachers who care about them get to know them well as individuals, far beyond their roles as students in the classroom. They want their teachers to be there to listen and respond when they have problems and to know enough about their family relationships that they can involve parents when necessary.

It appears that many teachers and students have reached an impasse in which students act out those feelings they do not understand to school staff who themselves may feel overwhelmed and dispirited. The question is how to provide each group with the opportunity it needs to connect comfortably and meaningfully with the other in a way that increases teachers' motivation to reach out inclusively to their students and increases students' motivation to express themselves most affirmatively. One way both goals might be achieved is to create an emotional common ground on which students and teachers can get to know each other more personally and meaningfully. Group interventions such as advisories can fulfill this intention.

Questions You Might Want to Ask Yourself About Your Attitudes About Adolescents and Your Own Experience as One:

As mentioned in this chapter, one way of checking in on our capacity to empathize with young adolescent students is to think back about our own experiences during this developmental stage. How might you respond to the following questions?

1. On a scale from 1 to 10, how would you rate your own early adolescence? Assume that 10 means that you recall it as a wonderful period in your life, and 1 implies that you would rather throw yourself in front of a truck than experience it again. Why would you rate it this way?

    1   2   3   4   5   6   7   8   9   10

2. If you could have changed one thing about your physical appearance between the ages of 11 and 14, what would it have been? What would changing it have done for you?

3. Were you "popular" in junior high or middle school? How did you know? How did your social status impact on you?

4. How influenced were you by what your friends said and did? Can you remember a specific incident in which you behaved in a way that was uncharacteristic of you because you felt it was expected? How did you feel about doing this?

5. What was the best thing about being an early adolescent? The worst?

6. When you had a problem, to whom would you go for advice? What made this person helpful to you?

7. Do you believe that young adolescents' problems today are harder or easier than what you recall facing at that age? What makes you feel this way?

8. Are you satisfied that your school strives hard to understand students holistically? How do you feel about your

own personal understanding of and level of interest in your students?

9. What is your reaction to the fact that a majority of middle school teachers today apparently lack confidence in their students' abilities to meaningfully contribute to society?

10. How do you demonstrate your own confidence in your students? What is the impact of your behaviors on their behaviors in class?

Chapter One

∿∿∿∿∿∿∿∿∿∿∿

Why Advisories?

Several years ago, a 13-year-old boy was stabbed to death at school by a fellow student. Word quickly spread to our school a few blocks away where many of our students knew both of those involved in the incident. What made this traumatic event all the more difficult for them to deal with was the fact that the victim had been a notorious bully who had tormented his attacker unmercifully for months and had bullied several other youngsters as well. The target of his bullying had finally decided he had enough; and unconvinced that school personnel could or would help him, he took matters into his own hands.

Our principal immediately suspended 7th- and 8th-grade period classes and asked that students report to their advisory groups, where they were given a chance to discuss this incident and how it left them feeling. School counselors were available to provide special attention to those who were especially traumatized. The intervention worked. Students were able to attain the support they needed; and with the help of one another and their advisors, they weathered the incident well.

There had been no advisory program in the other school prior to the stabbing; but when that principal spoke with ours and learned how the advisories had helped our students, he proposed the program to his staff. More than 20 teachers agreed to be trained as advisors, and I began working in that school as well. It is very unfortunate that it took a tragedy of such magnitude to promote this type of support for students, particularly since we know that students' perceptions of social support appear to be key to their belief that their school environment is a caring one.

Providing this support through group rather than individual interventions is often considered to be the most effective approach. The group is an excellent milieu in which adolescents can play out their most critical developmental concern: How to learn more about oneself and still be accepted by peers. Such activities promote adolescent empowerment, itself proven to be helpful in encouraging students to choose more positive roles as they develop personal identities. Indeed, a review of the literature of the types of interventions which build student resilience and protect them against acting out behaviors revealed that group approaches improve intrapersonal capacities, school attendance, peer acceptance, and anger managment skills.

The Advisory

Advisories are support groups for students. In some schools they are referred to as "family groups," because they potentially provide the unconditional acceptance to their members that is provided by a caring family. As this example illustrates, they have a powerful role to play in helping students to make sense of the incomprehensible. Could they help to prevent the type of violence illustrated here? Could they provide the necessary arena in which youngsters generally can tell us what concerns them rather than feeling they have no other choice than to act them out? Yes.

A principal recently told me that she wants to increase the size of her school's advisory program to include all students, although she is having difficulty convincing more teachers to become involved. The urgency she feels now is based on the gang activity within her area that has been steadily increasing over the last couple of years. She understands that adolescents often join gangs to belong, and she believes the advisory group provides a positive experience that can meet these same needs safely and constructively in school.

Although advisories can serve a vital early violence prevention function, more typically these groups allow their members the chance to belong and to express themselves about everyday concerns. They are ideally no larger than 10 to12 students each and are designed to help develop the aforementioned life skills of communication, problem solving, and decision making under the guidance of their advisor—a staff member who has agreed to become the "designated caring adult" (Cushman, 1990). Advisories are a means of redesigning large, impersonal schools into smaller, caring communities that promote closer relationships between students and staff.

Principals and teachers participating in a national study, who were asked to describe the elements of exemplary middle schools, ranked advisories fifth in importance out of 20. Many principals perceive supportive advisory programs to also have a long-term, positive effect by helping to prevent students from dropping out of school. George & Oldaker (1985) determined that 93 % of such exemplary schools had advisory programs for all their students and that 62 % of these children enjoyed "consistent academic improvement," while the schools reported an 80 % reduction in referrals for behavioral problems.

The goal of learning to appreciate the "whole" child is a hallmark of the middle school movement, and advisories clearly promote this opportunity; however, it would be a mistake to conceptualize advisory programs as exclusive to the middle school as they are often implemented in high schools as well. Indeed, the first high school advisory, established in the United States in 1924, still exists.

Differentiating Advisories From Other Group Approaches

Clearly, there are a number of possible group approaches to working with adolescents. Advisories share some qualities in common with each but are unique in many other respects. Here are some of the similarities versus distinctions between advisories and three other commoly used approaches: group guidance, discussion groups, and group counseling.

Group Guidance

Classroom group guidance is leader-centered instruction to students that is intended to help prevent developmental issues from becoming problems. Although advisory groups frequently address such issues, their purpose is to empower adolescents to think for themselves and to develop a mutual aid approach by which they help one another clarify what they are feeling, problem solve, and make decisions. The advisor's role is facilitative, not directive. An advisory group in which students are dialoguing only with the advisor is one that is not going as well as one would hope.

Discussion Groups

The discussion group encourages interactions among students facilitated by the leader to increase students' self-awareness. Although primarily educational in nature, they can in fact have a great deal in common with advisories but will differ in how the groups are led.

Advisors facilitate their groups without overdetermining them, whereas teachers may be more directive.

Devencenzi and Pendergast (1999) point out several ways support groups like advisories differ from classroom relationships:

- Teachers assume responsibility for their classes, but in advisories, students are responsible to and for each other.
- Teachers develop lesson plans, while advisors allow students to determine what they wish to address.
- Teachers' goals are to educate. Advisors support self and social improvement in terms which are defined by the students.
- Teachers focus on students' cognitive, physical, and social development whereas advisors focus affectively and socially.
- Teachers develop group activities which reflect the class's skill level, whereas students in advisories agree upon the skills they will develop through their group activities.[1]

Group Counseling

In the third type of group approach, group counseling, students learn skills that help them cope more effectively with both developmental concerns and specific problems. There are clearly circumstances in which students need and benefit from group counseling; and sometimes the need for more intensive counseling emerges from the advisory group itself, but an advisory is not a therapy group. It does provide an opportunity for teachers to react to student feelings which they might not see in class, however, as well as to encourage advisors to act as advocates for their students and as liaisons between the school and home.

Having said this, however, it is also true that depending on how the group is structured, the composition of the group, and the degree of cohesiveness it develops, the boundary between discussion and counseling becomes blurred. This is precisely the situation that frightens many prospective advisors.

You are teachers and administrators, *not* counselors. If you believe that your students have the ability to identify problems, forge close relationships with one another, and provide mutual assistance in making decisions, you will not be surprised when some advisory sessions become more emotionally charged and very personal information is shared.

If and when this happens, take a deep breath and sit back and remind yourself that your goal is to facilitate, not to solve your students' problems. If your instinct is that you are hearing material that reflects a serious issue, you will need to speak with that student and make the appropriate referral. Brown (2001), in describing an advisory program in an urban area in which students face serious family and environmental stressors, quotes advisors whose students routinely discuss issues like sex and drugs. One advisor commented, "I take my position as a teacher/advisor as a second parent."

In many instances, you will find that your students can genuinely provide support to one another in dealing with very difficult life circumstances. Much of what happens in your advisory group will depend on your personal comfort level and how you define your role as a facilitator. You must have the right to conduct yourself professionally in a way that feels appropriate to you.

Here are some general distinctions between acting as an advisor versus the role typically played by counselors.

- The goal of counseling is problem resolution/behavioral change, while that of advisories is support. This is not to say that students in an advisory might not help one another solve problems, but the presumption is that one enters counseling *because* of a problem that necessitates behavioral change. This is not true of students in advisories who are asked to participate supportively whether or not they are experiencing any difficulties.
- Counselors require advanced clinical training, whereas advisors focus on building their facilitational skills and can do so on either an undergraduate-, graduate-, or entry-level staff development level.
- Counselors must first assess and then treat problems, whereas advisors clarify and build individual and group problem-solving skills to address them.
- Counselors address deeper-seated clinical problems. Advisors identify students with problems and refer them to counselors.
- Counselors will more directly confront clients about behaviors that are problematic. In advisories, where such confrontation occurs it is often introduced by other students and becomes more an issue to be managed and facilitated by the advisor.
- Counselors tend to focus more on family and personal history, while advisors work more immediately in the here-and-now, focusing more on inter- and intrapersonal relationships at school.

- Counseling may entail an ongoing, long-term relationship while advisories are time limited.

Why and How Advisories Meet Adolescents' Developmental Needs

Of the numerous developmental needs of adolescents, eight are directly addressed by schools: competence and achievement; self-exploration and definition; social interaction with peers and adults; physical activity; routines, limits, and structure; diversity; opportunities to explore concepts and generate ideas from concrete experiences; and opportunities to explore values and decision making. The advisory is an ideal approach for meeting at least seven of these (probably, but not necessarily) excluding physical activity.

Advisories provide middle school students with the developmental guidance necessary to help them become "self-managers" capable of handling their increasing independence. The National Middle School Association (1997) also advocates strongly for advisories because it, too, believes that the groups meet a number of adolescent developmental needs by:

- providing social interaction and peer support in a safe environment,
- creating links between parents and school,
- supporting academic achievement by addressing personal and interpersonal factors and allowing for the practice of strategies to improve study habits and test-taking methods,
- increasing students' self-esteem and self-efficacy, and
- promoting positive student-teacher relationships.

Increasing Students' Self-Esteem and Self-Efficacy

Putbrese (1989) conducted a national study of the impact of advisories on 3,400 middle school students. Among its conclusions were that advisories

- impacted positively on how students viewed their teachers outside the classroom,
- gave students a feeling of greater control over their decisions,
- promoted an atmosphere of equality,
- provided opportunities for group work,
- improved students' willingness and ability to share their feelings,

- maximized early adolescents' sense of altruism,
- reduced the incidence of smoking, alcohol use and/or abuse, and
- appeared to make teachers more sensitive or attentive to students' behaviors.

His conclusion that advisories can meet early adolescents' needs to feel known and recognized was also demonstrated in a Michigan study which revealed that schools initiating middle school reforms such as advisories also achieved improved student behaviors, decreased alcohol use, and student reports of greater feelings of safety and self-esteem.

Given the literature on behavioral change, these results are not surprising. It is estimated that it takes a minimum of 50 hours of instruction to promote significant changes in health attitudes and behaviors. Providing students the opportunity to meet regularly in small, safe groups such as advisories where they can reflect on their personal choices and make reasoned decisions can only be beneficial, particularly if the groups continue throughout the student's school career.

The real "experts" here are the students who participate in advisories themselves. New York City junior high school students who met weekly in advisory groups for a year shared what they had gained from their experience:

"Because of this program, peers look out for each other more."

"The same groups and cliques still exist, but now they communicate with each other."

"I feel I can openly share and particpate in my advisory group."

"I have learned to be a better listener."

"I am more accepting of others' opinions, even though we do not agree."

"It helps us accept other people's feelings."

"I am learning to feel good about myself."

When we read their comments, we are struck by the fact that these students appear to have benefited both personally and socially. Several comment on intrinsic qualities within themselves which have changed positively. Others are touched by how the experience has helped them to express themselves more comfortably to one another. This is the potential power of the group experience when it is carefully planned and thoughtfully implemented.

Providing Social Interaction and Peer Support Within a Safe Environment

A visit to an advisory program at the University Heights High School in New York City several years ago demonstrated the potential power of advisories to nurture and protect students. Although many of the students attending this school had experienced problems in the institutions they had previously attended, the majority had done well at University Heights and were college bound. The school had created a close-knit, caring atmosphere for its students, in part because of its advisory program.

Students met in their advisories daily for an hour over the entire four years of their high school experience. After observing one group session for seniors and asking the students what they got out of their advisories, one student answered: "This group has saved my life. It's the only place in my life where I feel safe."

Not only can young adolescents in advisories feel cared for by school staff, as this student clearly did, but the groups also allow them to demonstrate caring themselves. Advisories can promote students' moral development because the social interactions encouraged by group participation allow students to really speak and listen to one another, to experience different viewpoints, to practice different social roles, and to learn to behave prosocially—a process which appears to be essential to enable adolescents to become more sophisticated in their moral reasoning.

Creating Links Between Parents and School Personnel

Middle school educators have long appreciated the importance of involving parents in their children's schooling. Teacher-advisors can effectively engage parents by acting as their liaison to the school: informing them if their children are having difficulties, helping them to negotiate systemic problems, and acknowledging students' successes. At least one study has shown that students flourish academically and personally when their teacher-advisors assume this role. Their attendance, grade point averages, and self-esteem all increased, while control groups reported a decrease in these areas over the middle school years.

School personnel considering the start-up of an advisory program invariably express concern about how it will be received by parents—it is rarely, if ever, a problem. One study of parents' reactions to their children's advisory program revealed that they believed that their children's transition to high school had been eased by their involvement in the program and felt relief that the advisors were looking after the students in this way.

Supporting Academic Achievement

A principal brought in to turn around a failing school sabotaged its fledgling advisory program, because she felt the time students spent in groups could be better spent in class preparing for standardized testing. She dismantled the program by forcing cancellation of the weekly groups first occasionally, then a couple of times monthly, and finally altogether. The students were very disappointed and not only expressed their feelings to their advisors, but on at least one occasion to the principal herself, who nonetheless disregarded their opinions.

Her concern that advisory time was "wasted" academically may have been ill conceived. Although there is a tendency to view advisories as promoting emotional and social well-being more than directly impacting on academics, in fact these groups appear to also contribute to students' classroom performance. In one Minnesota school the staff used their advisories to diagnose why their 8th graders had performed poorly on a standardized test. The results were very positive, and what teachers learned from students enabled them to make pedagogical changes that caused test scores to rise significantly the following year.

Two very different advisory programs in Newark, New Jersey, illustrate variations in advisory functions. Vailsburg Middle School offers a program which meets daily. Four days are devoted to subject matter enhancement, and Fridays are dedicated to group guidance. The principal is confident that this program has improved his students' grades. If so, perhaps it is because in this instance advisories seem to promote cooperative learning.

Promoting Positive Student-Teacher Relationships

On the other hand, staff at Camden Middle School, several blocks away, look to their advisory program to help them to identify those students at greatest need for emotional support. Their experience has demonstrated that teacher/advisors play a unique role in supporting their students in times of crisis, as well as those facing expectable adolescent problems. The experience of these staff members is consistent with findings from a study in which it was found that students in advisories often indicated that they felt as though they belonged to their school, enjoyed better relationships with their teachers, and had increased their decision-making skills.

In 1989, the Carnegie Council on Adolescent Development ascertained that the child who forges a relationship with a *single* caring adult is significantly more likely to complete a high school education than is the child who does not. The literature on dropout prevention strongly suggests that groups like advisories can provide proof that teachers and administrators care about students and that this support can maintain students in school.

Cautions

The caveat in developing advisory programs is that they vary widely in their quality and may not necessarily be perceived by students as being that helpful. Anfara & Brown (2000) studied 73 middle schools and found that only 14 had advisory programs, some of which appeared to exist in name only. Interviewing preservice teachers who reflected back on their own middle school experiences, the authors concluded that whatever the intervention—advisory or otherwise—students need "consistent adult contact to help meet the need of the 'fourth R,' to help bridge the gap between elementary school and high school, and to help build self-awareness and personal esteem" (p. 71).

Not surprisingly, much of an advisory's success or failure rests with the advisor's facilitational skills; thus unfortunately, not all advisory groups deliver the content or support they intend. When questioned, many teacher-advisors admit to often feeling ill prepared to address the social and emotional issues which can easily emerge in group discussions. Indeed, of all components of middle school reform, none is considered to be more difficult to implement or sustain than advisories, largely because so many teacher-advisors lack the necessary group skills and are confused about the purpose of advisories overall.

To address this problem many proponents of advisories insist that staff development is necessary to provide teachers the facilitational skills needed to run successful groups. Fibkins (1999) states, "A school that doesn't offer ongoing training for advisers is an accident waiting to happen" (p. 43). Unfortunately, to date, there has been little written about potential training programs for teacher-advisors.

Potential Impact on Advisors

In chapter 13, we will explore some of the ways in which the facilitational skills teachers use when they run advisories also impact on their classroom instruction. For the moment, however, let's consider only how the experience can affect teachers emotionally.

One teacher who had briefly run an advisory group two years earlier until scheduling changes forced her to disband it, mentioned that her experience as an advisor had changed the way she viewed her students. She believed that this change in perspective had made her more understanding of what they were experiencing and had positively affected her teaching.

Still another teacher attending a national violence prevention conference workshop on advisories discussed his school's now defunct advisory program. He looked reflective as he told the group that while he couldn't remember the name of a single student he had taught the previous year, he could still remember those of every student in his advisory group six years earlier. Becoming an advisor had clearly been significant for him, and he expressed regret that the school had discontinued the groups.

Finally, this teacher-advisor expresses what she has carried with her from her group experience:

> I recognize that the children are teachers, too. Why? Because although we may have greater knowledge and experience, they offer many new perspectives on life. If we are open to listening to them, we appreciate that many of our students live in the present and therefore bring a spontaneity that adults who are already flung into tomorrow's schedule seem to rush by.

These teachers' experiences are representative of the more than 200 I have trained to run advisories to date. Like the teacher whose school no longer sponsored these groups, many staff wholeheartedly endorse advisories and welcome the opportunity to know their students more fully, relating to them in more personal ways than they do as teachers.

A number of staff, however, justifiably question whether they can hope to gain anything personally from the advisory experience or indeed whether it is even appropriate professionally to want to do so. They are concerned that becoming advisors might require them to explore their private feelings, to enter uncharted affective waters, and to respond to their students in nontraditional ways. They wonder if the advisor role will somehow compromise or change their authority in the classroom. The question also arises about how close they want to become to students and how much they really want to know about their lives outside of the classroom.

While the literature may be persuasive that initiatives like advisory programs can help youngsters know their schools care about them and that this caring can build emotional resiliency, much remains to be done to reassure staff and to fully prepare them for yet another added school role.

> Young adolescents . . . need help—our help. I have found no better context for providing that kind of support at school than a well-conceived, conscientiously provided teacher advisory program. Alas, too few middle level schools have developed their full potential in this domain of our professional responsibilities. (Stevenson,1998, p. 307).

Delivering the William M. Alexander Memorial Lecture at the 25th annual conference of the National Middle School Association in 1998, Paul George (1999) addressed key concerns about developing viable advisory programs:

> The failure of teacher-based guidance or advisory programs has often brought discredit on our efforts as a whole. . . . In many schools, a majority of the faculty rejects the program either outright or by the silent sabotage of inadequacy. School leaders too rarely and with too little fervor act as advocates for advisory programs. A curriculum has never really been developed. Teachers have frequently been trained by those without real experience. Assessment of outcomes is almost nonexistent.

> Yet, I believe that it is almost impossible to find a successful ninth grade student whose positive experience in high school was not preceded by a warm and positive relationship with at least one middle school teacher. I suspect that you also believe that there is nothing as important as close and caring teacher-student relationships and a warm and supportive group of peers.

> The attempt to create nurturing relationships through our traditional advisory or AA programs has simply failed, except in very rare situations. Therefore, I urge the next generation of middle school educators to find a way to make advisor-advisee relationships and programs work well.

The key to a successful advisory program is that faculty believe it benefits students, are responsible for developing it, understand its goals, and feel confident in their facilitational skills. Students often demonstrate what they are feeling through their behaviors. The more we understand what these behaviors mean, and how they reflect adolescents' individual and collective developmental issues, the better able we are to join with them meaningfully both as teachers and advisors.

Your Attitudes About Advisory Groups

1. Does your school have an advisory program? If yes:

    – Are you personally involved in either its coordination or as a teacher-advisor?

    – How well overall would you rate your program's success in helping students to feel better known by faculty and staff? Why?

    – How much do you feel your advisory program contributes to students' sense of feeling supported by your school?

2. If you do *not* have an advisory program,

    – Are you interested in seeing one implemented? Why?

    – What role(s) would you wish to play in this initiative?

3. What makes you most curious or enthusiastic about imagining the role of advisor?

4. What is your greatest concern about being an advisor? Why?

5. Do you feel satisfied that you are reaching your students in all the ways you had imagined you would when you began teaching?

    – If not, what is missing for you at this time?

6. What is your reaction to the literature cited that suggests that advisories can make a difference in students' academic performance, as well as their psychosocial growth?

7. How do you feel about devoting school time to groupwork that isn't specifically academic in nature?

Endnote

1. Reprinted from *Belonging: Self and Social Discovery* by J. Devencenzi and S. Pendergast, 1999, p. 5, Jalmar Press. Used with permission from Jalmar Press.

Chapter Two

~~~~~~~~~~~~~~~~~~

Implementation

The principal of an urban junior high school, concerned about his students' poor academic performance and increasingly serious behavioral problems, decided to create a school-wide advisory program. Well intentioned, he nevertheless made a critical mistake by making this decision unilaterally without informing his staff or seeking their input.

Instead, he announced that in two weeks time all teachers would be assigned advisory groups of 15 to 18 students with whom they would meet weekly for 45 minutes. To educate them about the program he asked a social worker from a nearby community-based organization to address the staff and give them literature about the concept. She was then to be outstationed at the school to oversee this program and to provide whatever staff development she deemed necessary.

I was that social worker. I quickly (and ruefully) learned that the teachers I was to train were underwhelmed by this prospect. While some were curious about the groups and a few actually agreed with the principal that they might help address student concerns, there was so much resentment about the way advisories were initiated that it literally took years to overcome their resistance and to build a viable program. Clearly, this is not the ideal way for a school to undertake an intervention as challenging as advisories. The literature is emphatic that the programs that work are those built from the ground up by staff who are invested in the process. Such programs may be initially piloted on a small scale, but they must eventually be "owned" by all staff. If not, they are at risk of being sabotaged by participants and nonparticipants alike.

The experience of the teachers in the opening vignette mirrors what Cole (1994) found as she interviewed more than 200 middle

school teachers about their attitudes toward advisory programs before they were implemented in their schools. While more than three
fourths believed that their schools needed this initiative, fewer than
two thirds were willing to take on an advisory role themselves. Their
biggest concern was time—both that advisories would require significant planning and that the groups would result in a loss of instructional time. About one fourth were also concerned that they
lacked the knowledge and skills they perceived to be needed to
facilitate advisory groups.

The focus of this chapter is to outline the steps a school might
take in implementing an advisory program and the roles that district
staff, school administrators, teachers, and support personnel play at
each stage of the process:

- Conducting a needs assessment and determining the role of
  advisories in meeting them,
- Introducing the advisory concept,
- Determining programmatic goals and objectives,
- Addressing staff development needs,
- Piloting a program, and
- Evaluating its effectiveness.

Needs Assessment: Are Advisories Helpful to the School? How?

If you are thinking about beginning an advisory program in your
school, you are undoubtedly asking yourself one or more of these
questions: Would our school benefit from such an approach? How
can administrators and teachers be certain that initiating this program
will meet our student and staff needs? Are advisories better geared
for some schools than others?

Certainly very large schools will be well served by advisories that
create small, caring communities and promote intimacy. Other obvious possibilities are schools in which students struggle with a disproportionate share of problems that affect their academic performance,
school behaviors, or attendance. Yet is it only middle schools and
high schools with problems that need advisories? We have witnessed
the challenges adolescents experience as they make two critical educational transitions: the first from elementary to middle school and
the second as they enter high school. We have also all witnessed the
disastrous consequences which can result when students do not feel

they are accepted by peers or adult authority figures, as evidenced by the rash of student shootings over the past few years. It is difficult to imagine a school that would not be improved by initiating a program designed to support students in their collective journeys.

Administrators must first confer with staff, parents, and students to collectively determine the school's needs. Once these have been identified, prospective remedies can be researched both through the literature on school reform and through learning about programs initiated in comparable schools that seem to be having positive results in helping students to succeed. Assuming that consensus is reached on piloting an advisory program, the approach must next be introduced and fully explained to staff and parents.

Introducing the Advisory Concept

Advisories may be introduced to a school in numerous ways. In some schools, principals take on this role. In others, one or more teachers may propose them. The local district office might encourage principals to incorporate advisories, especially if they discern larger systemic problems that they believe this initiative could redress. A single parent in one middle school convinced the principal to create an advisory program there. In another instance, high school students requested the groups because they had participated in them in their feeder schools and wanted them to continue. Intrigued, the principal asked the middle school staff developer to address her faculty; and when 16 of them decided to be trained as facilitators, their advisory program was born.

The challenge, of course, is to fan the initial spark of interest into an enduring flame by building support for the idea among all involved. Advisories clearly do not thrive when imposed on staff, as graphically illustrated in the earlier scenario. They do not succeed when staff feel unsure about what advisories are in the first place, consider themselves to be inadequately prepared to facilitate their groups, or unsupported by their administration in their efforts to become advisors.

The Role of District Administration

Occasionally a district superintendent or his immediate staff perceives the potential advantage of advisory programs and insists that principals initiate them in their schools. The principals may comply without fully supporting their implementation. In my own district-wide experience several years ago, this was the case in one of the five schools in which I worked. Not suprisingly, I was least effective in building a quality program there even though the staff had seemed extremely interested and involved in the initial staff development and early phases of the program.

How can district administrators who want to see advisories initated encourage principals and teachers to do so without imposing the program on them? It would seem important for the superintendent to review with his/her principals the current satus of the district students.

- How are they doing academically compared to young adolescents in other, comparable districts?
- Within the district, how are students in different schools performing academically vis-a-vis one another?
- How do students' behavioral problems manifest themselves and where are they greatest?
- What is being done to address these problems?
- Are referrals increasing or decreasing district wide?
- Are behavioral problems particularly severe in any specific schools?
- What initiatives have already been implemented in respective schools, and how well are these working to increase student motivation to participate and succeed in school?
- Might there be room to try the advisory approach? If so, should it be piloted in one school and studied for a couple of years, then introduced into others if it proves effective?
- Is this an approach that might provide relief for all concerned?

To summarize, district staff who do not want to impose their programs, but seek instead to obtain a "buy-in" from principals, must find a way to build consensus for advisories which collaboratively a) identifes the issues with which schools are already struggling, b) acknowledges the very real efforts being made to date to address these issues, c) educates school administrators about the possible benefits of advisory programs, and d) introduces a plan to pilot them with adequate resources in the spirit of scientific inquiry.

The Principal's Role

Principals who want to establish a school-wide advisory program must themselves model the advisory role for their staff. They can do so by thoroughly explaining the concept of advisories and inviting staff to judge whether they meet the needs assessed. Facilitating this process via questioning, paraphrasing, seeking clarification as necessary, and actively listening is essential to setting the tone of acceptance and safety that staff-advisors are to establish with their students.

Realizing that an advisory program may be warranted and will need considerable preparation, the principal may appoint an advisory coordinator—ideally a staff person who has expressed interest in the position and volunteers for it. The principal might well bring in outside speakers, experts in middle school reform, and/or representatives from schools already implementing advisories to explain the purpose and potential scope of the program to staff. The principal also oversees the dissemination of information about advisories to parents and may wish to establish a fact-finding committee comprised of parents, staff, and students to consider whether this approach would benefit their school.

Finally, principals model exemplary facilitation by modifying their roles as the developmental process evolves. The roles a principal can play include conveying the importance of advisories to staff, parents, and the community; providing necessary resources; exhibiting an understanding of the program; providing sufficient space and time within the school schedule; promoting staff development; scheduling common planning time; and evaluating the program. Those principals who themselves are trained to run advisories provide the most genuine support of all.

Planning/Structuring the Advisory Program

Galassi, Gulledge, and Cox (1998) studied numerous advisory programs and discovered that they could be categorized based on the needs they addressed. They have identified six types of advisories:

1. Advocacy—meeting students' affective needs
2. Community—also meeting affective needs
3. Skills—meeting both affective and cognitive needs
4. Invigoration—affective needs
5. Academic—cognitive needs
6. Administrative—meeting administrative needs

Each type of advisory implies different time commitments, goals, advisor skills, and potential activities. Based on the their assessment, each school can determine which advisory approach will work best. It is also possible that different advisors may wish to take different routes, depending on their respective interests, strengths, and liabilities.

Burkhardt (1999) has compiled a checklist of questions that may help administrators, staff, and students plan and implement their programs:

1. What is the school's mission statement regarding advocacy?
2. What should the advisory program mission statement say to be consistent with the school's?
3. What are the basic responsibilities of an advisor?
4. Who will coordinate/maintain the advisory program for the school?
5. How will advisory groups be formed?
6. When will the groups meet?

The Principal's Role

The next step is to establish the goals for the prospective advisory program. Here, too, the administrator must take more of a facilitative role, encouraging the aforementioned committees to report back on their findings and encouraging them to take ownership of the advisory concept. This approach also sends a powerful message to teachers and staff that they possess the necessary abilities to solve the logistical problems inherent in beginning this program. As Bergmann and Baxter (1983) note, "Skillful leadership means that staff members do not perceive the advisory concept as administratively mandated. The principal should be viewed as an enthusiastic role model, coach, and facilitator of resources" (p. 51).

When the school-wide committee of one middle school had planned an advisory program, many staff rejected it as requiring too much in the way of counseling students. The principal then suggested that a steering committee be selected by the staff to rethink the program and to establish goals that the teachers could embrace. This step ultimately proved successful in gaining support for the program.

Staff Roles: Program Coordination

Gill and Read (1990) surveyed middle school advisory program experts about their opinions regarding implementation. The obstacle to effective advisory implementation most commonly cited was reluctant ownership of the initiative by staff. Staff development was critical in building teachers' sense of program ownership. They believed that a committee should be formed to supervise the advisory program, which most believed should meet three to four times a week for up to 25 minutes per session. Many also felt that advisories should meet in the morning and that an advisor should work with the same students throughout their middle school years. They agreed that the group size was ideally 11 to 15 students; but they split on the question of who should be advisors, with half saying all staff members and the other half listing only those who were certified.

Others contend that an advisory program is best coordinated by the school counselor to ensure a continuum of psychosocial services to students. From this perspective, the advisory might serve as a "prereferral system" to the counselor. One book that is very useful to school staff interested in either beginning or retooling an advisory program is *Adviser-Advisee: Why, What and How* by Michael James (1986). In it, the author details several different types of programs—how they are structured, staffed, scheduled—and also answers often-asked questions about their implementation. Ultimately, while organizational theory and others' experience offer substantive guides, school staff are going to have to make their final choices based on trial and error to determine what works best for them.

Finally, advisories have to fit into the school's existing support services infrastructure. Because advisors are advocates, not counselors, they represent a school's first line of defense against student problems that may impact on the system as well as the individual. These groups augment the services provided by guidance counselors, school social workers, and psychologists, who in turn must help teachers and other staff differentiate between the types of problems feasibly addressed in advisories and those that should be referred to the counseling staff.

Addressing Staff Development Needs

Staff development is essential and should encompass a number of different areas. First of all, advisors need to be experts about adolescent developmental issues to promote their students' academic achievement. Secondly, whereas most teachers who understand what this age group needs may appreciate the inherent value of the advisory group, they must also recognize the link between affective and cognitive learning. Without this understanding, they are likely to view advisories as an infringement upon classroom time that students cannot afford. Third, staff are primarily content experts and thus need to be trained in process observation to successfully facilitate these groups. This is probably especially true for secondary teachers who

may feel poorly prepared to serve as teacher advisors. Most
of their education focused on helping them become experts
in their areas of specialization. Typically they will have received less preparation than elementary-certified teachers
in understanding and responding to students' nonacademic
problems, interests and concerns: (MacIver & Epstein, 1993,
p. 594)

Advisory training must address what characterizes the advisory
group, include actual group participation, and provide practice in
facilitational skills and in selecting appropriate activities and exercises for students. This requires a considerable investment of time.
Too often advisory training is a rushed affair offered over a day or
two and thus fails to prepare advisors for the depth of the needs of
their advisees.

The scope and type of staff development should be tailored to
the overall advisory program goals. Helping students develop their
"life skills" requires that staff be trained in basic counseling skills
with follow-up supervision and booster in-service sessions. This type
of ongoing opportunity to share experiences and to give and receive
mutual support is key to a vibrant, growing advisory program.

Staff Development Provided by Community-Based Mental Health Professionals

Evaluations of programs designed to teach problem-solving skills
indicate that they do promote students' mental health when deliv-
ered consistently over a period of several weeks by staff who are
trained by mental health professionals. In some schools, staff social
workers or psychologists may be willing to train advisors and follow
up with regular support and supervision.

University Partnerships

There is much that can and must be done at the preservice training level of teachers and counselors to better prepare educators to
work with the whole child. Many states currently do not require
middle school licensure and their preservice teacher preparation may
be seriously deficient in the recognition of the needs of this age
group and how they might be met affectively and intellectually. In
one study of students graduating from the universities that provide
more than half of all middle-level teacher preparation in the United
States, nearly three fourths of the graduate felt they were not prepared to become advisors.

Nor can new teachers necessarily hope to gain a positive perspective on the value of advisories from their colleagues. Regrettably, it is often those teachers with the greatest number of years experience who are most negative about advisories, in part because their own teacher training did not prepare them for the responsibility. Ironically, college students who do their field placements in schools with advisory programs often say that this is the role they most enjoy.

Another alternative is for a middle school or high school to partner with a university that offers staff a course designed to prepare them as group facilitators on either a graduate level or as part of a school's continuing education mandate. For staff with bachelors degrees, training might be done at the graduate level, possibly paid for by the school or the district. Staff who are paraprofessionals and do not have an undergraduate degree, or those who have already earned a graduate degree, might opt to take advisory training to meet their continuing education requirements. This course might encompass the following areas:

- Defining advisories
- Identifying early adolescent concerns and issues and how these might be addressed in advisories
- Delineating the distinctions between classroom and advisory roles
- Addressing group process issues: atmosphere, participation levels, decision-making, influence
- Learning the stages of group development
- Practicing facilitation techniques: active listening, modeling
- Feedback, clarifying, questioning, reframing, deepening, partializing, generalizing
- Assessing one's leadership style
- Examining different roles group members play and their respective functions
- Understanding one's own reactions as a means to determine the motives for student behaviors
- Identifying and appropriately referring at-risk children for additional treatment

I currently teach a 3-credit graduate course on advisory group facilitation to middle school teachers on-site through Kean University in New Jersey. It requires that the staff run their own advisory groups simultaneously (beginning in the 5th week of the course) and provides ongoing feedback/supervision as they progress. In addition, the staff devote a portion of each training session to actually becoming an advisory group themselves. This enables them to better understand advisories from both an intellectual and emotional perspective and to further identify with how their advisees may be feeling. Although there is evidence that shorter courses can favorably predispose teachers to becoming advisors and increase their confidence as advisors, facilitation is a complex process that requires considerable practice over time.

Piloting the Program

Who Become Advisors?

Someone once observed that any time we try to effect systemic change, there will be 20 % of those involved in favor of it, 20 % who will never agree to it, and 60 % who will initially sit out and observe how it goes, reserving judgment until they are clear that the innovation is worthwhile. Advisories are no exception.

Time and again it has been demonstrated that an advisory program has a better chance of succeeding if it is piloted very carefully and thoughtfully with staff who are committed to its success, who then experience positive results, and become the program's champions to their peers. In one school in which I was asked to do staff development, a group of four 7th grade teachers decided to be trained as advisors. They were so enthusiastic about the results and the improvement in their relationships with their students that they encouraged their colleagues to get involved, and by the next semester an additional 16 staff had agreed to become advisors.

Not every teacher should assume this role, however. There are staff who don't want to take on this responsibility. There are others who do but whose personal issues compromise their effectiveness in facilitation. These individuals, fortunately, tend to eliminate themselves from consideration as advisors and to be supported in this decision by their colleagues. Staff who are not involved will have to assume other administrative responsibilities to alleviate the load on those teachers who do become advisors.

On the other hand, it is certainly possible that ambivalent or even negative staff can learn to enjoy the advisory role far more than they might have anticipated. One resource room teacher was initially very resistant to being forced to become an advisor and for over a year expressed strong resentment. Gradually, however, he began to see changes in his students' behaviors toward one another that he attributed to their advisory group membership. He started using structured activities; and when these were successful, he became much more positive about the advisory experience overall.

New schools have the advantage of hiring staff with the understanding that part of their responsibilities will include an advisory role. Most schools, however, begin this initiative long after the fact, with staff of varying lengths of service and certainly very different attitudes about groupwork. While there are pluses and minuses to beginning advisories on a school-wide basis, my experience is that overall it is advantageous to initially enlist only those staff interested and willing to participate. The most immediate problem with this approach is that working with a limited number of teachers and students in advisories creates tremendous scheduling challenges.

Sometimes administrators who strongly believe in the program may take very forceful steps in staffing advisories. One principal, who learned about the initiative at the National Middle School Conference, set up a coordinating committee at his school to study the program's feasibility, and to then implement it. At that time, he gave all his staff the option of either remaining at the school and being trained as advisors or transferring elsewhere.

The Advisory "Curriculum"

Many teachers are more comfortable as advisors if their groups resemble what is already familiar to them (classes), allowing them to draw upon skills they already possess (teaching/curriculum development). To accommodate these preferences, many schools rely on prepackaged programs or those developed in-house that may meet a school's overall needs but not necessarily those of individual groups. This approach creates the risk that advisors will not be responsive to what their group members most want to discuss and thus, these advisories become another missed opportunity. As Burkhardt (1999) notes, "Too many advisory programs foundered because advisory was seen as a curriculum to be covered rather than a relationship to be nurtured" (p. 52).

In some schools, advisories are structured so that certain topics are covered across the board in each grade (for example, getting familiar with middle school in 6th grade, building communication skills in 7th grade, preparing to transition to high school in 8th grade). There is nothing inherently wrong in this type of organization. It is well intentioned and based on teachers' understanding of what typical students will be experiencing at various points of their middle school and high school careers, but students' interest will be greatest when they determine the curriculum as the year unfolds and have a say in the topics they choose to discuss. Killin and Williams (1995) agree,

> The curriculum seems to work best when it changes to meet the needs of the students and the school. Students are surveyed to determine what issues are pertinent to them, and school-wide issues are identified by staff members. These concerns are then added to the curriculum. (p. 47)

This is surely riskier for all concerned and undoubtedly anxiety provoking to many staff, but it ensures that advisories are truly addressing students' needs. Given the fact that many adolescents find it difficult to articulate what's bothering them, advisors must be trained as process observers who can listen between the lines, attend to both verbal and non-verbal cues, and trust both themselves and their students to identify and express what is really on the latter's minds.

The bottom line is that the advisor deserves to feel comfortable in expressing his or her own style. If this means advising by using structured activities each session, at least until the process becomes more familiar and comfortable, then so be it. If it means consulting with the health education teacher to parallel what is being taught in that class in a way that promotes additional discussion, problem solving, and behavioral practice, this too is an option. If members of a school department or house feel they need to meet to plan general topics on specific dates, this is yet another possibility.

A computer teacher in one school with a new advisory program initially rejected the idea of being an advisor until he realized that he had excellent values clarification software and could structure his groups by asking students to work independently doing self-assessment exercises for 15 minutes and then convene as a group to talk about them. It isn't a classical approach to groupwork, but it was a start. Gradually, as he became more familiar with the process, he reduced and then ultimately gave up the computer time and focused solely on the group.

Staff who feel best using activities recommended by guidance or other counselors can certainly do so. In many schools one person— often a school counselor, prepares activities to be used in advisory— including worksheets, community service project materials, and so forth. Given what we are learning about multiple intelligences, it seems reasonable to assume that varying advisory activities increases group members' means of contributing to the group's success and enjoying increased acceptance as a result.

One might include role playing, using values clarifications exercises, watching films and discussing them, allowing students to take turns acting as leaders, using a box into which students drop their suggested topics and using these to direct discussion, challenging other advisory groups to sports or academic competitions, taking trips, preparing meals as a group. The possibilities are endless. What matters is that students come to feel that the group is theirs and that it has a clear identity.

> Advisory team-building activities—inter-advisory contests that involve car-pushing, bubble-gum blowing, name that tune, guess that teacher, and marshmallow/toothpick house building—occur throughout the year. Advisory teachers help their advisees start each day right, advise students on class schedules, hold conferences with advisees' parents, and assist advisees with developing their career plans. (Schoenlein, 2001, p. 29)

How Advisories "Fit" into the School Structure

In a middle school where I have worked for the past 2 years, the biggest obstacle is that the teachers who have been trained as advisors have decided collectively that they want to remain with their advisory students for all 4 years they are at the school. The program does not exist school wide, however; and each year, as students move on to the next grade, they are assigned to different homerooms. There are no periods dedicated to group sessions; and advisors find it virtually impossible to meet with their students during any one period, since everyone is in different classes.

There are other potential impediments. One advisor said she felt the experience to be somewhat stressful because of systemic obstacles:

> At times I was expected to incorporate new students into my group without warning. I've also had miscommunications with my advisory partner about who was supposed to work with what students. I have also had students removed from my advisory, then reinstated, with no prior notification, disrupting the continuity for that student as well as for the rest of the group. I hope that next year there will be more internal and external support.

Such experiences can lead teachers to believe that their advisory program is very expendable.

Likewise, sometimes unavoidable school events negatively impact advisories. One teacher wrote that the loss of several staff members during the course of the school year forced a restructuring of the school's advisories, with several students being redistributed to other groups. Many expressed their unhappiness about losing their groups, but scheduling problems apparently proved insurmountable.

Logistical concerns such as where the groups will be held and how much it will cost to provide coverage for teacher-advisors are always among the first questions staff ask, and to some degree the answers will depend on the facility. I have worked in schools where every child was in advisory, all groups met simultaneously, and groups used every existing space—the library, the cafeteria, the auditorium (in front of and behind the stage), administrators' offices, the nurse's office, and every classroom. In one badly overcrowded school one group actually met in a stairwell, although for obvious reasons this is far from ideal. Of course, in schools where only selected students participate or where groups meet at differing times, the space issues are more easily addressed.

Scheduling

There are countless ways in which advisories may be scheduled, ranging from once or twice a month to twice daily. Likewise the length of group sessions may vary from as little as 10 to 15 minutes to an hour each. Staff at the University Heights High School have chosen to make their advisory program a credit-bearing course. Another high school runs its advisory programs for only 13 minutes daily, but their teacher-advisors also stay with their students the full four years and actually present them with their diplomas when they graduate. Students' attention spans can vary greatly and sometimes longer sessions undoubtedly feel endless but if the goal of these groups is really to foster enhancement of the life skills described in chapter 1, it is difficult to understand how this can be accomplished in very brief group sessions. James (1986) suggests that the length of advisory time should be twice the number of participants involved (that is, groups of 15 students should meet 30 minutes per session).

One must also wonder what kind of systemic message is sent by school administrators when the groups are set to meet very briefly, more like expanded homeroom periods than real group experiences. In the school in which I worked for 3 years, the weekly advisory period became the dumping ground for all sorts of school-wide administrative obligations—that is, school pictures, returning forms to the office, and so forth The message to the students and staff was very clear: We're doing advisories because the superintendent and principal say we have to, but we don't really believe in them.

In some programs, advisories are scheduled daily but only 1 or 2 of these days are devoted to group discussion and the other time is spent reading, journaling, doing community service, meeting individually with the advisor, or doing academic enrichment exercises. The variety of approaches to advisories makes it both intriguing and difficult to grasp conceptually, because there simply is no one prescribed method for implementation.

There are a number of ways that group coverage can be provided. Teachers not assuming advisory roles can take over other administrative duties, freeing advisors to see their groups. Creative scheduling may be another solution. In one school, two 7th-grade homeroom teacher-advisors, who each wanted to work with all of the students in their official classes, were able to arrange for half of each class to go to physical education in one period while the teachers did advisories with the other half, then the following period, the advisory students went to physical education and the others came to group. In schools that utilize block scheduling, principals may allot a certain number of minutes from class for advisory. In other schools, teachers voluntarily forfeit a prep period. The list goes on.

Evaluating Advisories' Effectiveness in Meeting School Goals

When trying to evaluate and to possibly reconfigure an existing advisory program, it makes sense to ask students themselves to rate their groups. In one study conducted in an urban middle school, students who had participated in advisories told researchers that they wanted

- Their own, safe space where they wouldn't be overheard or interrupted by nonmembers or other staff;
- To talk and to have input into the topics discussed;
- Their advisor to talk to them because they felt that it was in this way that staff demonstrated that they cared about the students. They liked it when their advisors questioned them about their statements and also when their leaders talked about themselves personally;
- Variety and enjoyed it when discussion sessions were mixed with activities;

- The opportunity to do things as a group, taking field trips, competing against other advisories—experiences that reinforced their sense of group identity;
- Same-sex groups, even though girls were apprehensive that they might not be able to trust other girls to maintain confidentiality;
- Their advisors *not* to encourage discussion about the subject they taught and, in fact, some students weren't sure they even wanted to be in advisories with their teachers, especially if their classroom relationships were problematic;
- Not to discuss highly personal subjects unless or until they indicated a willingness to do so;
- The freedom to discuss subjects that were developmentally relevant to them, recognizing that by 8th grade they were interested in talking about subjects they wouldn't have felt comfortable discussing earlier;
- Advisors they could trust, who could relate to them, who cared enough to be a friend, who were respectful and funny;
- To avoid those advisors who were indiscrete, lacked control, or were disrespectful; and
- Advisors who were strong enough leaders to maintain control in their group and help them feel safe.

Another school developed a "card sorting" method of evaluating advisories with North Carolina University researchers (Galassi, Thornton, Sheffield, Bryan, & Oliver, 1998). Their results indicated that students across grades looked to advisories for "invigoration," having fun and taking a break from academics. Teachers' rankings delineated differences by grade. Sixth grade teachers ranked guidance in achieving academic, behavioral, and social goals as their highest advisor priority, whereas those working with 7th and 8th graders were most interested in developing one-on-one relationships with their students and fulfilling more of an advocacy role. Although the students' and teachers' interests do not closely align, neither are they mutually exclusive.

In many respects, evaluating an advisory program is much like measuring effects of other educational interventions. It is necessary to first recall the advisory program's goals and objectives . Advisories are dedicated to enhancing students' academic, emotional, and social well-being—goals that take time to achieve. In addition to the minimum of 1 year's planning time, it seems reasonable to implement advisories for at least 2 or 3 years, modifying the design throughout the process as needed, before making a judgment about whether your school, its students, and its staff have benefitted from them.

Evaluating an advisory program's success in meeting these goals suggests the benefit of following a student cohort throughout its school experience, comparing grades, behavioral referrals, attitudes toward school, and teacher attitudes at the end of their final year with those of students graduating the spring before the program was implemented. Thereafter, the program, like any other school component, should be reviewed and evaluated regularly, probably annually, by administrators, faculty, nonteaching staff, students, and parents.

Questions Frequently Asked by School Personnel and Parents When Considering an Advisory Program

1. If all students are not involved, how will the participating students be scheduled into advisories?

This is not necessarily a problem. What often happens is that advisors divide up official classes for their groups, then schedule group sessions based on times that are mutually agreed upon. Other teams do the same. Thus there are advisories meeting on different days, at a variety of times, but students can count on their group meeting consistently at the same time weekly.

2. Do advisors stay with the same group for the duration of students' school experience or does the advisory groups' composition change annually?

Every school looks at this question individually and, indeed, sometimes different houses within the same school will vary. In one urban junior high school which had implemented a house system, the teachers in one house elected to stay with their same students all three years and those in other houses switched annually. Many teachers believe it is advantageous to continue with the same group of students throughout their tenure at a school, but this works only if all students are involved in advisories.

3. Are advisory programs always group based or does the advisor also meet with students face-to-face?

There are proponents of advisories who believe strongly that one-to-one contact must also be built into this initiative. One approach, in programs that meet several times a week, is to schedule a silent reading session once weekly; and during that time, the advisor meets with 3 or more students individually to check on how they are doing and to provide some quality personal time. A study of one urban advisory program in New York City concluded that the absence of one-to-one advisor-student conferences compromised the program's ability to connect with students affectively. Many other programs do not include individual relationships, however, and still have a real impact on participating students and staff.

Those programs that do feature one-to-one relationships with students obviously imply greater responsibility on the part of the advisors. A study compared a well-run program in which advsiors met regularly in groups only with another program that included one-to-one meetings scheduled inconsistently. Students in the former program showed improvement in their GPAs, enjoyment of extracurricular activities, and decreased levels of depression. Whereas, their counterparts in the second school reported higher GPAs but no other positive results.

4. What is the optimal size advisory group?

Groupwork theory suggests that the optimal group size is 8 to 10 students. Realistically, this is difficult to accomplish in many schools in which class sizes can approach (or even exceed) 30 students. Ideally the groups should not be larger than 12 students, if the goals are to promote the kind of self-awareness, communication, and problem-solving skills discussed. When surveyed, several middle-level leaders felt the ideal size group was 11 to 15. Unfortunately, groups are often larger; and when this is the case, size may very well limit the intensity and type of discussion which take place.

5. What happens if an advisor is absent?

If at all possible, that advisor should try to make up his or her advisory group as soon as possible. No one else should try to substitute for him or her during the scheduled advisory session, however. To do this negates the powerful dynamics inherent in group work and also trivializes the meaning of the advisory. Group leaders are not interchangeable, nor are its members. The session should simply be rescheduled when that advisor is back in school.

6. Should advisors attend parent/teacher conferences?

This depends on the advisory model selected by the school's staff. In some advisory programs the advisor is the person who meets with parents, calls home when there's a need, and generally runs interference if problems arise for the student. In such cases, they would definitely attend parent conferences and, indeed, might be the only staff person to do so. In other schools, the advisor has a much smaller role and meets with students only once weekly. They might not ever meet parents.

My own opinion is that the advisor should be the one person to whom parents can and do contact to inquire about their child and to ensure that his or her school needs are addressed. Many parents find schools intimidating and don't know how to negotiate the system, particularly if their own school experiences were less than positive. Having one person to contact and to be contacted by is a much more "user friendly" approach to engaging parents.

7. Will groups be same-sex or mixed?

There is some literature on group process that suggests that girls prefer same-sex groups while boys are more comfortable with the sexes mixed. There is also evidence that the two sexes seek different qualities in advisors. One research team discovered that girls wanted advisors who demonstrated their caring by talking to them about what happened at school, and boys were most comfortable with advisors who used considerable, albeit respectful, humor.

The truth is that logistical issues often make it difficult to separate the sexes. My personal opinion is that it would possibly be beneficial to try running same sex groups for younger students who have a number of physical, social, and sexual questions which they might find easier to discuss with their same-sex peers than in mixed groups. One factor which might mitigate against this (or be one more reason why groups should be same-sex, depending on your perspective) is that girls often claim that they don't trust each other to keep secrets and feel more comfortable sharing with male friends. Truthfully, everyone has a different opinion on this; and there's no reason why different staff at the same school couldn't experiment with both types, then determine which seems to meet students' needs most effectively.

8. Should groups be multi-age?

You will make this decision based on what your objectives are for your advisory program. If, for example, you wish to create a strong sense of unity for students within a certain grade, particularly if you hope to maintain an intact group for more than one year, you will confine yourself to one grade per group. On the other hand, you might be hoping to develop a sense of mentoring or more of a peer advisory approach, in which case it may be advantageous to mix grades.

9. What do I do with a student who refuses to participate in my advisory and asks not to be included?

Any student may potentially feel this way at some point in the advisory group experience, and before you can decide how to address this issue you need to understand the student's underlying concerns. The basic facilitational skills we will cover in chapter 5, most fundamentally active listening, will help you to decipher what this student is experiencing; and hopefully your skills, in time, will help him or her to feel more comfortable in your group. If your student is one whose problems are considerable and exceed the parameters of what your advisory can provide, you have the option of making a referral for individual or group counseling; or, if your school resources dictate, it may be possible to organize a special advisory group for students with similar issues.

In one school in which I worked, there was an exceptionally gifted young male psychologist who thrived on working with disaffected students. He understood them, he appreciated them, and they returned the sentiment. Early on every year he would send a memo around to teacher-advisors asking them to send him those students with whom they were having special problems in their groups. They did and while initially some expressed a feeling of being stigmatized by being in the psychologist's group, he was so caring and adept that they quickly came to appreciate his involvement. It proved to be a win-win situation, particularly since he was also generous in his efforts to help staff work with students who acted out their difficult feelings.

10. How will issues of confidentiality be handled?

This is a very, very important issue in any type of groupwork, and must be addressed with students in the first group session. In general, what is said in an advisory group remains confidential. The only exceptions are if a student confides that he or she is thinking of hurting him or herself or someone else or if it is clear that a student is being abused physically or sexually. These potential issues will be addressed later in the book.

11. What happens if a student wishes to switch from one advisory group to another?

As a general rule, students are expected to stay with their advisory group but there are certainly exceptions. If there is a serious conflict between that student and the advisor which supervision fails to resolve or, similarly, if there are problems between that student and another which appear to be intractable, a move might be recommended. Before doing so, however, the advisor will want to use all of his or her facilitational skills to understand the nature of the problem and to try to resolve it, using the other students in the process whenever possible.

Conclusion

From the initial realization that creating an advisory program might be helpful to a school's culture, through its introduction to staff, students, and parents, preparing staff to run the groups, piloting the program, and finally evaluating it, the key to making advisories work is collaboration. Teacher ownership is critical to success. The bottom line is that this program will not succeed without teachers' and administrators' wholehearted endorsement. Moreover, staff must be part of the planning and implementation process.

It may be frustrating to some readers to continually hear that there isn't one specific way to develop an advisory program, but therein lies its challenge and potential. No two advisory programs look exactly alike. They can and must be tailored to meet the demands of individual schools to ensure that everyone's voice is heard and respected.

Chapter Three
~~~~~~~~~~~~~~~~~~~~~~

What Kind of a Leader
Will I Be?

Who was your most memorable teacher growing up? What was it about this person that made you like him or her so much? When teacher-advisors are asked this question in the facilitation training course, they often recall individuals who cared passionately about their subject matter, made learning fun, were respectful of students yet demanded a great deal academically from them. Almost inevitably, they also remark on the fact that these teachers went above and beyond the role of teacher to provide some kind of special interest in them as individuals. Is this true for you, too? Conversely, if you were to think back on a teacher you disliked, you might describe one who was uncaring, lazy, sarcastic, and seemed to enjoy publicly humiliating students—the antithesis of what we might look for in our educators and certainly those teachers who also shoulder the responsibility for leading advisory groups.

Not surprisingly, the same qualities we prized in our teachers and indeed try to emulate in our own classroom work are those which we carry with us to our advisory experience. The most successful advisors are those who are genuine, demonstrate unconditional positive regard for their students—whatever their behaviors—and exhibit congruence between what they are feeling and how they behave.

In this chapter we will review several different aspects of advisory group leadership. In addition to the qualities we would hope to embody as skilled facilitators, we will imagine how these might translate into different leadership skills. Next we will consider leadership styles, inviting you to decide which most closely describes yours and examining the potential benefits and liabilities associated with each.

Qualities Embodied in "Good" Advisors

While the following is not an exhaustive list of preferred qualities in an advisor, it does give us an idea of what we ideally "bring to the table" when we begin our groups. Above all, as teacher-advisors, we want to know our students better and to become a positive force in their lives by sharing our own broad life experience with different types of people and groups, exhibiting good planning and organizational skills, and demonstrating confidence in group process.

Whether we function as teachers, administrators, support school staff, counselors, or advisors, we are our own instruments. Our capabilities in working effectively with our students will largely depend on how well we know and accept ourselves. The better we do, the more likely we will be to embody these essential characteristics.

Many of us are familiar with the Johari Window and its illustration of the fact that we all have facets of our personalities that are open to us and to others, contrasted with other information that is known to others through what we say and do but, unfortunately, to which we ourselves are blind. Then there is that which we choose to keep personal and will not share with students or colleagues. Finally, there is deeper level material—repressed experiences or feelings which are genuinely unknown to either ourselves or to others. The assumption is that we seek to increase our "open" areas as much as possible to enhance our genuineness, tact, congruence, and unconditional positive regard for others.

	THE JOHARI WINDOW	
	KNOWN TO SELF	UNKNOWN TO SELF
KNOWN TO OTHERS	OPEN	BLIND
UNKNOWN TO OTHERS	HIDDEN	UNKNOWN

From Group Processes: *An Introduction to Group Dynamics,* Third Edition by Joseph Luft. Copyright 1984 by Joseph Luft. Reprinted by permission of Mayfield Publishing Company.

Genuineness

Genuineness implies honesty. When we are with someone who is genuine, we know we can trust that person. There are no hidden agendas, and it is a far more relaxing encounter than interacting with an individual who seems to be presenting a public persona that does not reflect what he or she may really be feeling.

Tact

Tact is essential in skilled facilitation, particularly in the timing of interventions and their focus. An advisor who is genuine is one who is able to access his or her true feelings and express them in an assertive, helpful manner which considers the feelings of others.

Congruence

Genuineness is closely related to congruence and may be thought of as the fit between what one is feeling and expresses. We have probably all been in the uncomfortable position of talking with someone who professes to feel one way, but gives off verbal and nonverbal cues which seem to belie what they profess. There are a number of reasons why individuals might act incongruently. They may be blind to their real feelings, or they may recognize them but not feel comfortable admitting them. They might feel that they are expected to act in a particular way under specific circumstances, regardless of what they are really experiencing. Whatever the source of the disparity between feelings and actions, it creates a dissonant and ineffective communication.

Unconditional Positive Regard

It is also imperative that as facilitators we are able to express unconditional positive regard to all our advisory students. This requires that at the very least we understand how we feel about each group member and that we strive to appreciate every student for the qualities that make him or her unique. In those instances in which we find ourselves unable to do this, we owe it to both ourselves and our student to again refer to the Johari Window's "unknown" area and try to take a closer look. What is it about this student that causes us problems? Does he or she remind us of someone else? Of some quality we suspect we ourselves possess that we're not thrilled about? Unconditional positive regard may be an ideal but it is one worth aspiring to; and if we can reframe such relationships positively as challenges to better understand ourselves, it will undoubtedly help.

Skills Demonstrated by Successful Teacher-Advisors

THE EFFECTIVE TEACHER ADVISOR:

1.   Sincerely cares about all students;

2.   Demonstrates enthusiasm toward all students;

3.   Listens to and values student opinions;

4.   Models respect and effective communication skills;

5.   Guides student self-reflection and group cooperation;

6.   Plans developmentally appropriate advisory activities;

7.   Identifies students needing more intensive guidance and support;

8.   Assesses the progress of the advisory program;

9.   Understands the teacher advisor's role and responsibilities; and

10. Participates in training to improve advisory skills.

The Middle Level Teacher's Handbook. From Hunt, G., Wiseman, D., & Bowden, S. (1998). Springfield, IL: Charles C. Thomas Publisher, Ltd.

Caring About/Demonstrating Enthusiasm for All Members of our Advisory Group

It is by demonstrating these skills that we apply the concept of genuine positive regard. Will there be those students you are fonder of than others? Of course. Will you always feel accepting of the behaviors your students exhibit in group? Probably not. A skilled facilitator, however, is able to appreciate the uniqueness in every group member and to separate the individual from the behavior; thus giving the message that although one may not approve of what a student is doing in the moment, he or she recognizes that the student has much to give that is positive. Our ability to express this skill to our group members frees them to step back and examine their behaviors, too.

As group facilitators, we possess the ability to provide emotional stimulation to our advisory students, defined as activity, risk-taking, and self-disclosure. One advisor, recognizing this fact, commented, "The more attracted and interested a student is to a group, the more the student will get out of the group. I try to make the advisory attractive to students and this takes the ability to connect all group issues, interactions, and process to all students."

Listening to and Valuing our Students' Opinions

To be able to provide this stimulation, we must demonstrate our emotional presence in the group through our listening to, eliciting, and identifying what our students reveal about their beliefs and behaviors. Drawing on our ability to find something about which we care in each of our advisees, we demonstrate our enthusiasm by being "courageous"—allowing our group members to see that we are affected by their actions and expressing confidence in the group's ability to promote change.

Modeling Respect and Effective Communication Skills

As an advisor, it is crucial that one be attuned to what he or she is feeling and able to articulate these feelings if it is in the service of the group's dynamics to do so. This extends to situations in which we might be angry, frustrated, or concerned. While we might not wish to express these feelings outright, we have to be able to recognize them and not act disingenuously. If we decide that we must express them, obviously it is necessary to do so in a way that promotes group member understanding and dialogue. Students are exquisitely sensitive to their teachers' and advisors' reactions and are going to find it difficult to relate honestly to a facilitator who is not able to return the favor.

Guiding Student Self-Reflection and Group Cooperation

One way in which we express this skill is by the aforementioned modeling of respect and good communication skills. These acts help to create a group atmosphere of safety and belonging which frees students to begin thinking about themselves and sharing as they are able to do so. Once this process begins and students themselves feel better able to be genuine and congruent, your group is well on its way. Members begin to care about one another and cooperation evolves very naturally.

Planning Developmentally Appropriate Activities

This skill is two-fold. First of all, this facilitator appreciates what students are experiencing because of their chronological age and seeks to create a group experience that meets their general psychosocial and cognitive needs. Secondly, such a leader also understands where his or her group is developmentally and tailors interventions accordingly.

Identifying Students Needing More Guidance and Support

At this point, suffice it to say that by maintaining a nondefensive curiosity about why students say and do what they do in groups, we can avoid reacting personally. We instead can surface potentially problematic behaviors in a way that helps group members to struggle with them and hopefully better understand their nature. As we do this, it becomes clear which problems are more serious, perhaps too serious to be addressed in the advisory group, but instead require more intensive intervention. We will discuss this topic in greater detail later on in the book.

Assessing the Progress of our Advisory Group

We do this both individually and collectively. We listen to our inner voices as they raise concerns about how our advisory is progressing. We also need to open this process to our students periodically (even weekly) to seek their input about how they feel the group is going. Ideally, we also meet with our colleagues on a regular basis to discuss this concern.

Understanding our Role and Responsibilities

Whatever our particular leadership style, a "good" advisor understands that he or she acts as an advocate for students and as such is responsible for assessing what their needs are both individually and collectively. We are then positioned to help our advisees address whatever might be of concern to them academically, socially, or personally.

Participating in Ongoing Staff Development

Teacher-advisors do not always realize their staff development needs until they are engaged in the process of group facilitation. Suffice it to say that advisement is a challenging and at times complex task, and it is incumbent on us as advisors or program coordinators to be sensitive to the fact that staff need to take care of their own needs first before they attempt this task. We need to know basic facilitational skills before we begin our groups, but we may well also seek additional training during our tenure as advisors.

Group Leadership Roles

These skills enable the facilitator to play a number of roles in guiding an advisory group. Although some of these are used consistently throughout a group's life, others will come into play more in certain stages of group development than others. Failure to adapt as the group matures can lead to a leader's demise. It is up to the advisor to assess and understand students' strengths and deficits and to introduce exercises and activities that meet their needs. This role is most essential during the preaffiliation and power and control phases, but later on the group takes on this function for itself. (Please see chapters 6–10 for an in-depth analysis of how leader roles change as a group develops.)

A related role is the advisor's continual interpretation of where the group is developmentally. This is very important in helping to create a sense of history for the group by reminding members of what they have done in previous sessions and by helping them set goals for upcoming sections throughout the group's life. To do this, the advisor must prepare for each session by reviewing the group's progress to date and by identifying issues or themes that appear to be impinging on the group's growth, with an eye toward helping the group to address these issues.

It is also the role of the facilitator to consistently educate students about the dynamics of their specific advisory session at that point in time. In this way, students are better equipped to assume more of the facilitative role themselves and develop a collective "group wisdom" that enables them to make interventions on their own. In effect, the advisor is like a parent who raises his or her child to become a competent adult.

To play these roles, Peterson (1995) suggests that facilitators

- Remind students about ground rules when interpersonal problems arise that affect the group negatively.
- Ask open-ended questions.
- Always allow students the right not to participate if they are unable or unwilling to do so, but explore the reasons for their reluctance.
- Avoid moralizing or judging.
- Relax and let the group process evolve naturally without feeling that something has to be produced by the end of the session.
- Strive for the best balance between self-disclosure and reflecting back, understanding that too much of the former can make group members feel that it isn't their discussion anymore.
- Model whatever behaviors you wish your group members to exhibit.

- Know when to step in and protect a member from others' comments and when to sit back and let them be heard.
- Offer verbal support to students who need it and encouraging other group members to do the same.
- Handle group conflicts immediately and honestly, using active listening and "I" messages to resolve these issues.
- Paying attention to the individual while also monitoring the verbal and non-verbal responses of the rest of the group.[1]

This last tip refers to what Sigmund Freud called "evenly suspended attention," and is one of the most important roles an advisor can play. It presumes that he or she continually seeks to try to balance the individual needs of students with those of the group as a whole.

If what a student says appears to bore or frighten other group members, for example, the advisor must be aware of this and be prepared to act. Knowing the stage of group development is essential here. In the earlier stages, for example, the facilitator might be aware that a student's behavior is having a negative effect on the others in the group; but because they have not yet become cohesive, he or she may not ask the members to react directly but instead might model an appropriate response.

This can be confusing for facilitators who are torn between trying to listen to students nonjudgmentally but wish to also be protective of students whom others attack. One advisor of a group wished she had "toned down" a student's "autocratic" rebukes toward another student and vowed that in the future she would try harder to let group members voice their opinions without being dominated by any one.

As we will see in chapters 6–10, groups go through very predictable stages. It is essential that as a leader, you understand where your group is developmentally and what is required of you. A student of mine recently told me about a group she had been in at work. During that group's last session, a disagreement broke out between two of the members and then escalated to also involve others. The leader broke down in tears saying, "I don't understand what's wrong with all of you," and then got up and left the group.

Had this facilitator understood that it is not uncommon for a group ambivalent about ending to resurrect previously-resolved conflicts, she would have been much better able to help her group members understand what was happening and work through it. As it was, she apparently personalized their behavior and by leaving the group, prohibited the participants' ability to put closure on their experience.

Leadership Styles

The research on group leadership does not conclude that any one style is superior to others. Although there are advantages and disadvantages to each style, probably the most important point is that every advisor needs to analyze his or her own personality and determine the style that feels most natural.

Imagine a continuum of leadership styles ranging from "leading" at one end to "facilitation" at the other. The advisor who leads is one who attempts to control the group's agenda and activities, much as a classroom teacher would. On the other hand, facilitation encourages students to assume responsibility for themselves and assumes that they have the capabilities to resolve many, if not most, of their problems with support and encouragement from the advisor and other students. It may be that as advisors, you assume more of an authoritative role initially and then gradually relinquish it as the membership feels more confident taking on these responsibilities, much as teachers often do in their classrooms over the course of a semester or school year. As one teacher observed about her own approach,

> I took on different leadership roles to suit the needs of the group. During preaffiiation my role was very directive. As the group became more established I became more democratic. I think my natural style falls between democratic and laissez-faire, but I would have to be sure that the group was ready to maintain itself to a large degree before I would looosen up.

Ballou, Fetter, Litwack, and Litwack (1992) appear to echo this point as they differentiate between effective and ineffective leadership by pointing out that group leaders who lecture, having to be the expert, are rarely successful facilitators.

Autocratic Versus Laissez-Faire Versus Democratic

One way of operationalizing these differences is to contrast autocratic, laissez-faire, and democratic leadership approaches. The autocratic leader determines the problems an advisory will address and decides how they should be resolved, being less interested in the group's process than in whether or not it accomplishes the "tasks" he/she believes the group faces.

A laissez-faire advisor, on the other hand, allows the group to determine both the problems they wish to address as well as their solutions. Such a leader keeps a very low profile. Democratic advisors use their process skills to determine which areas a group appears to need to focus on, then helps the group to do so with some degree of autonomy. Although it is generally assumed that the most effective advisors are more democratic than not, even a strict and highly structured leader who struggles with the question of how much autonomy to allow group members can be effective if they are genuinely caring.

One such teacher-advisor ran his group like a mini-class. Group discussions were mostly between himself and individual students in the group with very little interaction among the group members, which is not an ideal group format. Yet this teacher loved his students, and they knew it. He gave up lunch periods every day to provide them a chance to sit in the classroom and eat quietly with him. He was very strict and by-the-book in his teaching and did no cooperative learning activities in his classes, and he facilitated his advisory groups similarly. While his students would probably have gained considerably more interpersonally from a more democratic leader, they returned his love and respect and seemed to genuinely enjoy their advisory experience.

The autocratic leader is task oriented, competent, strives for excellence, and accomplishes a good deal. On the negative side, he/she often focuses too little on the goals of creating group cohesiveness and often fails to consider student feelings as they emerge, focusing only on the "work to be done." Such advisors are like the teacher who once commented that her advisory group frustrated her because she liked to end a session having accomplished a specific goal, and her group discussions were too open-ended and ambiguous for her comfort level.

The laissez-faire advisor strives most for group cohesiveness, viewing students as being responsible for virtually all decision making. The potential liability with this process orientation is that by refusing to provide any structure such a facilitator can create a leadership vacuum, particularly in the early group stages when no one is clearly responsible for structuring the group's functioning. This condition can initially provoke considerable ambiguity and anxiety among group members.

The democratic facilitator is often more maintenance oriented than either the autocratic or laissez faire advisors and actively tries to help create a comfortable group environment. In this respect, he/she is like a good parent who partners with students to create a sense of fellowship and support for individual group members but also attempts to stay focused on the task at hand. Ultimately, this leader provides structure as needed, with the overall goal of promoting student' "take over" as group decision makers.

There is evidence that the same students will act very differently depending on their group leader's style. Those whose facilitator is autocratic tend to be more dependent on him or her and also more egocentric and hostile than when led by laissez-faire or democratic leaders. Students in a laissez-faire led group also may act more hostilely than do those in democratically led groups, but will often express greater satisfaction with their group experience than those in autocratically led groups. When a group is led democratically, these same students begin to demonstrate more initiative, friendliness, and responsibility, even when working on their own. They like what they are doing more, work harder than do students in either of the other groups, and express the greatest satisfaction with the group experience. One advisor's experience reflects this theory.

> I believe that at various times I demonstrated all three leadership styles. Being a classroom teacher, I am more comfortable setting up a plan for the group to follow. I was very tempted to do just this but this would not have given them a chance to grow and learn. I also attempted to be democratic by trying to get them to suggest the skills they wanted and needed to learn. But my main leadership style was laissez-faire, because most of the time I allowed them to drive the direction of the meetings. This was evident in the fact that most of the discussions centered on what was bothering them at the moment.

It may also be that leadership style is situational to some extent. Depending upon how motivated a group is, how interested they are, and how challenging their task, the leader may need to adjust his style. He/she will assume a less active role as coordinator when members are very interested and challenged, act as inventor when tasks aren't challenging enough to find ways to make them more so, as enthusiast when members aren't that interested in the task, or as director for groups that lack motivation.

Interpersonal Versus Intrapersonal Orientations

One last way we can conceptualize leadership style is to gauge whether it is more interpersonal or intrapersonal. An interpersonal facilitator focuses primarily on interaction among group members and tries to foster this as much as possible. An intrapersonal group leader, on the other hand, focuses more on the needs of individual students.

Groups like advisories actually benefit from both approaches, since their goals are to help students develop personal skills while simultaneously increasing their comfort with peers. In the earliest phase of group development and again as groups move from intimacy into differentiation, it is very helpful for facilitators to assume a more intrapersonal approach; while at other times, we generally focus more interpersonally.

In conclusion, to be effective advisors we need to understand ourselves. The greater our own "open" area, the easier the task of facilitation will be. Whatever our styles and whatever our initial skill levels we must be prepared to be as honest and loving with ourselves as we hope to be with our group members. We must be willing to learn about our intrapsychic dynamics as well as the group's, and we have to be ready to collaborate in this learning process with the students whom we advise.

LEADERSHIP STYLES		
AUTOCRATIC	LAISSEZ-FAIRE	DEMOCRATIC
Task-Oriented	Member-Oriented	Maintenance-Oriented
Dominant	Very low-profile	Active as needed
Strives for excellence	Strives for cohesiveness	Strives for autonomy
Decides what the group needs to do and how to do it	Allows the group to make all decisions for itself	Listens for what members want to do and assists
Not concerned as much with member feelings	Not concerned with task completion	Seeks balance between task completion/ cohesiveness
Group cohesiveness not a concern	May create a leadership vacuum	Provides more structure initially in group life

What Is Your Leadership Style?

Please indicate whether you believe each of these statements is true or false.

1. I would feel most comfortable deciding the topic my advisory group members discuss in a session.   T   F

2. If two students got into a disagreement about what they wanted to talk about, I would say nothing and would let them settle it on their own.   T   F

3. If one student wanted to discuss a particular subject and another did not, I would ask the group to try to reach consensus about how to handle this.   T   F

4. If a student asked me for my advice on how to solve a problem, I would give it.   T   F

5. I would let students decide both what problems they wanted to solve and how they wanted to solve them.   T   F

6. When my advisees talk I would listen closely, share what I believed they were describing, and then ask them how they wanted to address this topic.   T   F

7. I would feel very comfortable talking about my own experiences with similar problems as my students shared in advisory.   T   F

8. It wouldn't be appropriate for me to ever talk about my own opinions or experiences with my students.   T   F

9. I would share my personal views if asked by group members and if I felt that doing so would help promote their own decision making.   T   F

continued

10. I would be more concerned about making sure our group accomplishes its goals for a session than with how they did so.   T   F

11. I believe that it's up to my students to decide what, if anything, they want to accomplish in a group session.   T   F

12. I would provide my advisees with a lot of structure in our first few sessions, then allow them to make more of their own decisions as the group progresses.   T   F

13. It's very important to me that my advisees learn from my example.   T   F

14. The most important part of advisory to me is that my students bond with each other.   T   F

15. I am most concerned with finding the best balance between addressing the needs of individual students with those of the group as a whole   T   F

Scoring

If you answered "true" to items 1, 4, 7, 10 and 13, you have a tendency to be more autocratic in your leadership style. Responses of "true" to items 2, 5, 8, 11 and 14 suggest that yours may be more of a laissez-faire approach. On the other hand, answering "true" to items 3, 6, 9, 12, and 15 would indicate that you are a more democratic leader.

Leadership Self-Assessment

Please read the statements below and indicate which number most accurately reflects your beliefs or behaviors, with "1" being "almost never true of me" to "5" representing "almost always true of me" as an advisory group facilitator.

1. I am enthusiastic about meeting
    with my advisory group.   1 2 3 4 5

2. I express my reactions to what is
    going on in the group.   1 2 3 4 5

3. I am able to help students stay
    on topic.   1 2 3 4 5

4. I understand group members and
    can convey this fact to them.   1 2 3 4 5

5. I can model behaviors which help
    promote communication in advisory.   1 2 3 4 5

6. I am aware of my group's stage of
    development and intervene accordingly. 1 2 3 4 5

7. I can challenge my initial assumptions
    and give them up if necessary.   1 2 3 4 5

8. My facilitational behavior is respectful. 1 2 3 4 5

9. I can often hear common themes and
    reflect these to help students make
    links to other group members.   1 2 3 4 5

10. I know generally what I want to
    accomplish before I begin a group.   1 2 3 4 5

11. I allow enough time to process
    activities and to summarize at the
    end of group sessions.   1 2 3 4 5

12. I can work effectively with students
    whose behaviors are self-oriented.   1 2 3 4 5

13. I provide support and reinforcement
    when appropriate.   1 2 3 4 5

continued

14. I know when to self-disclose in a way
    that is productive to the group.   1   2   3   4   5

15. I know why I am using the facilitational
    techniques I do.   1   2   3   4   5

Adapted from *Group Techniques, 2nd ed.*, by G. Corey, M. S. Corey, P. Callanan, and J. J. Russell, 1992, p. 77. Reprinted with permision of Wadsworth, an imprint of the Wadsworth Group a divison of Thomson Learning. Fax 800-730-2215.

Endnote

1   Adapted from *Talk With Teens About Feelings, Family, Relationships and the Future: 50 Guided Discussions for School and Counseling Groups* by Jean Sunde Peterson, 1995 (p. 16). Used with permission from Free Spirit Publishing Inc., Mineapolis, MN; 1-800-735-7323; www.freespirit.com. All rights reserved.

Chapter Four

~∾∽∾∽∾∽∾∽∾∽∾∽∿

What to Look for in Groups

I magine that you are facilitating a 7th-grade advisory group and the subject turns to bullying. One young male talks about the fact that although he is sometimes picked on by an older student, he isn't bothered by it at all. You hear the words and would like to accept them at face value, but his leg jiggles nervously as he speaks, and you suspect he's far more affected than he'd like anyone to know.

This is an example of the difference between process and content, and why it is so critical that advisors have a clear awareness of each. Content is the subject matter under discussion—what is being said. Process, on the other hand, relates to how it is being said, when, by whom, and to whom it is being said, and how the group as a whole reacts to it. We never simply listen to content, but always hear it within the larger context of what it appears to mean to both the speaker and to other group members.

As the facilitator, you will be trying to "read" the behavioral responses of several youngsters simultaneously. One may sit with his arms crossed over his chest, while another leans in and listens intently. Still another may giggle nervously. You're observing these behaviors, while trying to listen actively to the speaker yourself, always balancing the needs of the one with the group as a whole.

Becoming process observers is a fundamental necessity for those of us who choose to become advisors.

> The implementation of an advisory program requires reorganizing the school. . . . It demands that teachers see themselves not as curators of knowledge but as facilitators of learning, and that they pay as much attention to group process and group dynamics as to content. An advisory program is primarily about a change in the roles of teachers and students. (Ziegler & Mulhall, 1994, p. 43)

This chapter is devoted to process issues in group—what they may look, feel, and sound like to you, the facilitator, and how you can best understand and respond to them.

Parallel Process

When leading an advisory group, so much is happening at one time that it can be difficult to step back and assess what one is experiencing. It may not be until after the session has ended and we review what has happened that we are able to analyze our group's process. As we do, it is extremely helpful to review what our students discussed, understanding that nothing is said in groups randomly.

This is the concept of parallel process. When a topic is introduced and discussed by members, it is because it serves a purpose for the group; and it always tells us something about how the group is functioning psychosocially and what its concerns are. It is up to our faciliational skills to help students become aware of these issues and feel comfortable enough to discuss them openly. Consider the following examples of parallel process and see what you think.

An inexperienced and very skeptical 7th-grade math teacher, who had been forced to run an advisory group against his will, was asked about his first group session, during which half his students had left with another staff member to form their own group. He answered disgustedly, "Nothing happened. Nothing at all." When pressed further to reveal what his students had talked about in his advisory group he responded, "Nothing important. They just started talking about running away from home."

A more skilled process observer, of course, would have heard this discussion in a very different way, understanding that the students in question were responding to a unique circumstance in which their "home" group was now much smaller, several of them having "left home" to go with another adult figure. Such a facilitator might have encouraged students to talk about how it felt to be "left behind" and to wonder how their absent classmates' advisory experience compared with their own.

Parallel process often occurs when the group is struggling with difficult interpersonal dynamics that it cannot yet address directly. Listen to this White teacher's experience with his advisory group, comprised predominantly of Black students. In the first session, as he explained what the group was and outlined its goals, the students seemed enthusiastic about the concept. Immediately, however, they began to talk about experiences they had had in summer camps and in other planned activities with students from other races. Most of them talked about having difficult experiences with Whites and the discussion became animated and somewhat heated as they began to talk about how White people discriminated against Blacks.

This teacher was sensitive enough to understand that while these youngsters liked him personally and wanted to experience being members of an advisory group, they had real questions about how safe it would be to trust a White adult. Were they aware of this concern consciously? Perhaps not, but the advisor's willingness to hear them without judgment and his ability to attend to their process concerns by looking beyond the immediate content to their feelings, allowed him to give them permission to test out the group's safety.

Here's another example of parallel process. I recently began working with a group of paraprofessionals at a middle school where I had previously trained two groups of teachers. There was apparently a miscommunication between my present group members and their principal, who believed that they knew about the training and were enthusiastic about learning to become advisors. The staff, on the other hand, claimed not to know they were being asked to take on this responsibility or that they were to attend a 10-week course in preparation.

In our first session, I asked them to think about themselves as adolescents and how they might have felt if their homeroom teacher explained that they would begin meeting in weekly advisory groups. We discussed this, then I asked them how they thought their current students would react to being in advisories. Almost to a one, they said they felt that maybe students wouldn't really understand what these groups were or why they had been "singled out" to participate in them.

In listening to my group, I wondered aloud if their assumptions about how their students would feel participating in advisories was similar to their own feelings about being asked to go through this training to facilitate them. Apparently there was a connection, because the staff were able to then verbalize their concerns about why they had been "singled out" for this training, and it seemed as though they considered it to possibly reflect the administration's concern about their skills. It wasn't until the principal sat in with them and discussed her desire for them to participate in the program because she felt it was critical to the students' well-being, and that they had important skills to bring to the process, that they began to feel better.

Proxemics

Another cue about what a group might be experiencing dynamically is their proxemics, or how members seat themselves. Where do they sit? If a circle has been organized, can they tolerate being part of it or do they need to sit outside? Whom do they face? Do they sit sideways? With whom do they sit, and what is the impact of this seating arrangement on their participation? Do natural subgroups form which can be identified by physical positioning? Who chooses to sit opposite you? Frequently it will be students with a decisive personality and with whom you may want to ally because they often do take on important leadership roles.

Group Atmosphere

A group's atmosphere refers to its general feeling, which can range from warmth and acceptance on the one hand to hostility and rejection at the other. It is assumed that personal growth occurs most readily in an atmosphere that is open and inviting.

Establishing such a positive atmosphere requires time and the willingness and ability of the advisor to model two-way communication. It is only when students spend enough time together consistently and safely that they are able to experience interactions that allow them to begin to trust both the leader and one another. As individual differences emerge, there will invariably be disagreements and sometimes real conflicts that the members must be able to address and resolve. In the process their roles in the group solidify.

The group's atmosphere changes predictably from one stage to the next, and the advisor who realizes this and recognizes the changes as they occur is signalled to the fact that the group is facing critical choice points in their growth. For instance, a very new group tends to be polite, somewhat deferential, and willing to please. At the same time, they are very measured in their responses and the atmosphere can be threatened if they perceive the leader or a sole member to be intrusive or disrespectful. In such an instance they will become mute, and the atmosphere will feel very uncomfortable.

As the members begin to relax over the first few sessions and feel more interested in the group's life and their role within it, the atmosphere tends to become more alive and charged. Indeed, a facilitator may be alerted to the fact that their advisory is making this key transition from a group of disparate individuals into a real group by perceiving such atmospheric differences.

As a facilitator, you will need to ask yourself the following questions, understanding that in the first few sessions you are not only trying to lay the foundation for your group but you are also assessing your students' needs. Although you want to be aware of these process issues yourself, you may choose *not* to address them with the students initially, preferring to wait until you have a stronger bond with them:

- Do any students seem to prefer only a friendly, congenial atmosphere? Do any consistently attempt to suppress conflict as it arises?
- On the other hand, are there members who appear to thrive on conflict and instigate it at every opportunity? How do they demonstrate this tendency? How do they respond if successful?
- Do students seem interested and involved, both in what is being discussed and in who is discussing it? Do they generate their own discusion or simply answer questions passively?
- Is the group atmosphere lethargic or charged?
- Are certain topics avoided in the group? If so, what might these be? How are they avoided? Are there specific students who seem to reinforce this behavior? How?
- Are group members overly nice or polite to each other? Do they agree with each other too readily? What happens if they disagree?
- Are there obvious norms operating about the kinds of questions that are allowed and who will ask them (that is, do students nonverbally agree to let one or two speak for the group)?

Participation

Another vital process issue is the level of participation—the number of students actively involved in the group and their level of involvement. This is one of the easier process observations an advisor can make by analyzing such communication patterns as who talks to whom, for how long, whether or not they are interrupted, and how others respond to the discourse. One way to visualize these patterns is to diagram the group's participation patterns using a model called a sociogram at the conclusion of each session. You can do this privately, for your own information, or if you want your students to be actively involved in thinking about their participation, you can do it collectively.

Assuming your group has formed a circle, draw this circle,

indicating each person's seat. Then indicate to whom each person has spoken to during the session and note the quality of that interaction. For instance, if John talks to Sally but she doesn't respond to him, you might indicate this with an arrow pointing from John to Sally. If, on the other hand, she did respond, you could use a two-way arrow. If one student is misunderstood by another, this might be suggested by a dotted line. If a conflict erupts between two members, it might look like a line with slashes through it. Use your imagination and create a system that is clear to you. By looking at the illustrated sociogram, what do we see about this group's proxemics immediately? The males and females have formed separate clusters which may suggest, or evolve into, subgroups. As advisors, we would be very interested to see how their participation patterns unfold; and we might expect side conversations among members within each group.

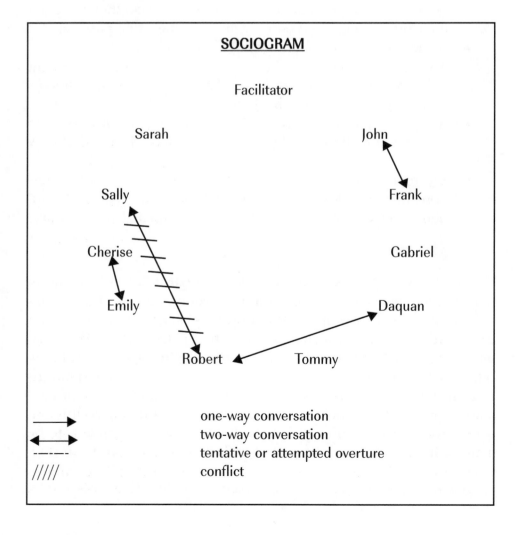

Only Daquan and Robert and Sally and Robert are communicating back and forth. The latter appear to be disagreeing about something. John and Frank seem to be engaging in side conversations, as do Cherise and Emily. You can see from this simple diagram that quite a bit appears to be going on; and as the advisor, your efforts to guide discussion will surely be impacted by your members interactions.

Considering the level of participation can help the leader gain some idea of the roles group members play, since the most vocal students are often—but not always—the most influential. The following are among the questions an advisor will want to address:

- Who participates more than others? Less?
- How often does each group member speak?
- Is there a shift in participation—for example, have frequent participants become quieter over time, or have quiet students become more expressive?
- How are silent group members treated? How is their silence interpreted by other students? Has this treatment changed over time?
- Are interactions determined at all by students' genders? If so, how?
- Who keeps the conversation going and by what means?
- What is the level of participation? Is it appropriate to the stage of development of the students and of the group?

We also want to be very careful to encourage intermember participation. Remember, students in your advisory have to learn to respond to you differently than they do in the classroom. The overwhelming tendency initially in advisories is for students to direct their comments to the facilitator, rather than to one another. You will need to continually help them change this behavior.

Decision-Making Procedures

All groups make decisions, sometimes explicitly and at other times without conscious awareness (such as, when a student introduces a subject that is too difficult for others to discuss, they will in turn ignore the statement). Because group decisions are hard to undo, the effective advisor should be aware of when and how they are made.

Decision making is required when problems emerge that require the group's attention. One example occurs early on when the advisor and students set the group's goals and ground rules. Once this is accomplished, these goals can be powerful guidelines for the group's discussion. Likewise, the ground rules can anticipate and prevent dynamic problems later on, such as breaking confidentiality or responding disrespectfully to one another's points.

There are four frequently used methods in decision making, which are presented here in order from the least desirable to the most advantageous:

- decision by one member
- decision by a minority
- decision by the majority
- consensus testing

The consensus testing method is generally preferred, because everyone is at least given the chance to express their feelings. Although students may not unanimously agree on a course of action, all members are generally comfortable with the group's process. In other words, whatever the actual course of action taken, all members feel included in the decision; and that is ultimately the most important consideration.

Zander (1982), however, cautions that groups must be careful not to engage in what he calls "groupthink," which occurs when members are so concerned with achieving consensus that they disregard the optimal decision in favor of another to which all can easily agree. As an advisor, you want to guard against this dynamic and help your advisory group develop its problem-solving and decision-making abilities; because the poorest choices are often made by very cohesive groups who lack these skills. Interestingly, the "best" decisions may be made by groups that are only moderately cohesive.

We probably all remember the movie "Twelve Angry Men" in which Henry Fonda successfully convinces 11 other jurors to change their votes. But as we might assume, in reality, group decision making is rarely accomplished by a single person swaying the majority. Rather, it is much more common that the opposite occurs. Indeed, the classic study on conformity in groups was that done by Asch (1955), in which he found that more than three fourths of the time one person could be convinced to perceive objects inaccurately if the others in the group unanimously did so. In general, group members do this either out of compliance (they secretly disagree with the majority view but want to be accepted) or conversion (they are persuaded to change their minds).

In gauging how group decisions are made, the advisor will want to consider the following.

- Does anyone make a decision and implement it without checking with others?

- Does the group drift from topic to topic with no apparent focus? Who initiates such topic jumping and why do they appear to do so?
- Who supports others' suggestions or decisions? Does this support amount to steamrolling by any two or three group members? If so, how does this appear to affect the other group members?
- Is there any effort made by students to enlist the participation of all group members in decision making? If so, how is this manifested?
- Does anyone make contributions that receive no response or recognition? What effect does being ignored have on that student? On other group members?

Influence

Although it is true that group members who actively participate are often influential, influence and participation are not always synonymous. Some people may say very little, but will capture the attention of the entire group when they do speak. Others may talk frequently but go unheeded. It is very important to members' overall satisfaction with the advisory experience that we be mindful of the relative influence exerted by different members, calling attention to it if needed. The advisor will want to consider

- Which members appear to be high in influence? How is this recognizable? What gender are they?
- Who is low in influence? Are there shifts in members' influence over the course of time?
- Do rivalries develop for group leadership? If so, how and what impact do they have on the other group members?

Influence can be demonstrated in a number of different ways. It can be positive or negative and used to enlist others' cooperation or to alienate them. There are those group members who try to impose their wills on others. Others may evaluate or pass judgement on their peers. Some students may try to block a group's action when it is not moving in their chosen direction, or they may push to get the group going. There are also students who consistently try to keep the peace and will do anything to avoid conflict. Such members may jump to support others' decisions or constantly act deferentially to those who appear more dominant. They may have problems in both giving and in hearing negative feedback.

Other group members may strive for attention by appearing to be uninvolved in the group. In assessing this possibility, the facilitator may consider if any student goes along with group decisions without seeming to commit him or herself one way or the other. Who seems to be withdrawn and uninvolved? Who never initiates activity, or who participates mechanically and only in response to another person's questions?

The student who consistently contributes to the group's development is the one who expresses genuine interest in what others have to say. This student tries to include everyone in the group discussion and decision making and expresses his or her feelings and opinions directly, openly, and without evaluating or judging others. When feelings run high and tensions mount, this will be the student who can be counted on to deal with the conflict in a problem-solving way.

Membership

A major concern for group members is the degree to which they are accepted by the advisory group as a whole. Different patterns of group interaction may develop that will yield clues to the degree and kind of membership which exists. To discern these possibilities, an advisor must ask:

- Who appears to be readily accepted by the other group members?
- Are there outsiders? Are these students scapegoated? If so, how?
- Are there any subgroups? If so, who? How do they interact with the larger group? What is their impact on the total advisory?
- What is the "price of admission" into this advisory; for example, what do members have to say and do to be accepted?
- What is the impact on those students who are not accepted?

Feelings

During any group discussion, feelings will be generated both by the topic and by interactions among members. Although these feelings themselves may not be openly acknowledged, students emit clear cues about what they are feeling through their nonverbal behaviors. Again, while the facilitator may only want to note these feelings and may not choose to openly raise them with the group, he or she will want to be aware of

- What signs of feelings they observe in their group members?

- Whether there are any attempts by selected group members to block the expression of feelings, particularly painful ones. How is this done? Does anyone do this consistently?
- If students can respond to a discussion of feelings by "deepening," by adding their own experiences and thoughts.

Our attention to these process elements is obviously essential in facilitating groups. It is also critical in helping us to identify students with deeper emotional issues—those who may be "at risk" for serious acting out (see chapter 10). By attending to all these group characteristics, a facilitator can feel generally assured that they are working with their group at their students' level of emotional and social readiness. Remember that at their best advisories offer students tremendous support. Advisors are helping their students to build their capacities to deliver constructive feedback to one another and to hear it for themselves.

Many students who have participated in advisories comment on how much they learn from one another. They feel good about being able to help each other. In this respect, advisees are responding to the group's "curative" factors and are discovering that they are not alone in their feelings, values, and beliefs.

Facilitation is not an easy task and can take considerable time to master. Individuals who choose to go into counseling careers work hard to build their process skills. It is no wonder that teachers and supporting staff, particularly those who view themselves first and foremost as content specialists, may be concerned about their abilities to enter this affective domain as facilitators of advisory groups.

It is a most worthwhile pursuit, however, because knowing our students both individually and collectively, and learning to hear the concerns behind the actions and overt statements, gives us a tremendous advantage in working successfully with them. This benefit is only compounded as we teach these skills to the youngsters themselves, developing students who are "group wise," invested in the group, and adept process observers in their own right.

Indeed, this becomes one of our most important roles and contributes greatly to an advisory's growing cohesiveness and its positive impact on members. Asking students periodically to comment on these elements of their group's process clearly gives them the message that they must stay focused in the here and now, and that each one of them bears responsibility for how meaningful the advisory experience ultimately will be.

Test Your Process Skills. What Might be Going on in Your Advisory Group if . . .

1. Each time a particular group member makes a comment, others in the group grow restless and begin talking among themselves.

2. One member of the group refuses to talk over a series of several sessions. Other students begin to question him about this.

3. In the early stages of the group's development, one student reveals strong negative feelings about herself. The other members of the group immediately begin acting out in physical ways by turning over a chair and dumping the contents of a female member's pocketbook on the floor.

4. A group is unable to untangle themselves during an ice-breaker even though they try to do so three times.

5. It is late May and your advisory, which has met weekly since September, will be terminating in a couple of weeks. In today's session, the topic is deaths of favorite pets.

6. Your group is comprised of 8 boys and 4 girls. The boys invariably want to talk about sports but the girls want to talk about relationships. Invariably, the boys prevail. The girls withdraw and talk among themselves.

7. Your group members, who are usually chatty and friendly with each other, are very quiet today. When you attempt to get conversation going by asking each student in turn how he or she is, one says she's angry and doesn't feel like talking. When you press her further, she reveals that she's mad at her sister for telling her mother something that was to be kept in confidence between them.

8. In your first session, your advisory students seemed eager to participate and had asked a lot of questions. They had also willingly set down the ground rules they felt they needed. Today, however, they are very reserved, sitting

back and saying little. One asks why they have to meet in the advisory on a regular basis.

9.   Two students in your advisory group have had an argument a few hours earlier. Still angry with one another, one confronts the other and begins the conflict again. A female student sitting in between them jumps up and asks to play a group game.

10. Your advisory group seems to be a hotbed of conflict. Virtually every week, at least one group member is annoyed at another and sessions are invariably spent trying to resolve conflicts. Over time, you gradually realize that one student is always involved in prompting these misunderstandings, although he does so indirectly and never directly expresses anger himself.

Possible Answers

1.   The student is low in influence in the group and the others have become impatient with his comments. It is not clear why his status is such; and how you will deal with this issue will depend on a number of factors, probably most importantly the stage of your advisory group's development. We will consider possible interventions in chapter 11 as we discuss how and when to make interventions.

2.   The student's lack of participation may be caused by a number of factors—it may be that he/she doesn't trust the other students in the group or possibly the advisor or general shyness might be a factor. Perhaps the subjects under discussion have felt irrelevant or on the other end of the spectrum, threatening. Some students act in a laissez-faire manner such as this for attention. You will need to watch and listen, reflect back what you believe may be preventing this student from contributing, and see if you're correct in your assumptions.

3.   On a process level, two different things appear to be happening. One is that this student has expressed feelings on a much deeper level than the majority of the group are

continued

able to acknowledge. If this is intolerable to them, they will wordlessly collude to isolate the member—in effect, scapegoating her—to bring her back into conformity with the rest of the group. This is also an example of decision making by the majority.

4.   A group that cannot master a relatively simple task, commonly used as an icebreaker, may well be one with communication problems that prevent them from collective problem solving. As their facilitator, you will repeatedly help them process what happened as they tried to untangle themselves: who did or didn't give suggestions; how these were responded to; who was or wasn't influential in the process; how it felt to stay stuck, and so forth. In doing this, you hope to then generalize as to what seems to be going on in the group as a whole, which likely parallels the problems they are demonstrating in this exercise.

5.   Your group is considering its own termination, although probably not consciously. This will be an ambivalent experience and actually sad for some of your members. They address this milestone indirectly via parallel process. Their conversation about losing pets who are dear to them and the grieving that attends these losses may well also be an expression of their sadness over the loss of their advisory group.

6.   Here, the majority clearly rules and the minority are dissatisfied. Feeling that their needs are not being met, and probably feeling also somewhat powerless since this has happened more than once, the girls form a subgroup and attempt to meet their discussion needs within it.

7.   This example is another one of probable parallel process. Your observations of a clear atmospheric change in the group alert you to the fact that something is amiss. In questioning the students individually, you hear this student's comment about her sister breaching her confidentiality by disclosing a personal fact about her to their mother. Given that the other members in your group are listening to her intently, you have to assume that she is in some way speaking for the

group. You might well wonder if, in fact, one of your advisees has broken the group's vow of confidentiality.

8. Again, you are aware of a clear atmospheric change as well as unanticipated negativity on the part of your students. You must wonder if such a dramatic shift signals the group's transition from one stage of development to another (see chapter 7). The students are expressing solidarity among themselves by collectively questioning/challenging you and the group's purpose.

9. What provokes this female student to attempt to divert attention from a possible conflict between her two male peers? At this point, you probably haven't a clue, but you will note this behavior and probably comment on it if you feel the group is cohesive enough to process what is going on. This female student is indicating that she is very uncomfortable with dissension and needs to try to prevent angry feelings from surfacing.

10. In this scenario, we see the virtual antithesis of the preceding example. You may find you are working with one or more students who are themselves angry but cannot allow themselves to express these feelings openly. Instead, they routinely foment conflict between other students. All roads lead back to their initial instigation.

Using the Sociogram to Assess Participation Dynamics: What's Happening in This Group?

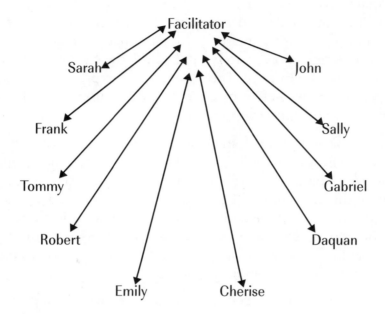

This advisor is facilitating his group much the way a classroom teacher might respond to students. Note that while he/she is careful to be inclusive by making contact with students and that they in turn respond back to the leader, at this point there is no communication among students. Given the consistency in emotional level of the students' responses, we might assume that the group is talking politely or matter-of-factly about a topic that is not particularly emotionally charged. Perhaps it is a new group who are measured in their responses. How might the leader encourage more interstudent dialogue?

Chapter Five

~~~~~~~~~~~~~~

Facilitation

In their fourth session, the facilitator of a 7th-grade advisory group noticed that one of her students, normally outgoing, today seemed quiet and withdrawn. The advisor had asked her group members to identify their favorite movie; and although the other students were participating enthusiastically, this student asked to "pass" when it was his turn to contribute. The facilitator allowed him to do so, and solicited all the other students' opinions. She then returned to this student and asked if he still wanted to pass or if he might now be comfortable participating. The student shook his head "no."

The advisor said, "You are still sure that you don't want to participate in this discussion." The student nodded briefly.

Not willing to move on, the facilitator persisted by commenting: "You feel disinterested in participating." The student said, "I'm not disinterested. I just don't feel like doing it."

The advisor then asked, "Can you help us understand why you don't feel like participating today, when you usually do?" The student replied: "I'm just in a bad mood. It's nothing personal," looking around at the group. "I just need my own space today."

The facilitator countered, "So you would like us to leave you alone." The student nodded. Then he shared, "I don't want to talk because I'm really angry at Mr. Edwards (the math teacher), and I don't feel like telling everyone why." The facilitator encouraged him to continue, saying, "You are angry at another teacher and aren't willing to talk about it here. It seems like it bothers you a lot to be angry at Mr. Edwards. Why is this?"

In reading this example, you may have noticed that in every interaction between the leader and student, the focus was on encouraging the student to express what he was feeling. The advisor managed to avoid any of these common facilitational pitfalls: ordering, commanding, warning, threatening, advising, giving solutions or suggestions, arguing, lecturing, praising, blaming, interpreting, reassuring, interrogating, and diverting, evaluating, analyzing, or interpreting.

The problems with some of these reponses are probably self-evident—clearly, we want to avoid asserting our authority by warning, blaming, or ordering, for example—but some may not be as obvious in their potentially negative effect. Reassuring, for example, may appear to be a benign response to our group members, but consider this: If a student chooses to share a concern and we hasten to reassure them that it's not that serious, we cut off that dialogue and leave the student unsupported.

Let's return again to the vignette and look more closely at each of the facilitational skills this advisor used. As the session unfolds, she is quickly aware that something seems off in the behavior of one of her students, who is uncharacteristically withdrawn. Concerned about what might be worrying him and aware that his silence will impact the group, the advisor asks him if he wants to participate. Upon receiving a negative answer, she allows him to pass. She decides to try again, however, and returns to the student and *paraphrases* or *reflects back the content* of what the student has said: "You are still sure that you don't want to participate in this discussion." The student nods briefly.

Not willing to move on, the facilitator then *reflects* back what he believes the student might be *feeling*: "You feel disinterested in participating." The student says, "I'm not disinterested. I just don't feel like doing it."

The advisor then *questions* the student by asking him: "Can you help us understand why you don't feel like participating today, when you usually do?" The student replies, "I'm just in a bad mood. It's nothing personal," looking around at the group. "I just need my own space today."

The facilitator then *seeks* further *clarification* by asking: "So you would like us to leave you alone and not try to get you to participate." The student nods.

The facilitator at this point has a couple of options, depending on the nature of the ground rules which the group has set. Often these include students' right to "pass" or not participate if they don't want to. If such a ground rule has been established in this advisory, the facilitator may choose to support the student by reminding the group members as a whole that they have the right not to participate, then continue the activity with those students who wish to participate.

If the facilitator senses that the student's nonparticipation has had a negative effect on the group, he or she might probe more deeply into what is happening for that student or may choose to table the activity temporarily to instead *generalize* from this student to the group. She can do this by asking if there have been times when other students haven't felt like participating—either here in advisory or in other group settings. Invariably, one or more students will acknowledge this feeling and the facilitator can focus on their experiences. This shifts attention off the one individual and also supports him by providing confirmation of what he is experiencing at the moment. The facilitator might then *summarize* these points made by the other students and, if appropriate, resume the initial activity.

Sometimes this technique in and of itself is experienced by the silent student as empathic enough to encourage him to share after all. Should this student decide to do so, the facilitator can then use additional skills to better understand what the student is feeling that made him want to withdraw.

For instance, this student said, "I didn't want to talk because I'm really angry at Mr. Edwards, and I didn't feel like telling everyone why." The facilitator can then again easily *reflect* back the student's *feelings*, "You are angry at another teacher and aren't willing to talk about it here." If this observation is accurate, the student might well talk more and reveal the source of his anger. At that point the facilitator might *reflect* back on the *meaning* this angry feeling has to the student. For example, the advisor might reflect, "It seems like it bothers you a lot to be angry at Mr. Edwards." Even if the facilitator's observation is inaccurate, what is most important is that the advisor has shown the student that he cares about how he feels, trusts him to decide for himself when and how to contribute, and has also supported him by encouraging other students to express similar feelings that probably reduce his sense of isolation.

When we facilitate advisories, we are doing two things: encouraging our members to learn more about themselves as individuals and helping them to become "group-wise" contributors to the overall functioning of the group. The foundation upon which we base our facilitational skills is self-awareness. Because it is so important that students feel safe in identifying and expressing their feelings, we must also be willing and able to do the same. Thus, we continually reflect about what we see happening to individual students, what we discern happening within the group as a whole, and how we are feeling as a result. We are aware that our effectiveness is nearly wholly dependent on the quality of the relationships we establish with our advisory group members.

Facilitation implies certain risks, however, because as we open ourselves to our students we risk caring more about them; and we may also feel more vulnerable once we drop our shield of professional distance. One teacher training to become an advisor acknowledged that she didn't want to run a group with her own students because she wasn't certain how much she wanted to know about their personal lives. Her concern was echoed by other teachers, too, and is one which must be honestly examined, for there is no way that one will facilitate groups like advisories without developing more personal relationships with the students involved.

Myrick, Highland, and Highland (1986) underscore the need for advisors to be adept facilitators, who not only need help in understanding group dynamics and facilitation but in how to help students think about and solve personal problems. What helps us to do so is our modeling of behaviors that enhance our students' communication in group. These include concreteness, appropriate self-disclosure, immediacy, giving and receiving feedback nondefensively, and staying focused on the here and now.

In this chapter we will discuss several skills which enable us to facilitate our advisory groups effectively. Some of these (active listening, reflecting, questioning, clarifying, self-disclosing) help us to engage our students and encourage communication. Others are used to help students look more deeply at what they're thinking, feeling, and doing (deepening, giving constructive feedback). Still others help students to achieve personal goals (problem-solving, conflict resolution). We also use techniques like modeling assertiveness, generalizing, linking, and summarizing to help us develop and maintain an optimal group atmosphere.

Active Listening

How do you know when someone isn't listening to you? How does it feel? Active listening is the cornerstone of facilitation. There is no single response a group leader can make that is more important than the ability and willingness to listen actively to his/her group members. Nothing is more powerful or means more to our students. Our undivided attention is the ultimate compliment we pay, the way we give our full respect to them.

We demonstrate active listening by making eye contact, nodding when appropriate, asking questions that tell others that we are listening to their concerns, or simply by listening silently. Our body language also encourages others to speak. We lean in or sit comfortably in an open way, sometimes mirroring the speaker's facial expression or physical position.

This concept is not new. Active listening is the basis of client centered therapy. Thomas Gordon (1976) applied these precepts to parenting relationships. Indeed, it is appropriate with all age groups, whether in one-to-one relationships or in groups. One woman recalled a memory that had taught her the power of actively listening, to her own child, then five years old:

> I was putting my daughter to bed one night when she began to cry and told me she was the only member of kindergarten class not invited to her classmate's birthday party the following weekend. I felt devastated and desperately wanted to say or do something to make her feel better, but I could not. I decided to try the active listening technique I had learned in the *Parent Effectiveness Training* book by Thomas Gordon, and forced myself to do nothing more than listen, reflect back (appropriately, I hoped), and to let my daughter vent.
>
> Eventually, she calmed down and went to sleep and I breathed a sigh of relief, thinking that active listening, indeed, did seem to help. I had no idea how helpful it actually was, however, until the next evening when my daughter announced over dinner that she had, in fact, been invited after all. When I said, "That's wonderful. What happened, had they lost your invitation?" She said, "No. I went up to Annie's mommy after school and I asked her 'How come you didn't invite me to the party?'"
>
> It wouldn't even have occurred to me to have given my daughter such advice, but by allowing her to think the situation through herself, I had facilitated her innate assertiveness skills. That was the day I developed a genuine respect for the power of active listening.

Active listening allows us to truly hear what it is our students need to express, helps us develop greater closeness with them, and also frees them to make decisions they are already in the process of thinking through. We've all undoubtedly had the frustrating experience of sharing upset feelings with another who feels obliged to give us advice on how to handle our problem. Far from helping us to feel better, it often instead makes us feel that the listener either isn't that interested in hearing us out or doesn't believe we can solve our own problems. In either case, the response is unsatisfying and antithetical to what we strive to do as advisors seeking to empower our students.

Modeling Assertiveness/Giving Constructive Feedback

Two other important facilitative roles which are often interrelated are modeling assertiveness and giving constructive feedback, both of which can be done effectively by sending "I" messages. Here again we turn to Gordon (1976), whose own work mirrors that of his predecessors Haim Ginott and Carl Rogers.

"I" messages are undoubtedly familiar to many of you. Deceptively simple in format, they can nonetheless be difficult to give because we are not often in the habit of being so honest with one another about how behaviors make us feel. An "I" message has three components: The speaker describes

- *what* it is the other is doing that affects him or her,
- *how* it has this effect, and
- *why*.

For example, I send an "I" message when I say to a student in my group with whom I am experiencing some discomfort: "John, when I ask you a question and you roll your eyes (the behavior), I feel uncomfortable (how it affects me) because I don't know what that behavior means" (why it has this effect).

Why is feedback so important in the advisory group? Because it is critical in helping our students to learn more about how they appear to others in an environment that they hopefully perceive as safe enough to allow them to respond nondefensively. What do we need to keep in mind as we first model this skill, then monitor our students' practice of it? There are a few fundamentals. One is to ask our students first if they would be open to hearing it. ("Can I give you some feedback about what you just said?") Secondly, we must express it as positively as possible. ("I know you were trying to be helpful in what you just said to Monique; but when you questioned her truthfulness, it seemed that you weren't ready to give her a chance to explain what had happened to her.")

Third, we give feedback about behaviors only; and we do so in as objective and neutral a way as possible. (An advisor might say, "Anita, you were late to group again. This is the third time this month," rather than saying something like, "Anita, your lateness again today—the third time this month, by the way—is disruptive and irritating.") We want to give feedback sparingly to avoid overwhelming the recipient; and when we do give it, accentuate the positive far more than negative.

Role playing is a technique that can be particularly useful with young adolescents learning to give feedback. This allows students to initially establish some personal distance by first practicing the skills in hypothetical situations and then applying them to real life circumstances. As some of these latter examples may well occur within the advisory, we are again called upon to model them ourselves as well as helping our members to do so.

Conflict Resolution

The simplest and most effective means of modeling and teaching confict resolution to advisory group students is to teach them to alternate active listening with sending "I" messages. Part of this process is also learning to compromise, and it is probably very well worth the effort to encourage students to talk about how they feel about compromising, what they see as its pluses and minuses, when they would or would not be able to compromise, and what is to be gained or lost if they do not.

Self-Disclosure

This is an interesting technique, one with which some facilitators are more comfortable than others. It can refer either to instances in which we share our own experiences or feelings because we believe that to do so makes a point in the moment and will be helpful in some way either to an individual student or to the group as a whole, or it can be in the form of direct feedback we are giving to one or more students because we believe that their behaviors in some way require it. A few cautions about self-disclosure: When we self-disclose we should do so briefly, infrequently, and without self-indulgence.

The first goal of interventions of any kind is to encourage learning among our group members about what is happening in group, and advisors do this not by telling but by questioning. With respect to self-disclosure, we have to continually decide when to share what we are experiencing and when not. The bottom line for us must always be to consider if what we have to share will help our students learn more about themselves individually or collectively.

In my experience, some students respond extraordinarily well to self-disclosure and appear to accept it as proof that you care about them. Although I have been unable to locate the source, I remember reading several years ago about working with two types of disenfranchised adolescents: instrumental and expressive. The former appreciate their advisor's self-disclosure. They hear what we have to say, integrate it, and may learn from it. Others who are more expressive, however, couldn't care less what happened to us or what our feelings about these experiences are. Every minute we speak is less time for them, and they don't appreciate our interruptions.

Linking

Linking refers to the manner in which we encourage our group members to form closer relationships with each other, and this can be accomplished both verbally and nonverbally. For example, you wish your students to communicate directly with each other in your advisory group sessions and not just to you. You may make this suggestion directly or you may do so non-verbally. When a group member talks to me, I often make a sweeping gesture with my arm to indicate that they are to direct their comments to the group. Another way we can do this nonverbally is to fail to make eye contact with the student speaking to us, but rather to look at the other group members. Human instinct will usually force the speaker to follow our example and direct his or her comments to them.

A way in which we "link" verbally is by illuminating similarities between what two or more students have said. ("Ginny, what you're describing sounds very similar to what Ann experienced when she tried to talk to Mr. Fishman.") Remember that of all the potential curative factors in a group such as the advisory, none is more potent than realizing that others share our feelings or our point of view; and linking is instrumental in helping our students gain this awareness.

Reflecting Skills

Young (1998) has written a book which is very useful in helping counselors and facilitators identify and practice the full complement of facilitational techniques. He helps us to understand the different levels upon which we may reflect what we hear our advisees say: content, feelings, and meaning.

Active listening also involves paraphrasing or reflecting what the person is saying. Reflecting is a way in which we verbally communicate empathy with the speaker. It also allows us to check that we are understanding him or her correctly and to provide feedback to this effect. When we are accurate in our reflections, our response often frees the speaker to probe deeper into what they are feeling, to be comfortable in expressing it, and even to recognize feelings that heretofore were not consciously accessible.

In chapter 6 we will consider the stages of group development through which advisories potentially pass, and at that time we will talk more about how reflection often changes and deepens as the group matures. As a general rule, however, we actively listen on the first level early on in our relationships; we then progress to level two as we get to know others better. It is only in our more intimate relationships that we tend to reflect back on the meaning level.

As an example, consider this exchange: A student comes in and expresses loudly that she's not in a mood to talk about anything serious today. She just wants to play a game. You comment, "You're interested in having fun here today and not having any kind of 'heavy' discussion" (content reflection). She says, "Yeah." At this point you might direct your questions to the larger group and observe that this student doesn't really want to talk today and ask how the others feel about this.

Let's assume that one of them questions the student by asking why she doesn't feel like talking today and she says, "I just don't feel like it. I'm bored talking about personal stuff. This group gets really boring." You might query her about this (reflecting back the feelings she's expressing), "You feel bored here talking about personal issues. What might feel more interesting to you?"

She replies, "I don't know. I just don't feel like telling other people here my business." You respond in a way that tries to reflect back the meaning of her statement, "You haven't always felt this way. Has something happened to make you uncomfortable about talking personally?"

If your observation is correct, your response empathic, and she cares enough about the group to take the chance, she may at this point deepen her comments to share what her feeling of unwillingness stems from and what it actually means to her. For example, she might reply, "I'm not going to be honest about how I feel here when there are certain group members who can't remember that we're supposed to keep what's said in group private."

So there it is. This student has revealed the content of her position (not wanting to talk personally), her feelings about not wanting to talk (her discomfort at doing so), and the meaning for her discomfort (someone has betrayed her trust by revealing what she said in group to nonmembers). Your reflecting responses were on target and revealed that you were hearing her empathically and correctly, and this has freed her to tell you what she needs you and the group to hear.

As a facilitator attempting to reflect feelings, you will want to try to avoid these potential pitfalls:

- waiting too long to reflect back the feelings you believe you have heard
- being judgmental in reflecting
- turning the reflection into a question
- focusing on the wrong person—for example, the person about whom the speaker is talking and not on the actual speaker
- allowing the speaker to ramble
- "undershooting or overshooting" by not matching the intensity of the feeling being expressed
- parroting the words and not the feelings behind them
- rambling in your response

Earlier, the point was made that reflecting feelings may help speakers to better understand their blind spots by encouraging them to not only identify their feelings but to struggle to understand their meanings. This is an extremely important intervention when working with adolescents; because more than most age groups, they will act out those feelings they cannot express verbally. We must be able to understand their perceived world view and to challenge it when necessary.

A model that can be useful to both ourselves and our students in better understanding our feelings and their connections to behaviors is the following cognitive approach, which can be readily adapted to use in the advisory:

1. An event has occurred between ourselves and another.
2. We interpret this event in a particular way.
3. Based on our interpretation we have an immediate feeling reaction.
4. Underlying our immediate feeling response is a much deeper level affect which reflects the meaning this experience has for us. This meaning tends to be a painful self-assessment which we may not be able to acknowledge consciously.
5. We respond back to the other individual in a way that protects us against this underlying, painful meaning.

Often, when we facilitate advisories, a student will tell us about his/her behavior; and we are then compelled to work back to its precipitant. In doing so, we often find that this individual has experienced some type of exchange with another that was upsetting because of how he/she interpreted it. Typically, the first reaction our student will be able to identify is one of anger; but if we can help him or her to look more deeply at what else they may have been feeling and if the group has established enough security for this task, the student may be able to acknowledge another, more potent feeling that was triggered. Usually this feeling is self-deprecating and thus painful, and it is not uncommon for us to "act out" without realizing we are doing so to protect ourselves from this feeling.

I remember once running a group session for a weight loss program, and it went very badly. Chagrined, I couldn't wait to get home and try to forget about how badly I felt. When I thought the situation through I realized that I believed the poor session resulted because I hadn't done a good job facilitating the group. My immediate reaction was embarassment, but the underlying feeling was that I was sure this was proof that I wasn't a skilled group worker. *That* was the underlying painful feeling I wanted to protect myself from. Realizing this allowed me to look at myself more objectively (and benignly), and I was able to soothe my feelings. This approach can be very effectively used in advisory to help our students deepen their feelings.

You may also find that other group members help you to reflect back to their peers on a meaningful level, and you will need to facilitate this exchange to both support the speaker and to help group members build relationships with each other. For example, two male 7th graders, Joe and Vinny, come into advisory and they are furious at each other. Joe has teased Vinny about his physical appearance in front of a girl they both like. Vinny became angry and cursed Joe out. Joe got mad and cursed back, escalating the incident.

It is immediately clear to you as the facilitator that something has happened between the two of them. Eventually, you comment on the fact that there seems to be some tension between them and ask Joe what happened. Joe says, "I don't know. He's a jerk. He got mad at me over nothing." Vinny retorts, "I don't consider it nothing. You insulted me by making fun of how I was dressed." Joe says, "We dis each other all the time. You do it as much as I do. Why'd you get so pissed off at me for it today?"

Let's assume that Vinny hasn't really thought this through for himself and may be surprised at Joe's question. Given this possibility, and the fact that he's already angry at Joe, he may well not be willing or able to answer. However, another group member, Jeanette, overheard the exchange. She says, "Vinny, maybe you got so angry because Joe dissed you in front of Roberta." Joe says, "What difference does that make?" Jeanette counters, "How would you feel if someone made fun of you in front of someone else, especially if you liked that other person?" Jeanette has identified a critical issue in this exchange.

Joe has teased Vinny (event). Vinny heard Joe's remarks as being insulting (interpretation). He became angry (immediate feeling response). Looking deeper, however, it is possible that the (underlying meaning) of this exchange to Vinny is that he is probably already self-conscious about his appearance as a young male adolescent; and in this situation he's particularly vulnerable because he was called out in front of a girl he likes and may want to impress. He counterattacks (response) to protect himself against acknowledging this deeper level meaning which is new to him and which he probably doesn't at all feel like admitting to anyone, least of all to Joe. Jeanette, however, has perceived its possibility and in a move that demonstrates caring for Vinny and Joe, has surfaced it in the group.

Deepening Feelings

As a facilitator, particularly of a more developed advisory, you will at times need to help students to deepen their feelings and to connect them with the underlying meaning described in step 4 above. To deepen feelings you will want to listen closely to what is said on a content level, listen for the underlying feelings being expressed, and reflect these back. If your assumption about the student's feelings is wrong, he or she will correct you; but if you are right, the student will respond by elaborating on what he/she is feeling.

Jacobs, Masson, and Harvill (1998) have developed a "depth measure," which ranges from 1 (deep personal sharing) to 10 (surface level). As groups progress developmentally through different stages, discussion generally begins to deepen; although in the authors' opinion, most school groups would probably not go to a deeper level than midrange. If students feel safe in their advisory group, they may talk very personally about serious problems including abuse and neglect, although this is usually not the case.

Generalizing

We generalize in two ways. The first relates to the process of deepening feelings we have been discussing. Once you have helped to identify the feelings a group member is expressing and have given him or her the opportunity to deepen their expression and understanding of them, you must generalize to the rest of the group. This means that you now ask other students if any of them have also had this experience or have felt similarly. This step is essential. While you want to assist individual group members to be expressive, you must always respect the group's balance and never allow one student to become overexposed and vulnerable. You always want to be sure that they know they are not alone in what they are thinking or feeling.

The second way in which we generalize is in our processing of what happens in group. Whenever we do an exercise or activity or conclude a discussion, we process it by first asking students to identify how they felt while participating. Next we ask the students to analyze what they saw and heard happening and to share why they believe events transpired as they did. Finally, we generalize by asking them to relate this experience to what goes on in their everyday lives. This last step is probably the most important in processing. Without it, activities are at best interesting diversions which don't impact on students' critical thinking.

Questioning/Clarifying

We will sometimes question as a part of active listening when we either need clarification on a point being made or if we feel that the speaker needs to look more closely at something he or she has said. When we question, we want to do so in a way that doesn't put the other person on the spot. Asking open-ended questions that encourage participants to look at their behaviors more critically are recommended.

Problem Solving

Much has been written about problem solving with young adolescents. Suffice it to say that, as advisors, we play a very important role in helping our students to reason through the concerns they share in group. The simplest model is

1. helping the student identify the problem he/she wants to solve
2. looking at alternative means of solving it
3. choosing one
4. practicing it
5. evaluating it
6. integrating it into everyday functioning should it prove to be successful

Reframing

Sometimes students present problems that appear to them to be very serious but which can be reframed in a much more positive light, thereby increasing student's confidence in addressing them. Reframing reminds me of the Chinese ideogram for crisis also means opportunity, and so it often is with the challenges with which our students are presented.

Once we have listened carefully, we are in a position to help our student first look at how he or she is interpreting the situation and whether or not this alone is making it unnecessarily problematic. For example, let's say that Sally tells us that she and Joan are no longer best friends; and the reason turns out to be that Joan has cancelled social plans with Sally for the third time in the last month. We hear from Sally that she believes Joan doesn't really want to see her; but when we ask if there might be any other explanations, we learn that Joan's mother has been quite sick over the past several months. Inquiring of Sally whether this might have something to do with Joan's cancellations helps her to reframe the situation differently and to agree to talk with Joan directly.

Sometimes our students respond to situations as though catastrophic because they don't know how to handle them. Reminding them of some of the techniques they've learned (that is, how to assert themselves) may help them to perceive their dilemma more confidently. By metaphorically encouraging our students to hold problems in their hands and look at them from several different perspectives, we are teaching them reframing and are building their critical thinking skills in the process.

Summarizing

One of a facilitator's most important tasks is to summarize what has happened, both after critical events have occurred during an advisory group session and upon the session's conclusion. To summarize well, the advisor must listen closely to the feelings voiced and recognize the underlying themes they express, tying these together in a coherent fashion.

We often summarize as we are actively listening to another to ensure we are hearing correctly and to keep the speaker focused on the topic. For example, "So what I hear you saying is that you're concerned about the weekend because your relatives are coming; and this means you can't see your friends and you'll have to spend time with your cousin whom you dislike."

We may choose to summarize as a student concludes his or her account of an experience before we go on to hear others speak. In this instance, summarization serves a dual pupose. It helps to put closure on one communication and serves as a transition to the next. Indeed, it will often be how we summarize that also helps us to generalize to others. ("Daveon, what I heard you say is that you feel really happy about what you gave your parents for Christmas and that it gave you a lot of satisfaction to pick out gifts that were meaningful to them. How about the rest of you? Is there anything anyone else who wants to tell us about how their holiday went?")

It is also extremely important that we leave time at the end of an advisory session to summarize what has transpired during it. Failing to do so is a common pitfall for newer group facilitators. Likewise, it is often very helpful to your advisees to begin a session with a very quick review or summary, of the preceding one. This helps to create a sense of history for your group. It also opens the door for you to be sure that there is no unfinished business from the previous session, and it can help to set the stage for what your group may want to do now. Initially, as you are "training" your students to become competent group process observers, you will have to assume most of the responsibility for reflecting back the essence of the themes which have emerged. Gradually, your students will take over this function very ably.

These underlying issues may not always be clear to you immediately, and you will have to summarize on more of a content level initially. You may find that over the course of the next few days you continue to analyze the session and are then better able to recognize themes. If so, when you meet with the group again you can open by reviewing the previous session and summarizing at that time.

All of the techniques described in this chapter are designed to help you to promote your advisory's development by freeing students to learn more about themselves and one another safely. Your willingness to listen and your efforts to reflect back what you have heard will help keep your students focused on what is of concern to them and will allow them to work through feelings that might otherwise elude them. Your efforts become steadily easier as your students learn what is expected of them as advisory group members and as they also become adroit facilitators in their own right.

Some Facilitational Questions to Ask Yourself

1. When is it easiest for you to listen actively to another person? Hardest? Are there those in your everyday life whom you find it difficult to listen to? Why might this be so?

2. If you had to characterize your responses in socially challenging situations, would you describe yourself as generally more passive, aggressive, or assertive? (The distinction between the latter two is that when we are aggressive we tend to send one-directional messages that are designed to coerce the other to do what we say. An assertive message lets the other know how we feel and invites him or her to respond.)

3. How easily could you model sending "I" messages to your advisory group students? Why? Do you believe in them or find them unhelpful?

4. Under what circumstances might you confront a student in your advisory with feedback designed to encourage him/ her to look at a behavior and to hopefully change it?

5. How do you feel about reflecting back what you believe a student's feelings might be or even possibly their meaning? Does this feel like a task you might assume comfortably as an advisor or does it feel too "therapeutic" to you?

6. Are there certain feelings that would be easier for you to address in advisory than others? If so, what might these be? Which would be harder to acknowledge and why? How might you handle a situation in which the more difficult feelings come up?

7. Do you believe your advisory students can handle their own problems? If not, why not? How do you envision your role in addressing their personal problems as they come up in group?

8. How concerned are you that conflicts may arise either between students or between a student and yourself? If very concerned, why? What is your worst fear about what might happen should such a conflict arise? How would you handle it?

9. How do you believe your students will respond to the technique of sending "I" messages? Why do you believe this?

10. What's the biggest mistake you're afraid of making as a facilitator? What might you do if this should happen?

Try This

1.   Sit down with a colleague, friend, or family member and tell them you would like to practice active listening. Explain the guidelines for doing so, then ask them to speak with you while you practice this skill. Once they have concluded, ask them for their feedback about how well they believe you were or were not listening and why they felt this way. Then ask yourself how it felt doing this. Was there anything especially difficult about it and, if so, what and why?

2.   Practice sending an "I" message to someone who is doing something that bothers you. Try a relatively low risk encounter with someone you know well and with whom you generally feel comfortable. Tell them something they're doing that affects you, how it's affecting you and, to the best of your understanding, why you believe it has this affect. Then sit back quietly, listen actively to their response, and see if you can both gain some satisfaction from the encounter.

3.   Recall an incident in which you reacted to another person in a way you wish you hadn't. Try to apply the cognitive model described earlier in the chapter by thinking through the actual event, how you interpreted it, how it made you feel initially, what deeper level feeling about yourself might have been triggered, and whether or not this might have caused you to respond as you did. In particular, sit with that deeper level feeling and try to make peace with it objectively and self-soothingly.

4.   Practice problem solving. Think of a situation that you are currently facing that's troubling you. Apply the steps to the problem-solving model and see how they feel. In particular, you will want to carefully evaluate how successful your approach appears to be.

5.   Try reframing an issue that feels especially challenging to you and see if you can't find a way of viewing it more positively or at least more proactively.

Chapter Six

~~~~~~~~~~~~~~~~~~~~~~~~~~~~~~

Introduction to Stages of Group Development

We have already determined that school-based interventions such as advisories can play a powerful role in building students' sense of emotional resiliency. In so doing, they encourage students to promote personal wellness and avoid acting-out behaviors. This is particularly so when facilitated by caring adults who understand not only their students' individual developmental needs but also those of the advisory group itself.

Building self-esteem and social problem-solving skills requires an ongoing, organized, and systematic group process and is more likely to occur when students perceive a sense of group cohesiveness. This collective identity builds slowly, yet predictably; and as it does, group members master increasingly complex levels of interpersonal communication.

Initially students in an advisory group are dependent on the facilitator for guidance, but they quickly become more challenging of the leader's authority as they become clearer about what the group means to them and more confident about the contribution they have to make. As they develop greater ease in sharing with each other, they often become more nurturing and eventually are able to engage in complex decision making with very little leader intervention. Finally, they tend to experience feelings of ambivalence and loss over the group's termination; and they need the opportunity to work through these emotions.

What drives the evolution of group stages is the continual tension between members' desires to become better known to one another and their fears of intimacy. If the group environment allows advisory students to confront and work through their individual differences to become closer, they will become able to engage in complex social problem solving.

As advisors, we work to help our students feel safe in becoming more open and in ultimately looking at their own self-defeating behaviors, even when this is difficult and painful. To accomplish these tasks, we must consider our students' chronological ages, their grade levels, whether or not they have had previous advisory experience, and their group's overall developmental level. To the extent that facilitators can do this, they will be able to understand what group members' behaviors mean, respond to them appropriately, and help the group to move forward in a healthful way.

Chapters 7–11 offer you a variation of a model of group stage development created by Garland, Jones, and Kolodney (1965). This model suggests that groups potentially go through five stages of group development: preaffiliation, power and control, intimacy with its sub-stage of disenchantment, differentiation, and termination. It views each stage's expectable content and process issues, roles typically played by members, recommended leadership skills, and specific interventions. A variety of activities appropriate to each stage are also included.

Member Roles and Their Evolution

Every group is a system with a unique homeostasis, and every member in it plays a characteristic role that contributes to this balance in some way. The roles members play are a function of their personalities and frequently mirror those they play in their nuclear families. A person who steps in to act as a buffer when his parents fight, for example, will likely play a similar role in group. Another who is an isolate within the family may instinctively refrain from participating in personal discussions in the advisory.

Member roles are also determined by what the group needs at that point in its development, for as homeostasis changes throughout the different stages of group growth, roles will also evolve. For instance, during Power and Control, the group needs to test its autonomy and one member may be called upon to "fight for the group" by challenging the authority figure. During intimacy, one member may elect (or be elected) to share personal feelings to satisfy the group's needs for closeness.

A particular role may be filled by different group members at various points in time, or the same individual may fulfill it throughout the group's life. As long as it meets a group need, the role will be played. Indeed, one of the more interesting issues in understanding group dynamics is to identify the principles that explain changes in a member's role over time.

In one group, a female student sat absolutely silently for the first seven or eight group sessions, resisting even the advisor's efforts to encourage her to comment on points made by other students. One day she sat down and began talking animatedly as though she had been outgoing from the start. When the leader commented on her behavior change, she simply said that she'd listened long enough to know that she felt comfortable with the other students and now had things she wanted to say. The other students were initially bemused by her change, but quickly accepted it. She continued to be a dynamic presence in the group for the remainder of the year and ultimately emerged as one of its leaders.

Sometimes the role a student feels compelled to play is ambiguous because the group has not clearly defined how it should be played. In an advisory, for instance, a student may play the role of informal leader, but if the group is uncertain about what they are supposed to be and do as an advisory, it will make this individual's "job" much more difficult.

Another potential role-related problem is role conflict, which develops when a group member finds him or herself playing multiple roles simultaneously. In an advisory, for example, one person may play an initiator role with a strong desire to see the group accomplish a particular task. Perhaps, however, this person also has a close friend in the group with an emotional problem he needs to discuss. The "initiator" now must play a maintenance role (an "encourager" to support his friend), but in so doing thwarts his own needs to stay on task. This is an example of "interrole" conflict.

"Intrarole" conflict, on the other hand, can result when a single role requires contradictory demands. Being a "harmonizer," for example, may require that a student calm disagreements but may create a problem for him or her if personal loyalties to one of the students involved in the argument compels him to support that student, whatever the circumstances.

Role Orientations

A group has to meet two basic demands: a) It has to accomplish its tasks, and b) it must maintain the relationships that develop among its members. Group members typically exhibit one of three different categories of behaviors in balancing these demands: task-oriented, maintenance, and self-oriented. Within each there are several characteristic roles.

Self-Oriented Roles

Self-oriented behaviors are exhibited by students whose own interests are dominant over those of other members or of the group as a whole. These individuals are not only unwilling or unable to work toward a common group purpose, but are far more concerned about how the group will meet their needs and do not hesitate to report when it doesn't. A group comprised of too many individuals playing such roles is unlikely to progress very quickly. It is unlikely that an advisory group will experience this problem, however, because these roles suggest more intensive problems; and while it is certainly possible that one or two students may fall into this category, it is unlikely that the majority will.

Self-oriented roles are those played by students who

- dominate by trying to make all decisions, not listening to others' points of view, and who try to monopolize the group;
- withdraw by isolating themselves from the group's process and making no effort to contribute to discussions;
- aggressively block through attacks on others' remarks, being excessively critical and hostile;
- seek help by presenting themselves as incompetent, belittling their own contributions, and frequently seeking others' opinions and advice;
- evade what's going on in the group by expressing only their personal interests, feelings, and opinions which are unrelated to the group's goals; and
- seek recognition by acting in a self-aggrandizing manner.

Maintenance-Oriented Roles

A group will progress more readily when a fair number of members play maintenance roles which focus on interpersonal dynamics and enable the group to develop strong working relationships. Maintenance-oriented roles are played by students who

- harmonize by attempting to reconcile disagreements, reduce tensions, and encourage other members to explore their differences;
- act as caretakers by supporting other individuals' points of view, making sure that no one is bullied or hurt in any way by others;
- are gatekeepers who keep communication channels open among all group members, facilitate other students' participation, and suggest ways to get discussion going;
- observe the positive and negative aspects of the group's dynamics and call for change if necessary;

- follow by accepting others' ideas;
- compromise if their ideas are conflicting with others, being willing to sacrifice their own needs in favor of group consensus; and
- encourage others through agreement, warmth, and praise.

Task-Oriented Roles

Task-oriented roles are demonstrated by members who actively work to meet the group's stated goals. Such students are also invaluable to an advisory group because they are the ones in concert with the maintenance-oriented students, who keep the group focused and make sure that it deals with issues of importance as they surface. Although not necessarily affectively inclined, such students can well contribute to personal discussions by fulfillling these roles:

- initiating discussion by proposing tasks or goals, defining the group's immediate problem, or suggesting a means for solving it;
- seeking others' information or opinions;
- giving their own opinions;
- coordinating by pointing out the relevance of different members' ideas to the overall problem at hand;
- energizing the group to continue working when it flags;
- mentally recording what has happened in past sessions and recalling it when helpful;
- clarifying and elaborating by interpreting ideas or suggestions, clearing up confusions, defining terms, and suggesting alternative interpretations as needed; and
- summarizing—pulling together related ideas, restating suggestions afterthe group has discussed them, and offering a conclusion about them.[1]

How well a group develops over time depends in part on the types of roles its members play and the balance among those in each of these three categories. Ideally, a majority of students play maintenance and task-oriented roles, while a minimal number are self-absorbed. If the opposite occurs, the group may never coalesce successfully into one which can achieve genuine intimacy. On the other hand, a group that is overly weighted with maintenance-oriented members may develop strong interpersonal relationships but have difficulty accomplishing its overall goals; and groups high in numbers of task-oriented individuals will be productive but may never attain real intimacy any more than the self-oriented groups.

A facilitator may feel very discouraged by students whose self-orientations dominate, but often patience and time persevere. A talented 8th-grade teacher who remained with her advisory over the course of 3 years, tells the story of one male student whose behavior was so disrespectful and disruptive that she wanted him removed from her group. He had been evaluated by a child study team, which had recommended placement in a special education class; but the wheels of public education can grind slowly and his transfer, though months in the works, had still not come through.

One day the advisor took her group bowling and to everyone's astonishment, this student turned out to be a natural. He won the match; and from that point on, his status in the group changed, with the others according him a respect they had not demonstrated earlier. His behavior in group began to shift; and he stopped being resistant and began joining in the group's discussions, eventually becoming an important contributor.

In February of that year he was told his placement in a special education class was imminent. Moving into it technically meant he would now also change advisories and join the one for his special ed class. The other students in his advisory revolted. They said to him: "You belong to us now." A special arrangement was made which allowed him to return to his original advisory group each week, where he had created his own special niche.

Although it is true that at any given point in an advisory group's life all three types of roles may be played, this is dependent upon the stage of the group's development. In the group's earliest stages more students behave in self-oriented ways as they strive to determine whether the group will meet their needs. As members begin to learn and care more about one another, a majority will begin to assume maintenance roles which promote greater communication and interpersonal understanding. Then, as the group continues to become more sophisticated and is able to engage in complex problem solving, the focus shifts again and a greater number of members may assume roles that are primarily task oriented.

Groups take care of themselves. They generally survive intact, and they do so because members will assume roles that ensure this survival. As an advisory group facilitator, it is helpful for us to remember this. If our advisees believe that the group is a positive experience, they will make sure it not only endures but ultimately thrives.

Leadership Roles

We have already considered a great deal about leadership styles and skills and will look more closely at how these change over the life of the group. Suffice it to say here that in general, your role as advisor changes in ways somewhat similar to that played by many classroom teachers over the course of the school year.

Quite possibly you begin in September in a structured manner, setting norms and making sure everyone is clear on what is expected of them. Gradually you begin to allow students to assume more responsibility for their self-monitoring. So it goes in advisories. As advisors we must adapt our interventions to meet the needs of our group; and these in turn are dictated to a large degree by their developmental stage.

Leadership functions must change as the group matures, moving from directive (geared toward task completion) to supportive behaviors (that promote group maintenance) as members become more independent and desirous of relationships with one another. A leadership style which emphasizes task or morale at the expense of the other for extended periods of time can be damaging to the group's growth.

Parallel-Process Themes

Parallel process provides cues which help us to determine our group's stage by the topics they discuss. It is probably an oversimplification, but in fact each stage will be characterized by different themes; and the topics students discuss will reflect this. Group development is rarely, if ever, a smooth process in which all members move collectively from one stage to the next. Indeed, listening while some members want to speak negatively about authority members, while others are ready to entertain more positive aspects of them, for example, helps us to discern when our group may be transitioning from one stage (power and control) to the next (intimacy). Likewise, it often happens that groups will regress periodically; and again, parallel process tips us to this event as well, as topics formerly discussed, and supposedly resolved, resurface for consideration once again.

Activities

Each of the following chapters will include several activities that are appropriate for an advisory group's respective stage of development. As might be suspected, these will reflect various goals, from building a sense of group cohesiveness in preaffiliation to helping students to evaluate the advisory group experience at termination. Sometimes, the content discussed in the activities reflects the theme of a given stage. Other times, activities are chosen because they enhance those skills required of students at that point in the group's life. So, for example, you might want to do activities during the intimacy phase that ask students to reflect on meaningful relationships. On the other hand, you might ask them to do an exercise in which they discuss feeling betrayed during power and control, since this is the stage in which they are struggling with the issue of trust in the group and whether or not it is safe to share personal feelings.

A reminder—It is essential that if we choose to do structured exercises, we process them adequately and leave sufficient time at the end of the group to do so. Beyond helping students to identify how they felt doing the activity, what they observed in the process, and what they can take with them into their everyday lives, we must also remember to put closure on both the activity and the session as a whole to help our students make the best sense of what they have done.

I would make two general suggestions to you as advisors that reflect what I have seen others do successfully. The first is to read to your groups periodically. Read to them from books that are slightly younger than they are, excerpts from newspaper or magazine articles, or books for their age group. The content can vary depending on the group stage, but regardless, reading itself is a powerful activity for students. For one thing, it simulates what hopefully they have gotten at home from their families. Secondly, it is a wonderful collective activity. Third, it encourages literacy and builds listening skills. Fourth, and to me most important, it opens the door to invaluable discussions of personal experiences and beliefs.

At a National Middle School Conference several years ago, I listened to Nancy Doda read aloud from the children's book *Love You Forever* to illustrate the appropriateness of reading aloud in advisories. Our group must have numbered 200 or more, and there wasn't a dry eye in the room when she had finished. Consider this activity for your own groups.

My second suggestion is that you encourage your students to keep logs. You can incorporate an excellent introductory exercise (see Preaffiliation Activities) through which students decorate the covers of their logs to reflect how they see themselves. More importantly, however, they can and should be encouraged to write in these logs weekly. You will keep them locked away in a file cabinet in your room. One advisor created a system by which she set up two piles. Once students had finished writing in their journals, they either returned them to one if they didn't want the advisor to look at what they had written, the other if they did. As the advisor read those in the second pile, she wrote back personal comments. She said that over the course of the year the size of the second pile increased steadily, as more and more of her students sought the opportunity to communicate with her privately.

The model you are being presented with is orderly and thus not very much like real life at all. Groups rarely if ever move harmoniously from one stage to the next, nor is their progress one of steady forwardness. It is much more often the case that some of our students move into one stage while the others remain in an earlier developmental position, much like adolescents do in all lines of development. It is also very common—probably the norm—that group dynamics are marked as much by periodic regression as by growth. Keeping the various cues cited in this chapter in mind, along with a willingness to be as flexible as you can to meet your students wherever they are, will help you create the kind of advisory experience that benefits you and your students.

Endnote

1   Adapted from material contained in Benne, K. D., & Sheats, P. (1948). Functional roles of group members. *Journal of Social Issues 4*(2), 41–49.

Chapter Seven

~~~~~~~~~~~~~~~~~~~~~~~

Preaffiliation

Overview

The first stage of group in this model is called preaffiliation and its dynamics reflect its name. Imagine a large scale with "individual needs" on one side and "group needs" on the other. When an advisory initially forms, this scale is tipped dramatically in favor of the former; although students have come together for a common purpose, they are not yet cohesive in any way. Students have little awareness, and even less interest, in their peers' concerns at this point and are focused solely upon themselves. Virtually all communications are between students and the facilitator, with little interpersonal sharing among themselves.

How long this stage lasts will depend on a number of variables. Most importantly will be your group's composition and its unique chemistry. Some groups are simply quieter and more dependent on others and may stay preaffiliated longer. Secondly, the time of year in which you begin your advisory is an issue. Those that start in September, particularly if students are new to the school and to each other, may develop more slowly. Third, our personalities are a factor. Those of us who prefer more structured groups, or who wish to relinquish the expert role for that of facilitator but are new to the process, may consciously or unconsciously strive to keep our groups in preaffiliation longer.

Sometimes this stage is extraordinarily brief, lasting no more than a session or two. You will know when your members are beginning to transition into the second stage because they will increasingly become verbal, and you will feel the atmosphere change accordingly.

Atmosphere

The atmosphere during this earliest stage tends to be polite if somewhat constrained, as students seek to better understand what the group requires of them. They will temporarily suspend judgment in favor of the possibility that this might be a positive experience and are initially willing to cede all leadership to the facilitator.

Influence/Decision Making

The facilitator has great psychological size for the group now, particularly for those students who have never before been in a group like an advisory and are uncertain about what it will entail. No one member is especially high in influence yet because students are assessing the situation from the relative safety of their own individual needs and have not yet begun developing a group consciousness.

At this point decisions are made by consensus, albeit a tentative one, under the direction of the facilitator. Some students will be more verbal than others and will take the lead in questioning the advisor, but the others allow them to do this more because it meets everyone's specific needs than because they have the status to make decisions for the group.

Membership

As advisors, we have to anticipate that in the first session or two, our students' roles will be self-oriented. They will have a number of immediate personal concerns that need to be addressed. Among these are

- what they will derive from the advisory experience,
- whether their needs will be met,
- if they will like the group and the leader,
- if they will be understood and liked in return, and above all
- if the group will be a safe experience.

They may wonder why they have been chosen for this group. One advisor said that in her first session students asked why they had been picked to be in her advisory and wondered if they had done something wrong. Although they want to please the advisor and do the right thing, and will seek ways to succeed and gain recognition, they are also worried about potential failure. Students are now very dependent upon the facilitator and may project their needs onto him or her, creating unrealistic expectations of how they will be cared for. They may says things like, "You really understand us," or

"I'm so glad we have you for an advisor and not teacher *X*." Such compliments are students' efforts to establish a relationship with the advisor and alleviate their anxiety about the upcoming experience.

Feelings

Students in the preaffiliation stage tend to be ambivalent about their group involvement. Although excited by its potential to allow them a chance to be themselves and "keep it real," and possibly intrigued by the opportunity to relate to their adult facilitator as someone other than a teacher, there is also considerable apprehension that the sharing entailed by group membership might be overwhelming. It is also probable that students are leerier of their classmates' reactions to what they have to share than they are of the facilitator's reactions.

This ambivalence may be manifested in a number of ways. Members may come late to the first few sessions. They may refuse to join in activities. They may term the group "boring" and ask the advisor to "do something about it." They may test to see if they can change their groups or ask that friends be allowed to join them in this group. They may sit with their jackets on, remain outside the circle, or state flatly that they don't want to talk.

Leader Roles

The leader's role in this first stage is to establish the group's ground rules, goals, and his or her own role in helping the group to meet these. To do this, he/she must provide considerable clarification about what the group is and how it will work. While doing so, the facilitator accepts the group members' dependency, but strives to create activities that allow students to begin to explore both themselves and others safely, and eschews the opportunity to become too controlling.

We do all in our power to include everyone equally and safely, while giving the message that such ambivalence is absolutely natural and understandable. Some advisors ask their students what it might take for them to begin feeling more comfortable and relaxed in the group, and this question often segues into a discussion of ground rules. Above all, the facilitator presents him/herself as interested and eager to participate, and willing to do so at the group's level and to allow the group to move at its own pace.

As advisors, we also continually strive to mold members who are "groupwise" with good facilitational skills. For this reason, we work hard to help students build their cohesiveness, shaping behaviors in such a way that those students playing roles that express maintenance and task functions are encouraged. Those involved in self-oriented behaviors are supported to the extent possible and are given certain latitude in the earlier group stages.

We have different tasks in preaffiliation. First and foremost, we must begin to teach students what these groups will provide and what they will require. The issue of safety is paramount, and to reinforce it students must be given the chance to establish their own ground rules for participation. Traditionally these include maintaining confidentiality, acting respectfully toward one another, and giving students the right not to participate if they so choose.

It is also essential during this initial stage that advisors make the point that if students reveal behaviors or experiences suggestive of physical or sexual abuse, or if they position themselves as being either a threat to themselves or to someone else, the facilitator will have to refer these students for additional, intensive assistance. (If such an occasion should eventually arise, the facilitator must take the individual student aside and tell him or her the action to be taken before making a referral.)

Leader Strategies

This is the facilitator's "honeymoon" phase during which he or she can do very little wrong. Advisors must appreciate the depth of their power now and take special pains not to give feedback to students that can be negatively construed. Activities, if they are to be used, have to be chosen with care. They must be designed to encourage inclusion on an easy, fun level that does not threaten the participants.

As the advisor you will also immediately begin modeling positive communication skills, with a special emphasis on active listening and sending "I" messages. Exercises in this initial stage can safely, and helpfully address active listening, as it is paramount for your group's success that all members believe others care enough to really listen to them.

Themes (Parallel Process)

In their effort to orient themselves to the advisory group, students will often recall previous group experiences, even those that don't immediately appear to be such. They may talk about teams they have played on, camp experiences, scouting, school, community organizations to which they have belonged, or times they have gathered more informally with others their age. Without realizing it, students bring their earlier frames of reference about group experiences with them to the advisory, and these definitely shape their feelings about their current group experience.

We do the same thing, and it is important to realize this. In a training group with which I recently worked, one staff member had been in a therapy group many years earlier and it had not been that positive an experience for him. He was able to verbalize about this in our first session and, with a little encouragement, to acknowledge that given his dissatisfaction with it, he was not only leery of facilitating an advisory group, he wasn't too thrilled about being in a training group that itself had an advisory group component in which he would be asked to discuss personal feelings.

CHARACTERISTICS OF PREAFFILIATION

Atmosphere:	Polite, Deferential
Feelings:	Ambivalence
Participation:	Limited, Student To Advisor
Decision Making:	By One Or A Few
Membership:	Self-Oriented
Influence:	No One In Particular
Theme(s):	Earlier Group Experiences

Ask Yourself

1. How do you typically feel when in a newly forming group?

2. How would you go about helping the students in your advisory group begin to feel comfortable?

3. What ground rules would you hope to see your students develop?

4. How do you feel about these coming from the students rather than yourself?

5. What would feel like safe topics to begin discussing in the first session?

6. How would you explain to students what an advisory group is?

7. How do you feel about the fact that your students will initially be very dependent upon you for structure and support?

8. What can you do to both acknowledge and address your students' ambivalence about being a member of your advisory?

9. What do you believe is your greatest strength as an advisor of a group in the preaffiliation stage?

10. What most concerns you about the role you will initially have to play as an advisor of such a new group?

Exercises and Activities for Advisories in the Preaffiliation Stage

I Like People Who . . .

Goal: To help students begin to see what they have in common in a fun, relaxing way.

Objectives: At the conclusion of this activity students will be able to

1. identify at least three ways they are similar to several other advisory group members,

2. describe how it felt having to take a risk in front of others, and

3. demonstrate their ability to assert themselves in a group.

Activity

This activity resembles "Musical Chairs" in that there is one chair fewer than there are participants. In the first round, the students sit in moveable chairs arranged in a circle with the advisor standing in the middle. The advisor says, "I like people who _____," describing a characteristic that may be physical, emotional, or social. (Examples: like music, like to dance, like sports, are wearing sneakers, are wearing glasses, are wearing the color blue, don't like homework, and so forth.). Students are directed to get up and change seats if the adjective describes them. They, as well as the advisor, strive to find a seat. The last person to do so is "it" and moves into the middle to give the next "I like people who . . ." description. This is repeated as many times as desired.

The activity may be processed by asking

1. How did it feel to have to risk your seat to find a new one when you heard yourself described? (Identify feelings)

2. What did you observe in the group as we played the game? (Analyze what happened in the activity)

3. Are there times in real life when you have to take such chances? (Generalize to real life circumstances)

Assessment Of Personal Skills

Goal: To enable students to begin identifying their strengths and weaknesses.

Objectives: At the conclusion of this exercise students will be able to

1.   identify as many as 10 personal characteristics,

2.   clarify these characteristics as strengths and weaknesses, and

3.   describe how they feel about each.

Activity: "I am" Statements

The advisor hands out 10 index cards to each participant and asks them to describe somethng about themselves by completing the statement "I am . . ." on each. The students should write down the first things that come to mind.

When they have completed these, the advisor asks them each to order their descriptions, from what they consider to be the most important to the least.

Once they have prioritized their qualities, the advisor asks students to examine them closely to see if they can see any patterns in what they consider to be most important versus less important.

Are there any cards they would like to discard? What do they gain or lose by holding on to them?

This activity can be processed by asking

1.   How did it feel to think about their personal qualities, then prioritize them? (Identify)

2.   Did they notice any pattern in what they considered to be important traits? If so, what? (Analyze)

3.   Is it possible that we may have many different aspects of our personalities and that we need all of these to succeed? (Generalize)

Find Someone Who . . .

Goal: To help students begin to learn about one another in a fun, unstructured manner.

Objectives: At the end of this activity students will be able to

1.   identify at least three characteristics of each group member,

2.   describe as many personal characteristics of each group member as you can, and

3.   demonstrate the ability to talk personally to the other students one-on-one.

Activity

The students are each given the handout "Find Someone Who . . ." and are asked to get up and circulate around the classroom, speaking to each of the other students and writing each student's name on the appropriate lines of the form. Once their forms are filled out, they return to their seats.

This activity can be processed by asking

1.   How did it feel doing this activity? What was it like having to get up and move around to talk to everyone else? (Identify)

2.   What did they notice about their fellow group members as they talked to one another? Were there some facts that surprised them? What did they learn about each other? (Analyze)

3.   How is it for them in real life to meet new people and to begin to learn about them? What are some ways they do this? (Generalize)

continued

Find Someone Who . . .

Has always lived in this neighborhood _____

Loves to dance _____

Hates cats _____

Wants to learn to swim _____

Has gone to sleepaway camp _____

Loves to read _____

Believes that women are the stronger sex _____

Has been out of the country _____

Wants to be an actor or actress _____

Has a pet _____

Is the oldest child in the family _____

Likes school _____

Loves pizza _____

Likes to play sports _____

Is superstitious _____

Has won an award _____

Listening Skills

Goal: To help students begin to learn more about one another while simultaneously promoting listening skills.

Objectives: At the conclusion of this activity students will be able to

1. describe at least three characteristics of their partner and themselves, and

2. explain at least one reason why it's important to be able to listen to others individually or in a group.

Activity

The advisor asks students to pair up. (If there is an odd number of group members, the advisor may either form one group of three or choose to partner with one of the students him or herself.) Each pair has five minutes in which the students describe themselves to their partners. They may give their name, age, family information, favorite school subject, favorite activity, musical performer, movie, and so forth. How they describe themselves is at their discretion. Then each student introduces his or her partner to the group.

The activity may be processed by asking

1. How did it feel to pair up with another student and to both talk about themselves and to listen to their partner? How did it then feel to introduce their partners and have to remember what was said? (Identify)

2. What kinds of things did they find themselves talking about to one another? Why do they think they chose these topics? (Analyze)

3. Why is it important to begin thinking about how we listen in our advisory group? How is it similar to or different from meeting people for the first time in real life? (Generalize)

The Name Game

Goal: To help students to learn each others' names and personal qualities.

Objectives: At the conclusion of this session students will be able to

1. name every member of the group, and

2. describe at least one quality of each member.

Activity

This activity is excellent for the first or second advisory group session if students aren't already acquainted. The facilitator begins by saying that we are going to play a game to help us remember one another's names and then gives his or her name. He/she then does so again, this time adding an alliterative adjective (e.g., I'm Serious Susan, I'm fabulous Mrs. Foster, Excellent Ed, Javelin-throwing Mr. Johnson, and so forth).

Each student then introduces themselves in a similar manner. Then the group as a whole says the names of every member.

This activity may be processed by asking

1. What did it feel like to introduce yourself to other students in the group? (Identify)

2. How did they decide on the adjective they used in describing themselves? What did they think about the adjectives other students used? (Analyze)

3. How do they handle meeting new people in real life? How do they describe themselves in such situations? Is it easy or hard to do? Why? (Generalize)

Listening Diagram

Goal: To teach listening skills and to help students become aware of some of the difficulties in doing so effectively.

Objectives: At the end of this session students will

1. demonstrate their ability to listen to verbal instructions by creating a visual image, and

2. identify at least two problems in listening carefully and how these might be resolved.

Activity

Ask one student to describe the diagram below without letting anyone else see it. The others in the group are to draw it as they hear it being explained. The students then compare their drawings with the original one, as well as with one anothers'.

This activity may be processed by asking

1. How did it feel trying to duplicate a design you couldn't see by relying on a verbal description of it? (Identify)

2. What made it easy or hard for you to do this? Why do students' pictures look different from one another? What problems might have prevented better communication? (Analyze)

3. Is this activity similar at all to what happens in the classroom when you take notes on a subject your teacher describes? How well do you do under those circumstances? What might help you to make sure you're understanding verbal instructions as well as possible? (Generalize)

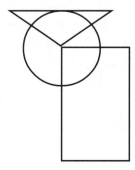

Name Catch

Goal: To enable students to learn one another's names while also practicing their listening skills.

Objectives: At the conclusion of this activity students will be able to

1. identify every other member of their advisory, and

2. demonstrate their listening skills by following specific sequences.

Activity

The group members stand in a circle. The advisor holds a small rubber ball and says that he/she will throw it to a member who will catch it while saying his/her own name. That student will then throw the ball to another student while saying that student's name, and so forth, until it has been caught by every group member.

Once this has been done, the facilitator asks the group to repeat the same process—in the same order—but faster this time. (Eventually, group members will probably voluntarily move in closer to complete this task more efficiently.) The exercise continues for a few minutes until the group can complete it to their satisfaction.

The activity may be processed by asking

1. What did it feel like playing catch and stating their names and those of other group members? How did they feel about doing it repeatedly, faster each time? (Identify)

2. What helped them to accomplish this task? What kinds of skills did the group need to use to be able to accomplish it? (Analyze)

3. Is there anything students can learn from this activity which might tell them what they will need to do to make this advisory group a successful experience? (Generalize)

The Tangle Game

Goal: To illustrate the need for teamwork.

Objectives: At the end of this activity students will be able to

1. physically untangle themselves without releasing one another's hands,

2. identify the verbal and nonverbal types of communication necessary to solve a group problem, and

3. give at least one example of the kind of teamwork necessary to accomplish collective goals.

Activity

Group members stand in a tight circle, shoulder to shoulder. Each student takes the hands of two other students. They may choose any two students in the circle *except* those standing on either side of them. They are then asked to "untangle" themselves without loosening their grip on one another's hands. The facilitator observes only. The participants will then have to try a variety of strategies of turning, stepping under arms, possibly over legs, reversing their direction, and so forth, to accomplish this task. The facilitator will want to watch and listen carefully to see how the members do this.

The activity can be processed by asking

1. How did it feel doing this task? (Identify)

2. What did they do that either allowed them to succeed or prevented them from doing so? Which members of the group were particularly helpful? How? What did they have to do collectively to get untangled? (Analyze)

3. Will the same teamwork be necessary to make the advisory group work? How? How about in team activities in their everyday lives? (Generalize)

Designing A Group Logo

Goal: To encourage your advisory to begin to develop a sense of grop identity.

Objectives: At the conclusion of this activity students will be able to

1. identify a collective characteristic that should be reflected in the logo,

2. describe two feelings they have about working together in this group, and

3. design a logo representative of this group.

Activity

The facilitator will need to supply certain materials: pens, paper, markers, crayons, and so forth. Students are asked to think about who they are as a group and to work together to design a logo that reflects their identity. The session is devoted to their discussion of the logo and the assignment of tasks to those who will actually design and create it. The advisor needs to observe closely to make sure that all participate in some way.

The activity can be processed by asking

1. How did it feel thinking of, designing, and creating a logo? How do they like what they've created? (Identify)

2. How were they able to do this task? How was it decided who would do what and how well did this strategy work? (Analyze)

3. In real life, how do they work with others to create finished products? (Generalize)

Active Listening

Goal: To help students enhance their active listening skills.

Objectives: At the conclusion of this activity students will be able to

1. identify three characteristics of active listening,

2. disclose how it feels not to be listened to versus being heard,

3. demonstrate their ability to listen actively to a partner.

Activity

This activity is twofold. You will first model poor listening skills, then discuss ways to demonstrate active listening. Next, your students will talk about times they didn't feel listened to and how that felt. Then, in pairs, the students will practice listening actively to one another.

Part 1

Tell your group that today you will be discussing active listening, then ask for a volunteer to share a personal experience with you. (Ahead of time, ask one member if they will help you with this exercise without revealing your arrangement to the other students. This student will volunteer to tell you something that happened to him or her while you intentionally show that you are *not* listening. I have found this to be preferable to being inattentive to an unprepared student.) Demonstrate your nonattentiveness to this student.

This part of the activity can be processed by asking

1. How did it feel to them that you weren't listening to their peer? How did it feel to the speaker? (Identify)

2. How did they know you weren't listening? What behaviors of yours showed this? How do we show that we are listening? (Analyze)

3. What's it like in real life not to be listened to? (Generalize)

Part 2

The second part of the activity requires your students to either pair up or work in triads, depending on your number and whether or not you want observers. In this exercise, students will take turns talking to their partners and sharing personal experiences while their partners practice active listening.

This part of the activity can be processed by asking

1. How did it feel being the speaker? The active listener? (Identify)

2. How did your partner let you know he or she was listening to you? What were you aware of trying to do when it was your turn to listen? What was easy/hard about listening actively? (Analyze)

3. In your everyday interactions, how does it feel to be listened to? What does this help you to do? (Generalize)

We're All In This Together

Goal: To help students begin to appreciate what they have in common and how as a group they will be interconnected.

Objectives: At the conclusion of this activity students will be able to

1. name at least two other students who have something in common with them and

2. identify their feelings about being a member of the group.

Activity

The facilitator states that this is an activity in which they will get to know more about each other and that they will take turns telling the group about themselves. The facilitator begins the exercise by taking a ball of yarn and, while holding one end, tosses it to one of the students. In doing so, the facilitator asks that student a question that requires him or her to do some personal sharing. Then that student holds on to his/her segment of the yarn and tosses it to another, who does the same. The effect is to create a "web" in which all are a part.

Students get to decide what they want to ask one another. Questions might include: "What's your favorite food? Who's your favorite singer? What teacher here do you like the most? If you could be an animal, what would you be"

The activity can be processed by asking

1. How did it feel asking questions of one another? Sharing about yourself? (Identify)

2. What did you hear when we all shared? Were there things we had in common? (Analyze)

3. How do you find out what you have in common with others who might become your friends? (Generalize)

Gravity Circle

Goal: To demonstrate how group members depend on each other for support.

Objectives: At the conclusion of this activity students will be able to

1. identify what it felt like to be an integral part of this circle and

2. describe what is involved in supporting and being supported by others.

Activity

The students form a circle of chairs, at first sitting normally. The facilitator then asks them all to turn to the right. Next, they each lean backward and put their heads on the knees of the student behind them. Once all are in position, the facilitator walks around and, making sure students are secure, instructs them to raise their backs slightly as he/she removes their chair. Their positioning will keep them in place even as all chairs are removed. They hold this final position for several seconds, then stand up and retrieve their chairs.

This activity can be processed by asking

1. How did it feel to first form the circle? To lean back on another student's knees? To feel your chair being removed? (Identify)

2. What was necessary for you to be able to support each other without your chairs? Why did/didn't this work? (Analyze)

3. Is there a parallel between what we did in this activity and what we will need to do as members of this advisory group? What? (Generalize)

The Person Whom I Admire Most

Goal: To help students think about the qualities they admire in others and why these are important to them.

Objectives: At the conclusion of this activity students will be able to

1.   identify a person they admire and explain why, and

2.   enumerate three positive personal qualities of the person they admire which they also try to embody

Activity

The facilitator asks students to complete this statement: I would admire a person who . . . After all have done this, ask them to think about the person they most admire and why. Each student then shares this information.

The activity can be processed by asking

1.   How did it feel to think about the qualities you admire in a person. To decide who you most admire? (Identify)

2.   What made you pick the person you chose as most admired? Does he or she embody the characteristics you described? (Analyze)

3.   Is this person someone you strive to be like in your own life? How might you begin going about being similar? (Generalize)

Chapter Eight

~~~~~~~~~~~~~~~~~~~~~~~~~~

Power and Control

Overview

The power and control phase may be imagined as the group's "adolescence," marked by members' needs to assume autonomy and to establish hierarchical relationships among themselves. It is considered to be a "preintimacy," and the presumption is that members are beginning to feel as though they really are a group and that the advisory is potentially a very meaningful experience for them. The psychological "stakes" are thus raised because of their deepening investment in the group's process. This can provoke feelings of both exhilaration and anxiety since group members now care more about being viewed positively by the facilitator and by other members than they did initially.

Students often feel that they have been asked to surrender too much of their own individual identities to become members of the group, and during power and control they make efforts to reclaim their individuality and to find a more realistic and comfortable balance of power with the advisor. Indeed, it is during this phase that students may at times view the advisor as a hindrance to the group's process rather than as its facilitator. They may challenge his/her authority but, ironically, usually still feel safer with the leader than they do with fellow students whose opinions matter more to them. Although this phase can feel stressful to advisors, it is important to remember that one has to care to fight and students do care a great deal.

It is also now that advisory members will attempt to create a social hierarchy and compete with one another for status. "Putdowns" are common and students can easily hurt one another's feelings. This is one reason why it is so important that your group create its ground rules in the first session (and that at least one of these addresses how students will communicate with each other) and that these be invoked as necessary.

Atmosphere

During power and control, the atmosphere is charged and discussions often become heated. As the advisor, you may at times feel uncomfortable as students challenge your authority or as discussion becomes more confrontative among members. In a training session recently, we were role playing what might happen if a problem developed between two members. I asked the staff participants how they might handle such a dynamic in their own advisory. A few suggested separating the two students, but why? Isn't this an ideal opportunity to provide these students a safe opportunity to express what they're feeling to one another in a manner they can both hear? Rather than trying to stop this, the facilitator again must help students understand what they are doing and why.

Influence/Decision Making

Students who tend to be highest in influence during power and control are those who are most willing to be confrontative and "fight" for the group. They may take the lead in initiating discussions of unfair practices by teachers, administrators, and parents. They may directly confront you on your interventions. (If this happens and no one comes to your aid, listen closely. Remember that nothing happens in group without a reason; and if you're challenged and no one defends you, the others are either as yet not assertive enough to dissent or they agree with the challenger.)

You may witness one or two students becoming particularly dominant and trying to make decisions for the group. If this occurs, observe it at first and see how the group responds. Generally, your students themselves will correct this dynamic by becoming more assertive themselves. If they do not, you can bring attention to it. See chapter 12 for more strategies related to this situation.

If these dominant behaviors begin to impede the group's growth, however, you may wish to send "I" messages that confront them on behalf of the group as a whole. In this way, you model the negation of these behaviors and advocate for group growth, giving members permission to do the same. Eventually, other members will become strong enough to assume this function; and they will attempt to bring those students who withdraw, dominate, monopolize, or aggressively block into compliance with the wishes of the majority.

Membership

During power and control, student roles are often a mix of self- and maintenance oriented, which tend to shift over the course of this stage. Although not consciously aware of this, group members are now actually questioning whether or not the advisory is a safe place emotionally—that is, one in which they can genuinely express their feelings without being censured by anyone else. They need to know that "feelings are spoken here," even the angry ones, and that the advisor is strong, smart, and caring enough to help students to hold these feelings until they are understood and worked through. Subgrouping is common, and this makes it very difficult for groups to achieve any kind of consensus or to problem-solve collectively.

Feelings

Members, although still ambivalent about how close they want to become to each other, can put tremendous pressure on each other to conform to the emerging group norms. Scapegoating may occur as students seek to solidify their group membership by creating "in" and "out" groups. In a recent group in which one member stayed silent the first four sessions, except for occasionally signalling nonverbally when she was unimpressed by something that was going on, a few other participants confronted her vigorously and told her how her attitude was affecting them. Their overture to her was an effort made in frustration to compel her to participate with the other members who had made a commitment to the group.

Leader Role(s)

We must work hard to help our students understand what is happening dynamically during this phase. Making process observations about how students feel about what is going on in the group, their opinions about what the facilitator is doing and why, what they would like to do, and how they feel about the way students are relating to one another are very helpful now in helping students to make sense of the changes that are occuring during power and control.

This phase represents a "normative crisis" in the group's development. As advisors, we must create an atmosphere of "supported autonomy," much as parents of adolescents do. This enables students to feel free to state their opinions, to establish interpersonal relationships, to voice dissent, and to test the safety of the experience for themselves. Those of us who engage in power struggles with our group members because we feel threatened by students' attempts to become more autonomous, do our groups a tremendous disservice. Without the opportunity to assert their own individuality, students will be unable to move forward into closer relationships with one another.

Leader Strategies

Understanding that our advisees are well positioned in this stage to reflect on their respective strengths and weaknesses and are willing to talk about both, we must work especially hard to model strong communication skills, particularly active listening and sending "I" messages, which help students to assess how their actions are affecting others. These skills also are the foundation for conflict resolution, which will likely be required now.

Exercises which encourage them to assess their skills, to compare themselves with others, to practice giving one another constructive feedback, and to vent their feelings about those in authority are especially appropriate now. Again, we want to be mindful of the need to encourage students to talk with one another, and not only to us, as much as possible.

Themes

During power and control the predominant theme is, in fact, power and the perceived lack of it. Students will criticize other teachers, their parents, or others whom they believe are at an advantage in some way and will often cast themselves as powerless and disregarded victims. Listening without judgment, and from the perspective of what the dialogue reveals about the group's developmental needs, is critical now. Often advisors become unsettled by the criticism of colleagues, feel guilty that they're participating in such discussions, and move to quash them. A much more helpful intervention is to focus on what the students are feeling and to help them struggle to understand these emotions and their underlying meanings.

The progression from one stage to the next is rarely smooth and that from power and control to the third phase of intimacy is no exception. What frequently happens is that some students in your advisory will be eager to become closer faster than others. When intimate issues are brought up in a group in which most members are still in power and control, the results can be very challenging.

One advisor recalled an instance in which his group had spent several sessions complaining bitterly about a teacher whose classroom management techniques were at best questionable. Ultimately she was removed from her responsibilities, and the students' behaviors worsened temporarily. We might interpret this as happening because they still had a need to maintain a social distance among themselves.

In one particularly trying group session, a student shared that his cousin had been accidentally shot and killed the previous weekend.The advisor worried that the other students were not affected by this tragedy because they began sharing their own losses in a manner that seemed to him to be almost competitive in nature. He writes, "I was happy that the students were able to share all this information. . . . (but) was very appalled by their lack of compassion for one another." In this instance, it is more likely that the students' apparent efforts to "one-up" each other reflected their efforts to begin drawing closer to one another but their needs to establish a group hierarchy were not yet met. As the advisor, you can always make an observation about what you're seeing and hearing and ask your group members to reflect on what they think might be happening. Again, this is a key part of our responsibilities in helping our students to become "group wise." Ultimately, the "normative crisis" is resolved. Students feel assured enough that they can speak freely to begin to explore the other side of their ambivalence about closeness, and the stage is set for intimacy.

CHARACTERISTICS OF A GROUP
IN THE POWER AND CONTROL STAGE

ATMOSPHERE:	CHARGED
FEELINGS:	ANGER, EXCITEMENT
PARTICIPATION:	ALTERNATES—FEW TO MOST
DECISION MAKING:	OFTEN BY A MINORITY
MEMBERSHIP:	MIX OF SELF-, MAINTENANCE-ORIENTED ROLES
INFLUENCE :	MOST CONFRONTATIVE
THEME(S):	POWER

Ask Yourself

1. How would you feel if your authority is challenged?

2. Which might concern you more: being confronted by students yourself or listening to them confront each other?

3. How do you think you would handle a situation in which two students have a serious disagreement?

4. What is your reaction to the possibility of one student being scapegoated by others in the group?

5. How might you respond to scapegoating? Why?

6. What is your reaction to "I" messages? How comfortable might you feel sending them?

7. Do you think your students will adopt communication techniques like "I" messages? Why or why not?

8. Of all the emotions which may be expressed during power and control, which do you think would be easiest for you to handle? Hardest? Why?

9. How do you think you might respond to the dynamic of subgrouping? What do you see as its effect on the overall group?

10. What would you like to see your students emerge from this stage thinking and feeling about the advisory?

Exercises and Activities
for Advisories in the Power
and Control Stage

Designing An Adolescent Bill Of Rights

Goal: To encourage group cohesiveness while simultaneously highlighting some of the power/powerlessness issues with which adolescents contend.

Objectives: At the end of this session students will be able to

1. identify at least two ways in which they believe they are viewed by adults,

2. describe one feeling they have about being adolescents, and

3. demonstrate the ability to work together to complete a task.

Activity

Give a brief introduction on what the Bill of Rights is and ask students their reactions to it. Then follow up by asking your advisory students to think about what an "Adolescent Bill of Rights" might consist of and why, inviting the group to collectively write it.

Given the newness of the group all suggestions should first be brainstormed, then the group can decide which to retain and/or modify, collectively giving reasons for each.

The activity can be processed by asking

1. How did it feel thinking about and and creating your group's Bill of Rights? (Identify)

2. What made you think of the rights you included? What kind of group rules might we need to protect these rights? (Analyze)

3. How well do you feel that adults respect these rights? Why? What can you do in real life to assert these rights in a way that elders will tolerate? What are some of the misperceptions adults have about you? How might they be corrected? (Generalize)

Design An "I" Message

Goal: To enable students to practice sending "I" messages.

Objectives: At the conclusion of this activity students will be able to

1. identify the three components of "I" messages,

2. develop their own "I" message responses to three situations, and

3. describe how they would feel behaving assertively, rather than passively or aggressively, in these situations

Activity

The facilitator will review what an "I" message is—a means of responding assertively when someone does something that bothers us. It always has three parts: (a) describing the behavior that's bothersome, (b) how the person feels when the other engages in this behavior, and (c) why the person feels this way.

He or she will then ask the group to think of three possible situations (or real life ones) they have found themselves in that upset them. Consider each of these one at a time in the large group. Ask students to put themselves in this situation. If they had to confront the person who was upsetting them, how would they

1. describe the offending behavior,

2. explain how it makes them feel, and

3. share why they would feel this way.

After each situation is presented and the students have time to personalize it, ask them how they would feel talking in this way to the person with whom they were upset.

1. Would it feel comfortable or uncomfortable? Why?

2. Do you feel the approach would work? Why or why not?

3. When might you be most likely to honestly tell another person that what they were doing was upsetting and to explain why?

continued

4.   Have you tried sending "I" messages in real life? Can any-
       one give an example? How did it work?

This activity can be processed by asking

1.   How did it feel considering these three situations? (Identify)

2.   Which of them would be hardest for each student to deal
       with? Why? (Analyze)

3.   How well do you believe that sending "I" messages would
       work for you in your everyday lives? (Generalize)

Assertiveness Power Line

Goals: To enable students to differentiate among aggression, assertion, and passivity and to examine the pros and cons of each.

Objectives: At the conclusion of this activity students will be able to

1. define assertion, aggression, and passivity;

2. give at least one example of when they might be inclined to engage in each of these responses; and

3. identify possible consequences of each.

Activity

Ask for three volunteers to come up to the front of the room and explain that there is an imaginary line running across the room. You will give the students examples of potentially stressful social situations and ask them to position themselves on the line based on how they would respond. (Construct your scenarios so that there are always three possible responses, "1" passive, "2" assertive, and "3" aggressive. After each scenario is presented, students position themselves to the far left if they agree with response 1, in the center for response 2, or to the far right for response 3 and to explain why they are standing where they are. Then invite other students to comment and ask questions. Scenarios might include: someone cuts in front of you in lunch line, your best friend snubs you and hangs out with someone you don't like, a teacher accuses you of cheating, and so forth.

This activity may be processed by asking

1. How did you feel while participating in (observing) this activity? (Identify)

2. What are advantages/disadvantages to responding passively? Assertively? Aggressively? (Analyze)

3. In real life, when are you most likely to act passively? Assertively? Aggressively? Why? (Generalize)

I Am Not My Description

Goal: To encourage students to consider how they view themselves and whether this perception is realistic.

Objectives: At the end of this activity students will be able to

1. describe four ways they perceive themselves and why and

2. compare their self-perceptions with those others have of them.

Activity

Ask your students to each anonymously write down two adjectives that positively describe them and two that are negative. These are all put in a box, and the facilitator draws them out one at a time. Students listen to the adjectives and then discuss why they feel this student may have described him or herself in that way. (A variation is that students might guess who wrote these self-descriptions. Students have the perogative of choosing to reveal this or not. In this instance, students would be asked to give the authors feedback on their adjective choices.)

The facilitator then asks students to consider whether the ways in which we see ourselves can affect how we act. If we believe we are "bad students," for example, will this affect our willingness to try? If we see ourselves as "angry," might this color our relationships? Where do these self-perceptions come from?

This activity can be processed by asking

1. How did it feel writing down self-adjectives? Hearing others? (Identify)

2. What kinds of adjectives did students hear? Where do these come from? (Analyze)

3. Are we always how we are described? (Generalize)

Two Opinions To Share

Goal: To allow students the opportunity to give and to receive constructive feedback.

Objectives: At the conclusion of this activity students will be able to

1. give three examples of positive comments about themselves,

2. identify three areas in which others believe they could make some personal changes, and

3. express their opinions in the form of "I" messages.

Activity

This exercise can either be done verbally or in writing, directly or anonymously. Students take a few minutes to reflect on their feelings about one another and to write these down. They then use their notes as a reference while they address each other student in the circle by giving him or her two "I" messages each. The first is positive feedback, and the second points out a behavior the student engages in that either confuses or disturbs the speaker.

As facilitator, you will again review what an "I" message is and coach students as needed while they give their feedback. By the conclusion of the activity, each student will have heard positive and negative comments from every other student in the group.

This activity may be processed by asking

1. What did it feel like giving this feedback? Receiving it? Using the "I" message form? (Identify)

2. Were there any common themes in qualities we either liked or had difficulty with? What? Why might this be true? (Analyze)

3. How do you give or receive feedback from people who matter to you? Would "I" messages work for you? (Generalize)

A Time When I Succeeded Against All Odds

Goal: To remind students that they have skills and opportunity to cope successfully with difficult life circumstances.

Objectives: At the end of this activity students will be able to

1. recall one life event in which they persevered against very difficult circumstances and

2. identify at least two personal qualities which enabled them to do so.

Activity

Ask your students to try to recall a time in which they had to face something very difficult but were able to do so successfully. (These should be events that they don't mind discussing in group.) Each will describe the circumstance and the personal qualities that enabled them to cope with it. If they begin to talk about external supports, encourage them to focus on themselves. Students may question one another as needed, but should not be allowed to divert the focus off the speaker. Make sure all students are equally heard before processing.

This activity may be processed by asking

1. How did it feel recalling this life event? Talking about it? Why? (Identify)

2. What qualities did students describe that seemed to help them prevail? Did students realize they possessed these qualities before this event? (Analyze)

3. Has having this experience and realizing more about your coping skills changed your lives in any way? If so how? (Generalize)

What It's Like To Be My Gender

Goal: To enable students to identify what they do and don't like about being male or female and how these beliefs affect them.

Objectives: At the conclusion of this activity students will be able to

1. describe two qualities that they like and two that they dis-like about being their gender and

2. identify two qualities each that they feel to be positive/negative about being the opposite sex.

Activity

Divide your advisory into two same-sex groups and ask each group to think about what's good about being their gender and what's bad. Then ask each group to do the same for the oppo-site sex, creating lists of positive and negative qualities about being male/female.

Then compare lists. Ask the females to first share what they feel is positive about their gender, then ask the males to share what they feel is positive about being female. Compare lists. Next, ask what females think is positive about being male and males' opinions of the same, again comparing. Then repeat the pro-cess for perceived negative perceptions, that is, ask each gen-der to describe what they don't like about their sex and com-pare their answers with perceptions of the opposite sex.

This activity can be processed by asking

1. How did it feel working in your same-sex group thinking of benefits and disadvantages of each gender? (Identify)

2. How did the two sexes compare in what they saw as positive and negative? Why might this have been true? (Analyze)

3. How do your perceptions of what's good and bad about be-ing your gender affect your behavior generally? (Generalize)

Try To Convince Us

Goal: To encourage students to think critically and to argue persuasively.

Objectives: At the conclusion of this exercise students will be able to

1. articulate an opinion they hold,

2. identify three elements present in a persuasive argument, and

3. give constructive feedback to at least one other group member.

Activity

You will read a statement to each of your advisees and in turn each will be asked to either support or refute the statement. Students will then take a vote to determine whether or not the person convinced them of his/her point of view and discuss why or why not. Suggested statements might include: You should never let other people know that you have a problem. Teachers are entitled to get angry at students. The principal is the most important person in a school. Parents should feel proud of their children. Boys are stronger than girls.

This activity can be processed by asking

1. What did it feel like trying to convince other students of your point of view? (Identify)

2. What did you notice to be true about the arguments that were most persuasive? What was it about the person arguing his/her point of view or how he/she did so that convinced you? (Analyze)

3. How important is it for you that other people agree with your opinions generally? How do you usually go about trying to get them to go along with you? What if they don't? (Generalize)

I Was Pressured To Do Something I Didn't Want To Do

Goal: To introduce the concept of refusal skills and when a student might need to use them.

Objectives: At the end of this activity students will be able to

1. identify at least one real-life situation in which they have felt pressured to act in a way they didn't like and

2. demonstrate one way in which they might refuse to do so.

Activity

You will ask your group members to recall a time when they were pressured to do something they didn't want to do and then ask them to write it down and hand it in. The responses will be shuffled and then redistributed. Each student will read the scenario as though it were their own and will a) describe the situation, b) explain why they were tempted to engage in it, c) then discuss what would concern them about doing so, and d) then explain how they would refuse it. (Students will react to each scenario and give feedback about the refusal techniques being suggested.)

This activity can be processed by asking

1. How did it feel recalling a real life situation and writing it down? Reading someone else's scenario and trying to figure out what that student was experiencing? (Identify)

2. What were some of the common reasons why students were tempted to engage in these behaviors? Any commonalities also in what concerned them about doing so? (Analyze)

3. In real life, when is it especially hard to resist doing what others want you to do? How do you handle this? (Generalize)

What Would You Do?

Goal: To ask students to consider how to assert themselves and the possible consequences of doing so.

Objectives: At the conclusion of this session students will be able to

1. describe their own responses to each of seven hypothetical situations and

2. identify at least one consequence for resisting/cooperating in each of these.

Activity

As facilitator, you will first distribute sheets describing each of the seven hypothetical situations to your advisees, ask them to read the scenarios, and then ask each participant to share with the group which scenario would be the hardest one for them to refuse to participate in and why. Try to elicit some of the core values/concerns which your students express and ask the group collectively to comment on them.

Then, ask each student to take a turn describing how, in fact, they would respond to the situation they've identified and why. The scenarios are

1. Some friends of yours are going to the park to smoke weed. You don't do drugs yourself, but these friends are important to you and you want to be with them.

2. Your friends want you to sneak out Friday night after the curfew that you and your parents have agreed upon. Your parents trust you, and you don't want to betray this trust but you have a crush on one of the people going.

3. Your group of friends is ganging up on someone and has started a rumor about him or her. You don't like this person very much yourself but you're sure the rumor is false.

4. Your friends are wearing clothes that make you uncomfortable but you feel pressured to look like them.

5. Several friends shoplift while you're with them at the mall. They encourage you to do the same.

6. One of your friends brought a can of spray paint to school and wants you to guard the door of the rest room so that he can graffiti a wall.

7. As you are walking through the school parking lot, you see several of your friends smoking cigarettes. They offer you a drag. You don't smoke.

This activity can be processed by asking

1.   How did it feel putting yourselves into these scenarios? (Identify)

2.   Were there any that were easier to respond to? Harder? Why? (Analyze)

3.   What did the assertive answers have in common? (Analyze)

4.   How well do you think such assertive responses would work in real life? Why? (Generalize)

Degrees Of Anger

Goal: To help students differentiate among various degrees of anger and to modulate their responses accordingly.

Objectives: At the end of this session students will be able to

1. identify three different circumstances which anger them to varying degrees and

2 describe their reactions to each circumstance and discuss why they vary.

Activity

You will hand out out a sheet divided into three areas marked "I would feel mildly angry if . . .", "moderately angry if . . .", and "severely angry if . . ." and ask students to complete the appropriate statements with scenarios from their everyday lives. Students are then asked to share their situations with everyone else. They may do so by sharing all three levels in their turn or you might ask everyone to first address mild anger, then moderate, then severe. Students will share why they respond with the degrees of anger they do to each, while other students ask questions or comment freely.

This activity can be processed by asking

1. How did it feel recalling three different situations which can make you angry? (Identify)

2. What differentiates a situation which makes you only mildly angry from one that has a stronger effect on you? How do your responses change as the anger you feel grows stronger? (Analyze)

3. In real life, when are you likely to show this anger and when are you likely to hide it? Why? How does not showing it work? (Generalize)

What I Do And Don't Like About My Family

Goal: To assist students in expressing balanced feelings about their families.

Objectives: At the end of this session students will be able to

1. identify one positive and one negative feeling about their families,

2. describe why these feelings are positive or negative, and

3. suggest a way to handle the negative feeling.

Activity

Ask each of your students to give the group a quick overview of their families—who lives with them and their relationships to these individuals. Then ask each to describe one quality they enjoy about their families as a whole and another they do not. Encourage them to explain why they hold these feelings. Ask the other students to listen carefully and, if possible, to suggest a way each student might build on their positive feelings to begin to address or to reframe the negative ones.

This activity can be processed by asking

1. How did it feel to describe their families to the group? To identify positive/negative feelings about them? (Identify)

2. Was it harder to talk about the positive feelings or the negative? Why might this be so? (Analyze)

3. Having done this exercise, can they see any ways they could reframe their negative feelings over the next few weeks? How might they begin to do this? (Generalize)

Chapter Nine

~~~~~~~~~~~~~~~~~~~~~

Intimacy

Overview

Once students perceive their advisory to be a group in which they can safely express themselves, they tend to relax and draw closer to each other, becoming particularly interested in their similarities to one another. Indeed, relationships among group members are key during intimacy; and their focus shifts away from the advisor. No longer needing to prove themselves to you or to each other, they instead tend to view their advisor benignly as an important presence but not one they're particularly concerned with at the moment. Students will support one another now, and one of the most beneficial of all the curative factors in a group's dynamics is in play: The realization that one is not alone in his or her feelings or experiences.

This group stage is initially pleasurable to its members and there may be subtle pressure exerted among them to maintain this sense of harmony and well-being. The caveat here is that the sense of intimacy is relatively short-lived; and the longer students attempt to hold onto it, the more elusive it becomes. There is an unreal quality to this phase, much like that experienced by lovers who are initially infatuated with each other. Indeed, it is more of a "pseudo-intimacy"; and eventually differences that were at first overlooked become apparent, and students again feel ambivalent about their closeness to other group members.

In fact, intimacy actually encompasses two substages: the closeness described above and the ultimate realization that it is transitory. This gradual awareness represents a second normative crisis. Your advisory students have taken a big risk in revealing personal information about themselves, having temporarily felt close to one another; but as this stage begins to end, they are aware that something has gone awry that they don't understand. It is not uncommon now for students to attempt to "change the rules" by restricting the type of sharing they will do henceforth.

One group in the intimacy phase initially demonstrated their closeness by successfully "untangling" themselves in the tangle game (described in chapter 7). They had been able to do this successfully in one session and the advisor was pleased that they worked cooperatively with no regard to gender. In the following session, they asked to play the game again. This time it wasn't as much fun and players dropped out or failed to cooperate with one another. The group was very upset and confused about why things had changed in a way that they perceived to be negative.

Atmosphere

You will readily know when your advisory moves from power and control into intimacy because the atmosphere changes markedly from one of confrontation to that of peace and harmony. As the facilitator, you, too, will feel relaxed and engaged in the discussion. Students often draw their chairs closer together, creating a tighter circle. They will laugh more, and at times act more flirtatiously with one another. If food is ever introduced into the group, it will be now.

Indeed, several years ago a colleague conducted a training course in group counseling based on these stages of group development. The group he was working with was quite small (three men and three women) and the members apparently had considerable social interest in one another. On the day he anticipated the group moving into the intimacy phase, he noticed that the men had dressed with far more care than in the earlier sessions. The women, too, all looked their best and were wearing more makeup than they had previously.

One of the men announced that although he realized that the group was theoretically ready to go into intimacy he didn't see why they had to, and he wondered if they couldn't just skip to the next stage of differentiation development. My colleague said, "How dare this train not stop at intimacy when the ladies have so obviously dressed for the occasion." It's a funny anecdote, but it underscores the power the promise of intimacy holds for us.

Feelings

Emotions run the gamut from *A* to *Z* during intimacy. Initially, members experience a near-giddiness in the promise of sharing and closeness. They really care about one another and revel in finding ways to express this. As students begin to realize that they cannot sustain the pretense of commonality, however, pleasure changes to disillusionment and disappointment.

Although this is a common, and indeed necessary, occurrence in group development, it can feel disheartening to students because they may experience this shift as a loss, possibly even a group failure. If so, they may again express disappointment or anger toward the facilitator for not protecting this good feeling, or they may seek scapegoats among themselves. Indeed, many of the dynamic issues that appear toward the end of the intimacy phase are a recapitulation of power and control issues.

Themes

Discussions tend to focus on families' positive aspects, and sometimes there are even overt references made to the advisory group feeling like a family. (Indeed, in some schools, advisories are referred to as "family groups" because they represent the best of what families do have to offer to their children.) It is also frequently during this stage that students will ask questions about personal accomplishments or disappointments, relationships, sex, or possibly feel comfortable enough to talk about sexual experiences. Should the latter be true, it is important that the facilitator not feel that he or she is being asked to play the role of expert and answer these questions, nor feel pressured to share personal experiences if asked by students: "Did you ever . . . ?" or "Is it normal to . . . ?" Rather, facilitators faced with such questions should listen for students' underlying concerns and reflect the question back. For example, they might respond by saying: "It sounds as though you might be wondering if it is "normal" to . . . Are you concerned about this?"

Decision Making

Given the ascendance of group needs over individual needs, it is not surprising that decision making becomes very much more a group process than it may have been previously. It will be important to your students that everyone participate in any such process. Decisions are made thoughtfully now, by consensus.

Influence

Those students who tend to be high in influence during intimacy are those who are willing to share personally. Because the students are now expressing the procloseness side of their ambivalence, they eagerly encourage their peers to share, although they may still have reservations about how much they themselves want to personally reveal. Those willing to take this chance are appreciated.

Membership

In power and control, we saw membership roles encompassing both self- and maintenance orientations. During intimacy, these shift from self-oriented to maintenance oriented, then back to self. The group in intimacy has developed a very positive valence. Students will nurture one another and, in the process, may also learn how to better nurture themselves. The primary risk now is that students may feel pressured to share more than they are comfortable doing; and although they may succumb to the temptation to do so (particularly as it enhances their group status), they may ultimately regret having done so, feeling overly exposed and unprotected.

They are willing to support others but definitely need this support reciprocated. Students who take the chance of revealing personal information need to know that they are not hanging from a limb by themselves. It's not uncommon to see more vocal students challenge silent members to talk more now, feeling that a failure to do so is unfair to those who are committed to participating.

As intimacy progresses and students are forced to admit that they don't really have as much in common as they had initially assumed, self-orientation again prevails. Members retreat from one another emotionally, standing back a bit as if to say "I don't know what I was thinking wanting to be so intimate with the rest of you. I'm really very different than you."

Leader Roles

Facilitators may feel that they are less needed now than in previous stages because the focus has shifted off of them to interpersonal sharing among students, but this is hardly the case. We advisors assume less directive roles now but continue to be active, encouraging the group members to take certain risks, of sharing more personally and helping students to identify commonalities. We also act protectively, attempting to balance the needs of individual students with those of the group as a whole by preventing any one student from becoming too vulnerable. We do this by closely monitoring discussion and protecting students from revealing too much too soon.

As the stage ultimately shifts, as it must, from one of heady togetherness to a kind of disenchantment in which students withdraw emotionally, our roles also change. We now must "take our group's temperature," by addressing each member individually and asking how he or she is feeling at that moment. If students are unwilling or unable to respond, we may have to take the lead and reflect back what we are seeing, hearing, or feeling in the group's demeanor that suggests that our students are feeling in someway more ambivalent about their closeness to the others.

Leader Strategies

It is during intimacy, probably more than any other phase, that we practice our deepening and generalizing skills. Remember our discussion in chapter 5 about how much of our work involves identifying students' underlying feelings and deepening them, then generalizing to the other members by asking them if they, too, have experienced these feelings. This technique not only protects the individual student, but it also fits in dynamically with the group's needs to establish commonalities. Students are therefore receptive to its practice.

Advisors will want to encourage their group members to identify their respective needs and to seek the group's help in problem solving how these might be met. A student with low self-esteem who learns to speak respectfully to peers and is addressed respectfully in return, for example, can be affected in a tremendously positive manner by this experience.

One advisor described doing the "trust fall" when she sensed her group had moved into the intimacy phase. She asked two students, best friends, to stand in the middle of the circle and then requested that one stand with his back to the other and allow himself to fall into his friend's arms. When he did this successfully, the other 9 students cheered for them. She writes, "This was the point when we emerged into intimacy." What members cannot yet see, but what we as facilitators must help them to understand, is that this pseudo-intimacy based only on what they perceived themselves to have in common must be experienced but then outgrown for them to truly have the chance to be themselves openly with each other, as they are about to in the next stage of differentiation development.

CHARACTERISTICS OF A GROUP
IN THE INTIMACY STAGE

Atmosphere:	Relaxed, comfortable
Feelings:	Elation changing to disenchantment
Participation:	All are engaged
Decision Making:	By consensus
Membership:	Maintenance oriented to self-oriented by end
Influence:	"Sharers" high in influence
Themes:	Family, relationships

Ask Yourself

1. How will you feel during this stage when the emphasis shifts from students' relationships to you to those among themselves?

2. What are you likely to feel if students ask you questions about sex?

3. How will you handle questions on this topic?

4. What family-related topics might you be comfortable addressing?

5. Are there family topics that would make you uncomfortable? If so, what might these be and how will you handle them?

6. How will you feel when the group realizes it must abandon its illusion of intimacy?

7. How will you help students to understand what is happening when they can no longer sustain the illusion of commonality?

8. If power and control themes reemerge, how might you handle them?

9. Can you give up your role of being more directive, including introducing exercises to your group, in favor of allowing them to take more responsibility for deciding what they want to address?

10. Do you feel confident in your ability to protect your students from over exposing themselves? How will you do this?

Exercises and Activities for Advisories in the Intimacy Stage

If I Could Do It All Over Again

Goal: To help students recall an incident in which they regret how they behaved, reflect on why they feel this way, and discuss what they learned from the experience.

Objectives: At the conclusion of this exercise students will be able to

1. acknowledge a past behavior which they regret,

2. explain what they had hoped to achieve from the behavior, and

3. describe how they might act differently in a similar situation today to achieve their desired goal.

Activity

Ask students to form pairs and to think back to a time when they had a problem with another person and responded to him or her in a way that didn't work out well. They will share this experience with their partner, focusing on

*   What triggered the incident.

*   How they were feeling at the time.

*   What they actually said or did that they now regret.

*   What they hoped to gain by saying or doing this.

*   If they could replay this event, would they do anything differently? What? Why?

This activity can be processed by asking

1. What did it feel like sharing this experience? (Identify)

2. What did you learn from doing so, both from your own reflections and from what your partner said. (Analyze)

3. Do you think you acted as you did to protect yourself in some way? If so, how? (Analyze)

4. How easy or difficult is it for you to admit mistakes to your friends, teachers, or family in real life? Why? (Generalize)

The Christmas Stocking

Note: This exercise should be done right before Christmas break. It's listed in the stage of intimacy because that may well be where your group is by this time of the year. Regardless of your group's stage, however, this is a very powerful and, ultimately, a very helpful activity at this time of year. Christmas is difficult for many children and this "gift" means a lot.

Goal: To enable students to both reflect on their positive feelings about other group members and to learn how others feel about them.

Objectives: At the conclusion of this activity students will be able to

1. identify at least one positive feeling about every other group member and

2. describe at least five positive feelings other students express about them.

Activity

This activity may take more than one session. It requires green, red, and white construction paper; scissors; glue; markers; and possibly sequins or colored dust for decorations. Each student makes a Christmas stocking with his/her name affixed.

Then each student writes a brief message to every other student in the group, describing one positive quality of that person. These are given to the facilitator, who then checks them and puts them in the appropriate stockings. If the facilitator wishes, he or she might also participate in the exercise both by sending messages to group members and by making his/her own stocking and receiving messages from the students.

This activity can be processed by asking

1. How did you feel doing this activity? (Identify)

2. What did you realize about the other students in the group? (Analyze)

continued

3.   How do you usually give one another compliments; and if you don't, why don't you? (Generalize)

4.   Why is it important to both give and to receive compliments? (Generalize)

The facilitator might conclude by pointing out that Christmas is often a time when we have high hopes of receiving certain gifts. Sometimes we do, and at other times the holidays can be disappointing. Whatever else the youngsters do or don't get this Christmas, the positive responses from their fellow group members are all theirs, earned and deserved.

What Scares Me

Goal: To encourage students to think about what's frightening to them and how they handle these fears.

Objectives: At the conclusion of this activity students will be able to

1. identify at least three things that scare them and why and

2. relate how they have handled each of these threats.

Activity:

You ask the students simply to think about something that is frightening to them and to share it with the rest of the group. In doing so they will identify

1. the scary situation,

2. what makes it scary to them,

3. why they believe it is scary to them, and

4. what they've found that helps them to handle this fear.

This activity can be processed by asking

1. How did it feel sharing this fear with the others? (Identify)

2. What did you learn from doing this activity. (Analyze)

3. Did you hear any other strategies for handling scary situations that you think you, too, might use? What? (Analyze)

4. In real life, to whom do you go if you're fearful? Does this help? (Generalize)

5. Could the advisory be such a safe place? (Generalize)

When Someone Let Me Down

Goal: To encourage students to reflect on what helps them to trust others and how they respond if this trust is broken.

Objectives: At the conclusion of this activity students will be able to

1.   recount an experience in which their trust was violated and

2.   describe the impact of this betrayal on them and what they learned from the experience about relationships.

Activity

You might preface this activity by pointing out that all of us have been disappointed in relationships when someone we care about lets us down by not being trustworthy. If comfortable doing so, you might begin by sharing a personal example of such an event, how it made you feel, and how you responded. Ask your students if they can recall similar experiences that they might feel comfortable sharing. (Anyone who wishes to may pass.)

Students are encouraged to ask one another questions and to make comments as they desire.

This activity can be processed by asking

1.   How did it feel hearing others' experiences? Recounting your own? (Identify)

2.   Were there any similarities in what different students shared? If so, what? (Analyze)

3.   How did this experience affect your attitude about trusting others? (Generalize)

4.   Might it have an effect on your willingness to take chances here in the advisory? If so, how? (Generalize)

What Confuses Me About The Opposite Sex

Goal: To provide students the chance to ask questions about the opposite sex safely and anonymously.

Objectives: At the conclusion of this activity, students will be able to

1. identify three behaviors the two genders find confusing about one another and

2. articulate possible reasons for each of these behaviors.

Activity

Split your advisory into same sex groups and ask them to make up a list of 10 questions each which they would like to collectively ask the opposite sex. Depending on your comfort level, and that of the group, you may do this in a completely open-ended manner or put limits on the types of questions allowed.

Set ground rules for answering one another, reminding students how to give constructive feedback and making sure students talk one at a time, since discussion tends to become very animated. Then ask your groups to alternate their questions and facilitate the discussion they engender. Help your group to avoid gross generalizations a much as possible.

This activity can be processed by asking

1. How did it feel to make up your list with other members of your sex? To ask these questions? (Identify)

2. Why do you think you chose the questions you did? (Analyze)

3. Did you hear any patterns in the responses by gender? If so, what? Anything that particularly surprised you? (Analyze)

4. In real life, how do you get the answers you look for about the opposite sex? (Generalize)

One Thing I Am Enjoying About This Group

Goal: To enable students to evaluate their feelings about the advisory group to date.

Objectives: At the end of this session students will be able to

1.   identify a positive feeling they have about the group and/ or specific group members and

2.   relate at least three positive feelings expressed by others.

Activity

This is a very straightforward exercise in which you will ask students to each think about one thing they really enjoy about the advisory group at this time. You might also ask them to compare this group with another group experience in which they had also felt like they belonged.

This activity can be processed by asking

1.   How did it feel to think about your reactions to the advisory? (Identify)

2.   What's the best thing about feeling like you belong to a group? Is there any possible negative to it? (Analyze)

3.   Are there any similarities in what students find enjoyable about this group? (Analyze)

4.   How do students' feelings about the advisory compare with their previous group experiences? (Generalize)

What I Have To Offer

Goal: To give students an opportunity to think about how they present themselves to others and why.

Objectives: At the conclusion of this activity students will be able to

1.   identify three personal characteristics they value in themselves and

2.   contrast their self-perceptions with others' perceptions of them.

Activity

Hand out sheets of paper to your students and ask them to imagine that they are advertising for new friends by writing personal ads that will appear in the school newspaper. Go over some of the common abbreviations for such ads first. Collect and redistribute these and ask students to each read an ad. Students then comment on what this student sounds like, what he or she has described about themselves. (If you wish and, if this meets with overall approval, students can guess who wrote each ad.)

This activity can be processed by asking

1.   How did it feel writing a personal ad about yourself? (Identify)

2.   How did it feel to hear your ad read and analyzed? (Identify)

3.   How did you choose to portray yourself? What qualities seemed to best describe you and why? (Analyze)

4.   In real life, how do you present yourself to others with whom you would like to develop a relationship. Why? (Generalize)

What I Would Look For In Different Types Of Relationships

Goal: To help students begin to differentiate among the attributes they seek from different types of relationships.

Objectives: At the conclusion of this activity, students will be able to

1.   identify the qualities they seek in friends, in romantic relationships, and in life partners; and

2.   describe why these qualities may or may not be the same in each.

Activity

Ask students to first write down one quality they appreciate the most about their best or a close friend. Was it this quality that first drew you to this person? If not, when did you discover it? Next, ask the students to imagine that they were ready to fall in love. What quality would be most important to you in this relationship? Finally, can you think ahead to adulthood and imagine that you are now looking for a life partner with whom you may wish to have children. What would you look for in this relationship? Once students have committed to these qualities, ask them to begin discussing what they look for first in a friend, then in a lover, and finally in a prospective spouse or significant other.

This activity can be processed by asking

1.   How did it feel to think about the qualities you look for in a friend, lover, partner? (Identify)

2.   Did the qualities you would seek in each stay about the same or did they change? If the latter, how and why? (Analyze)

3.   Did your qualifications for a life partner have to do with what kind of a parent he or she might make? (Analyze)

4.   How might this relate to qualities you see in their own parents? (Generalize)

The Trust Walk

Goal: To provide students an experience in which they must depend on each other.

Objectives: At the conclusion of this activity, students will be able to

1. describe how it felt being dependent on another person and

2. identify at least one responsibility they assumed as guides.

Activity

This is a classic groupwork exercise in which students are paired, one is blindfolded, and the other leads him or her around for several minutes. The guide is responsible for ensuring that his/her partner is safe at all times.

This activity can be processed by asking

1. How did it feel being blindfolded and led around by your partner? (Identify)

2. As the person leading, what did you have to do to? What did or didn't help you do this? (Analyze)

3. Was it easier guiding or being led? Why? (Analyze)

4. How important is it to be able to trust other members of this advisory group? (Generalize)

5. Are your relationships within the group different from relationships you have outside of the group? If so, how? (Generalize)

Questions About Sex Fishbowl

Goal: To allow students the opportunity to anonymously ask questions about sex.

Objectives: At the conclusion of this activity, students will be able to

1. answer at least two commonly asked questions about sex and

2. identify different reasons why people might be curious about different aspects of sexuality.

Activity

The questions for this activity can be gathered all at once at the beginning of this session or students may be invited to think of them over a week's time prior to it. In either event, you will ask students to think of at least one question they have about sex and write it down anonymously.

Then collect all the questions in a basket and ask students to each draw one slip of paper, read the question, and comment on why they feel this student may have been curious about the topic. Then you will ask students collectively what they feel the answer is. If they don't know, you will answer. (Bring a text with you to which you can refer quickly as needed.)

This activity can be processed by asking

1. How did it feel to ask questions about sex? (Identify)

2. What were some of the most common concerns expressed? (Analyze)

3. Why might students your age be so curious about these particular questions? (Analyze)

4. How do you get your information about sex in real life? How accurate do you believe it is? (Generalize)

Success Sharing

Goal: To help students identify and disclose their accomplishments.

Objectives: At the conclusion of this activity students will be able to

1. identify at least one personal accomplishment and how it felt and

2. share this with the other members of the advisory.

Activity

Begin by pointing out that we all enjoy successes but may not always allow ourselves to acknowledge them. Today we will. Students will each recall at least one personal accomplishment of which they are particularly proud. (No one will be allowed to pass today. Those students who claim not to have any to report will be coached by the advisor and other members until they have been helped to recall one such experience.) Other members are invited to ask for more information, to give feedback, or to share similar experiences.

This activity can be processed by asking

1. What did it feel like recalling a success? Sharing it? (Identify)

2. What made this particular accomplishment stand out for you? (Analyze)

3. How has this success affected who you are and how you feel about yourself? (Generalize)

Autobiographical Sharing

Goal: To allow students to reflect upon and share important life events.

Objectives: At the conclusion of this exercise students will be able to

1.   identify at least three experiences which have shaped their personalities and

2.   explain to others how these events have impacted on them.

Activity

You may start by making the point that for any of us to know where we are going in life, it is helpful to look back to where we have been. Today we will do an exercise in which we recall three experiences that we believe to be very important in shaping who we are today. Each member recalls these experiences and shares them with the rest of the group. Other members are invited to ask questions and to seek clarification as needed.

This activity can be processed by asking

1.   What did it feel like recalling these three experiences? Sharing them with the group? (Identify)

2.   Why did you pick these particular events? What significance have they had on your life? (Analyze)

3.   How do these experiences, and the students' reactions to them, affect you in your everyday life? (Generalize)

How I Am Independent

Goal: To enable students to realize how they are their own persons.

Objectives: By the end of this activity students will be able to

1. identify three ways in which they act on their own despite pressures to do otherwise and

2. describe why it is important to them to be their own person.

Activity

You will ask students to reflect on their everyday lives and to think of the ways in which they take responsibility for themselves and possibly others. Did they learn to do these things on their own? Have life circumstances dictated that they needed to become independent in these ways?

This activity can be processed by asking

1. How does it feel to think about how you act independently and how you learned to do so? (Identify)

2. What have students heard in the experiences they have shared today? Are their similarities? Differences? (Analyze)

3. How does it feel to act independently in your everday life? How do you feel if your independence is challenged in any way? What might challenge your sense of independence or responsibility? (Generalize)

Chapter Ten

~~~~~~~~~~~~~

Differentiation

Overview

D ifferentiation embodies the group's most productive "work" phase. Students in an advisory that is in this stage are able to discuss a wide range of topics constructively, because it is now that they can view both themselves and their peers realistically. Whereas in earlier stages group members glossed over their differences, they now recognize and celebrate their diversity. Groups in this stage are disclosing more personal information, demonstrating their abilities to communicate assertively, and giving constructive feedback to one another.

Students in differentiation need opportunities to practice decision making and problem solving and are far more capable of doing so than in earlier group stages. If a group leader were to have asked students in the power and control phase to do a collective exercise—for example, the classic one in which students are told they are going on a moon mission, are given a list of 20+ items, and are asked to rank order them on the basis of their usefulness in this operation—the group would not be able to complete the task. Their discussions would break down because of the conflicts inherent in that stage. However, a group in differentiation could accomplish this task easily. They could allow themselves to acknowledge one another's knowledge and to take direction from others as needed to meet a common goal.

They are also better able to reflect upon and learn from previous experiences and to better understand the connection between thoughts, feelings, and actions. If they are disposed to practicing new behaviors, they will now do so with a minimum of reliance on the advisor, for at this point group members are autonomous. Students in this stage are inclined to think about who they are, what they want for themselves, and the resources they possess to help them attain their goals.

Atmosphere

The atmosphere now is relaxed and comfortable but also stimulating. Students are able to achieve more collectively than they could individually, and they have an accurate appreciation of one another's talents. They tend to be flexible, trusting, and more cooperative. They can compromise and problem solve effectively.

Influence

The overall style of influence is a democratic one. There may be multiple informal leaders who have emerged by now because of their investment in the group's success, their abilities to analyze what needs to be done, and their willingness to facilitate decision making that is representative of the group as a whole. The group realizes it possesses potential for "success" and will listen to those members with helpful insights and strategies for achieving it.

Decision Making

Decisions are made by consensus. This is related to an appreciation of each members' individuality and the fact that by now they have come to realize that it is their differences—in points of view, temperament, and talents—that makes them as strong a group as they are. They no longer fear these differences. They, indeed, embrace them.

Membership

Members are very aware of the distinctions between them; and, in particular, who has the intelligence, motivation, and skills to help the group be most productive. Although students in the differentiation stage play roles that are generally task and maintenance oriented, the end of this stage may be marked by a resurgence of individual needs. Members may now seek recognition for what they have contributed. They may also begin to emphasize differences between one another and to use this as an excuse to once again move apart, rather than continuing to embrace these differences as a source of their collective problem solving strength as they did earlier in this stage.

Feelings

When you ask students how they are feeling at the end of a session in this stage, they will often seem almost surprised by the question, as though it were understood that they feel fine. They feel easy with one another, clear about their roles in the group, and confident that collectively they have found a balance that accommodates everyone's needs.

Because groups in differentiation are now able to make the most of their personal attributes, many facilitators consider this to be the ideal stage of group development. Not only do members work well collectively, but individually they begin to consolidate many of the intrapsychic gains they have made previously, maintaining a growing sense of self-esteem. They have already identified their respective strengths and liabilities in power and control and developed nurturing strategies in intimacy. Now they strive to integrate what they have learned and, in the process, to hopefully derive a more realistic and loving appreciation of themselves.

Leader Role

The role of the advisor now shifts from being directive to letting go of the leadership and encouraging students to assume it. He/she now helps the group to clarify its goals and to support the importance of the members' initiative in problem solving and decision making. Taking on such a pure facilitative role allows the advisor to confront the group honestly about their processes and the feelings which they express. You will find that you are still listening and processing what you hear, see, and feel as much as always; but you are probably speaking much less now as your members can assume more and more of the leadership roles the group requires.

Because of their developmental status and capabilities in giving constructive feedback, this is an ideal point for you as the advisor to assess how well the group is going. How well is the group meeting members' needs? How do they like the structure of the sessions? Are there any additions or suggestions they might make? What are their participation levels?

Remember that you have continually been focusing on both process and content issues since your advisory began, and all the while you have been "training" your group members to do the same. You should be able to reap the harvest of these efforts now. Get your students to help you evaluate how well their needs are being met on both levels; and if there are difficulties, now is the time to allow them to suggest solutions.

Leader Strategies

What will not work now is for you to continue trying to run the sessions unilaterally. Your members neither need this direction from you nor do they want it, and they certainly won't tolerate it well. They will likely demonstrate their resistance, to what on some level they probably experience as infantilizing, by becoming less active and more withdrawn. Now, as always in your facilitation of your advisory, you must listen closely to your members to understand where they are and then move to meet them there.

As Gitterman and Schulman (1994) remind us, "Note also, how much help is available from members in the group. This is a relief for the worker, who does not have to provide all of the help but can concentrate instead on releasing the group's inherent potential for mutual aid" (p. 45).

On the other hand, there are several possible mistakes we can make as advisors during this stage. We can underlead or overlead, as described above. We can fail to hear the underlying concerns and follow up on them as well as necessary, instead allowing the group's focus to shift around with no real exploration of key issues. We may spend too much time on one or two group members at the expense of the overall needs. We can also not allow enough time to process whatever activities or discussion has ensued in a particular session.

If you choose to do activities, let them be loosely structured ones that require meaningful problem solving and decision making by your students. If you begin such an activity but one or more students bring up personal issues and the group seems more invested in dealing with them, let your activity go and work with the real life problem. Your students will still be building the same skills but in a way that is more relevant and powerful to them.

If you are asked your opinion on a subject, it is invariably most helpful to turn the question back to the group, paraphrase it, and then ask your students what they think about it. Remember, that often student questions to you aren't really concerned with your point of view but rather are their way of letting you know that this is an issue they are struggling with in some way. Your job is to hear this and provide the forum in which they can exercise their own abilities to make sense of the issue.

Themes

The topics students in differentiation might wish to talk about are varied, but among others you will probably hear themes related to autonomy, future school plans, possible career directions, and family separation issues. Listen carefully to how your students discuss these, because in all likelihood they will do so from the perspective of problems that have emerged and how they might be resolved.

CHARACTERISTICS OF GROUPS
IN THE STAGE OF DIFFERENTIATION

Atmosphere:	Relaxed, comfortable
Feelings:	Accepting of/interested in one another
Participation:	High on part of most if not all members
Decision Making:	Via consensus
Membership:	Task- and maintenance-oriented roles prevail
Influence:	Democratic members with strong problem-solving skills
Themes:	Autonomy, future plans, differentiation from others

Ask Yourself . . .

1.   How readily will you shift your facilitational goals from being more directive to being much less directive?

2.   What kinds of problems would you comfortably hear your advisory students try to solve for themselves?

3.   At what point might you become concerned that a problem being expressed by your students requires more clinical interention than the advisory can provide?

4.   How might you help students recognize the natural shift from this stage to the group's ending in termination?

5.   How would you describe your primary purpose as an advisor during the differentiation phase?

6.   How might you most helpfully contribute to your students' problem-solving or decision-making attempts now?

7.   Knowing yourself, what do you believe you will enjoy the most about facilitating your advisory during differentiation?

8.   What might be least enjoyable to you now?

9.   How might your students in this phase show signs of the kind of regression so common in any group experiences?

10. How might you most helpfully address such regression to enable them to work through this dynamic?

Exercises and Activities for Advisories in the Differentiation Stage

The Advisory Group Challenge

Goal: To utilize the talents of every advisory group member by challenging another advisory group to a competition a la TV's "Survivor."

Objectives: At the end of this series of activities students will be able to

1. identify one personal skill/talent,

2. identify personal skills/talents embodied by other members, and

3. demonstrate team cooperation and sportsmanship.

Activity

This activity builds on the concept of multiple intelligences and borrows shamelessly from TV shows such as "Survivor," not to mention events like camp color wars. Understanding that we all have capabilities in various areas including mathematical and scientific reasoning, linguistic abilities, music, art, interpersonal skills, intrapsychic awareness, natural phenomena, spatial relations, and physical fitness, students will be asked to develop a competition which taps all these areas and to challenge another advisory group to participate.

The task has several facets. First, advisory students have to decide whether they will address all eight areas. Secondly, they must create activities that illustrate each area. Third, they have to decide which team members will participate in each area, making sure that every member has a role to play. Then they will need to determine how to construct the competition. Will it be against one other advisory group? Will all groups be included in a field day type of event?

Planning and execution may well take several sessions and requires that students have a good understanding of one another's strengths and the ability to collectively problem solve. Some possible activities include basketball shoot-outs, design and create a piece of art or a structure, softball games, musical competitions in which groups write and/or sing their own songs or perform original raps, spelling bees, spelling baseball, geography bees, jeopardy-type competitions, contests in which students have to match their self-perceptions with those of other group members, or other activities in which participants are asked questions about things other group members have said or done over the course of the year that tap their interpersonal skills.

This activity can be processed by asking

1. How did it feel to a) prepare for this competition, b) assume the role you personally took, c) engage in the competition as an advisory group team, d) win or lose the competition. (Identify)

2. How did you as a group a) prepare, b) assign roles, c) actually compete, d) win or lose. What do you feel contributed to your win or loss. (Analyze)

3. If you had it to do again, what would you do differently and why? (Analyze)

4. In real life, how do you decide what your strengths are? How do you display them? When in a group or a team with others, how do you know how to show off one another's abilities? (Generalize)

How I Make Everyday Decisions

Goal: To present a decision-making model to students that they can apply to their own lives.

Objectives: At the conclusion of this activity students will be able to

1.   identify at least 3 decisions they commonly make for themselves,

2.   describe the steps they take in making these decisions, and

3.   evaluate whether or not they have thought out their decisions carefully.

Activity

Ask your students to each recall and share three decisions they have made for themselves in the past 24 hours. Give some examples (such as, deciding whether or not to do their homework, what TV shows to watch, whether to answer a question in class, and so forth).

This activity can be processed by asking

1.   How did it feel thinking of these decisions? (Identify)

2.   Were any of these decisions harder to make than others? If so, which ones and why? (Analyze)

3.   In real life, do you make these decisions pretty automatically or do you ever have to stop and really think about what to do? (Generalize)

Developing A Problem-Solving Model

Goal: To help students think through the steps they take when trying to solve a problem.

Objectives: At the conclusion of this activity students will be able to

1. identify the five classical steps to problem solving and

2. apply these steps to a real-life problem.

Activity

(If this activity immediately follows "How I Make Everyday Decisions," you might ask your students to recall the three decisions they made for themselves that day and pick one to analyze.) When you do this activity, you will explain to your students that they are to think more carefully about how they make decisions. What steps do they go through? Try to get them to do this work, but supplement as needed to develop a model that resembles the following:

1. Define the problem or situation at hand.

2. Think about the different approaches which might be taken to address it.

3. Choose an approach.

4. Act on your decision.

5. Evaluate whether your decision worked as you hoped it would.

Ask if any students are wrestling with a decision they have to make now? If so, ask if he or she would be willing to talk about it with the other students and to go through these decision-making steps. (If no one comes forward, be prepared to share a problem of your own to demonstrate this model.) Test the model out by using it to solve this problem.

Then ask students to pair up and apply this model to a problem they are currently struggling with or a decision they need to

continued

make. They should help each other do this task for their respective issues. Then every one comes back to share what happened.

This activity can be processed by asking

1.   How did it feel developing the model? (Identify)

2.   Was the model helpful in solving your problem? Why or why not? (Analyze)

3.   In real life, how do you solve problems or make decisions? Do you think through these steps? Do you act automatically without thinking? Which works better for you and why? (Generalize)

Group Collage*

Goal: To provide members an opportunity to understand how groups make decisions.

Objectives: At the end of this session students will be able to

1.   pick a theme and create a collage which expresses it and

2.   give three examples of the kinds of group decisions that had to be made first before the collage could be done.

Activity

Hand out scissors, magazines, oaktag paper, and glue; and ask your students to make a collage that represents a specific theme that expresses who they are as an advisory. They will then choose images and text that express this theme and decide how these should be arranged on the paper.

This activity can be processed by asking

1.   How did it feel first thinking of the theme, picking the images and text to express it, and then arranging it in a way that was agreeable to all of you? (Identify)

2.   Was this task easy or hard to do? Which part was most difficult? Why? (Analyze)

3.   Can you think of real-life situations in which you are called upon to work together? How do you make decisions with others? Is the advisory one example of such a situation? How? (Generalize)

* If possible, reserve this for about a month before the end of school. It's a good transitional exercise into the termination stage, and it helps group members begin to evaluate the overall experience for themselves.

Risking

Goal: To help students to identify and to evaluate specific behaviors they would consider risky and to determine how they might handle these risks.

Objectives: At the conclusion of this exercise students will be able to

1. rate 10 hypothetical behaviors as being low to high risk and

2. identify what feels risky about one of these behaviors and determine how they might handle it.

Activity

Give students the *Risk Inventory* and ask them to read each item and rate the degree of risk it carries for them. Once students have done this, ask them to pick out one that is a "*3*" or higher and then to discuss with the group why this situation feels particulary risky to them and how they would respond to it. After each finishes his or her statement, others may comment or ask questions of them as needed.

This activity can be processed by asking

1. How did it feel considering the riskiness of each of these behaviors? (Identify)

2. What was it like for you to share the behavior that felt particularly risky with the rest of the group? (Analyze)

3. What is it about taking risks that is often so important to adolescents? How do you feel when you take risks? (Generalize)

4. What tells you when a risk is worth taking versus when it is potentially too dangerous? (Generalize)

Risk Inventory

1	2	3	4	5
Low Risk				High Risk

Read each statement and fill in the blank with the number representing the degree of riskiness this behavior would entail for you.

_____ 1. Start a new project at school.

_____ 2. Visit a city to which you have never been.

_____ 3. Express anger at someone important to you.

_____ 4. Admit you are wrong about something.

_____ 5. Ask someone whose opinion matters to you for a personal favor.

_____ 6. Ask directly for attention.

_____ 7. Hug someone you care about other than a family member.

_____ 8. Ask someone to tell you how he/she sees you.

_____ 9. Go to dinner or a movie alone.

_____ 10. Make a change in your group of friends.

Three Mental Drawings

Goal: To enable students to identify three different perceptions they have about themselves.

Objectives: At the conclusion of this activity students will be able to

1.   illustrate three ways in which they see themselves and

2.   identify at least one way they might positively modify a self-perception.

Activity

Ask your students to close their eyes and breath deeply for a minute or so to help them relax. Then ask them to think about three images: how they see themselves now, how they would like to imagine themselves as young adults, and what it will take for them to make this journey from present to future.

Then give each student a sheet of paper and ask them to draw three sketches which illustrate each of these images. Each participant then shares his or her images with the group, who in turn are invited to give feedback.

This activity can be processed by asking

1.   What did it feel like to think about how you see yourself now? What would you like to imagine 10 years from now? What step(s) will you need to take to achieve this future image? (Identify)

2.   How did your self-perceptions compare with other group members? What struck you about how they saw themselves? (Analyze)

3.   How easy/difficult will it be for you to do what you feel you have to to reach your adult goal? What will help you? What may be an obstacle to your success? (Generalize)

It Was Hard To Make A Choice

Goal: To encourage students to think about what factors come into play when they have to make difficult choices.

Objectives: At the conclusion of this activity students will be able to

1. describe a difficult decision they had to make and

2. identify the factors that helped them to make this decision.

Activity

Ask your students if they've ever been in the position of having to make a choice between two people or activities or opportunities that are both appealing. Ask each student to reflect on the hardest choice of this type they have ever had to make which they could comfortably share with the group. As each participant shares his/her experience, the other students are invited to ask questions, give feedback, and share similar personal experiences.

This activity can be processed by asking

1. How did it feel to recall this difficult decision and then to share it with the other group members? (Identify)

2. How did you make your choice? What factors came into play for you? (Analyze)

3. Did you hear any similarities in how your fellow group members made their choices? If so, what? (Analyze)

4. Knowing what you do now, if you were faced with a similar decision today, would you make the same choice? Why or why not? (Generalize)

Sexual Decision Making

Goal: To help students consider different alternatives when making sexual decisions.

Objectives: At the conclusion of this activity students will be able to

1.   offer at least two alternatives for each of the sexual decision-making situations presented and

2.   make a personal decision for each situation and give their rationale for it.

Activity

Sex is a topic which may very well come up in advisory and is certainly an area in which students can benefit by thinking about how they make decisions. If your students have given you indications that they would like to talk about sex in group, this activity might be a useful introduction.

You will tell your students that you would like to present three scenarios youngsters their age might encounter in real life. Read each scenario to the students. Ask them if they would like to do a role play and then discuss it or if they would like to simply discuss it with a partner, in small groups, or in the large group. Give them as much choice here as possible to ensure the greatest comfort level for them. For each of the scenarios, ask the students to consider,

- What would you have to feel certain about before you could make this decision?

- To whom would you speak to obtain the information you need?

- What do you believe the consequences of your decision might be?

It would be helpful to put these in writing either on the board or in a handout prior to presenting the scenarios.

Scenario #1

Your are 13 and have never had sex. Some of your friends tell you that they have and encourage you to lose your virginity. You are seeing someone you like a lot and both of you are curious about what it would feel like to have sex, but you don't really feel ready to take this step. How would you decide what to do?

Scenario #2

You have become sexually active. In speaking with friends who are also having sex you discover that no one seems to use birth control. You know about the risks of unprotected sex, but your partner seems unconcerned. What do you do?

Scenario #3

A close friend asks to see you. She is very upset and tells you that she was forced to have sex the previous weekend by the boy she has been dating. What would you do? What action, if any, would you advise her to take?

This activity can be processed by asking

1. How did it feel listening to each of these scenarios? Being asked for your opinion about how to handle them? (Identify)

2. Which of these situations would be hardest for you to know how to handle? Why? (Analyze)

3. Did you hear any suggestions from other members that you felt were particularly helpful? If so, what and why? (Analyze)

4. Are these scenarios realistic for what students your age face in real life? How are they realistic or unrealistic? To whom do you go for advice if faced with a sexual question? (Generalize)

The Baseball Team Experience

Goal: To provide a collaborative problem-solving experience for students.

Objectives: At the conclusion of this activity students will be able to

1. determine the nine individuals who play on this baseball team and

2. identify at least two problem-solving techniques used to complete this task.

Activity

Explain to your students that they will be asked to figure out which men play which positions on this baseball team. They will be given certain facts and must work together to determine the roster. Distribute a copy of "The Baseball Team" fact sheet to each student.

(Solution—Catcher: Allen; Pitcher: Harry; First Baseman: Leroy; Second baseman: Jerry; Third baseman: Andy; Shortstop: Ed; Left Field: Sam; Center Field: Sean; Right field: Mike).

This activity can be processed by asking

1. What did it feel like to be given this task initially? (Identify)

2. What steps did you have to take first to begin to solve the puzzle? Who was particularly helpful in putting the clues together? How? (Analyze)

3. What did it feel like doing a collective problem-solving exercise as an advisory group? What did your success (failure) at doing so tell you about how the group is functioning? (Generalize)

The Baseball Team

a.　Andy dislikes the catcher.

b.　Ed's sister is engaged to the second baseman.

c.　The center fielder is taller than the right fielder.

d.　Harry and the third baseman live in the same building.

e.　Leroy and Allen each won $20 from the pitcher while playing hearts.

f.　Ed and the outfielders play poker during their free time.

g.　The pitcher's wife is the third baseman's sister.

h.　All the battery and the infield, except Allen, Harry, and Andy, are shorter than Sam.

i.　Leroy, Andy, and the shortstop lost $150 each at the racetrack.

j.　Leroy, Harry, Sean, and the catcher were beaten at pool by the second baseman.

k.　Sam is undergoing a divorce.

l.　The catcher and the third baseman each have two children.

m.　Ed, Leroy, Jerry, the right fielder and center fielder are bachelors; the others are married.

n.　The shortstop, the third baseman, and Sean each won $100 betting on the fights.

o.　One of the out fielders is either Mike or Andy.

p.　Jerry is taller than Sean; Mike is shorter than Bill. Each of them is heavier than the third baseman.

Reprinted from *Treasure Chest: A Teachers Advisory Source Book* by Cheryl Hoversten, Nancy Doda and John Lounsbury with permission from the National Middle School Association.

What I Like About . . .

Goal: To provide students the opportunity to reflect on their attitudes about their own gender and the opposite sex.

Objectives: At the conclusion of this activity students will be able to

1.   identify three characteristics about their own gender they like/dislike,

2.   identify three characteristics about the opposite sex they like/dislike, and

3.   describe at least one way they try to act differently than the stereotypes of their gender.

Activity

Ask your students to take a sheet of paper and divide it into quadrants. Label each in the following ways: What I like about girls is; What I like about boys is; What I dislike about girls is; and What I dislike about boys is. Ask them to write three qualities in each quadrant. Then have the students take turns sharing in whatever order you choose. Ask students to listen carefully for common themes and to be prepared to comment on them. Once this phase of the activity is completed, ask students to each think of one behavior they engage in that is *not* stereotypical of their gender and to share this with the group.

This activity can be processed by asking

1.   What did it feel like thinking about what you liked and disliked in each gender? (Identify)

2.   How would you sum up your likes and dislikes about each? Did you hear any common themes in what others seemed to like and dislike? (Analyze)

3.   Where do these stereotypes of gender come from? Do they affect students in their everyday relationships? (Generalize)

Chapter Eleven
~~∿∿∿∿∿∿∿∿∿∿∿~~

Termination

Overview

Regardless of what stage an advisory group ultimately reaches during its life cycle, there comes a moment when the academic year concludes and group members are forced to acknowledge the end of their group. If the advisory has been a positive experience, students' sense of commitment and closeness to one another helps them to reconcile themselves to this eventuality.

Their most important need now is the opportunity to evaluate what they have learned from the experience, to discuss how they will incorporate this knowledge into their future experiences and expectations, and to put some closure on it. "What has been accomplished and how the group moves to disband become central issues during this period" (Berman-Rossi, 1993, p. 78).

This is also the phase in which it is critical that any unfinished business be addressed; and for this reason, termination must be started a few weeks in advance of the group's last session. Sometimes there is regression to power and control issues now, particularly among members who don't feel ready for the advisory's ending but cannot articulate these feelings. Instead, they may act them out. In one group, two members who had always gotten along very well picked a serious and painful racial argument with each other in the second to last session. In processing their exchange, the facilitator was able to help them identify the feelings of both sadness and frustration about the group's demise which had underscored their conflict.

Termination is therefore the only stage that does not necessarily evolve naturally, but instead falls to you to initiate. If you fail to do so and there are indeed such unresolved issues hovering, they may well come up on their own in the last session or two when there may not be adequate time to address them. These unresolved issues may negatively impact the entire termination process.

I remember my own failure to adequately prepare a group for its termination. When the last session came, two of the most vocal and influential members didn't show up until more than halfway through the meeting. I reacted very poorly, becoming angry with them—very angry, in fact. I tried to recover, to tell them how badly I had felt that they didn't show up earlier and how my anger toward them had reflected my personal sadness about the group's ending and my fear that their absence would have a negative effect on their group. Needless to say, this intervention was an inadequate substitute for handling the situation more evenhandedly. Had I done the preparatory work this group needed, these students might not have acted out their own separation difficulties as they did and the last session would have progressed in a closer, nonconfrontational manner.

Atmosphere

In general the group atmosphere is somewhat low keyed now. Even so, there can be considerable variability in the moods students express both within individual sessions and throughout the course of this phase. At times they may express sadness, at other times elation. Do not be fooled or disheartened if students appear disengaged or profess a lack of concern about the disbanding of the advisory. Absorb what you're experiencing about the tone and overall feeling of the group, rather than what may actually be said. Process speaks louder than content.

Influence/Decision Making

No specific member types are particularly high in influence now. Interestingly, your skills are especially needed now; and you may find that you have to provide more structure now than you have for many weeks. Your group members will allow you to do so because they instinctively know that they need help saying goodbye to one another and to the experience itself. As Corey and Corey (1997) state: "The potential for learning permanent lessons is likely to be lost if the leader does not provide a structure that helps members review and integrate what they have learned" (p. 266).

The willingness to work for consensus in decision making may or may not decrease now. Certainly it is true that there is a natural inclination among students not to bring up matters of great importance that require close collaboration now, since time is so short. Thus, it is now that you literally "jump into the fray," working hard to make sure that members do the work that's needed to help them terminate most successfully and to help them give voice to their emotions.

Membership

Role orientations during this final stage tend to revert back to being self-oriented as students prepare themselves for the discontinuation of this experience. This does not occur to the exclusion of task and maintenance orientation, however. The group has grown together, weathered many critical incidents, and has developed its own history. Students care about one another and about you, the advisor. All of these realities converge now to create a particularly potent dynamic.

Some may express a desire to see the group continued in some fashion over the summer or in the next academic year. Although continuing from one year to the next may be a possibility in some schools, for the most part it is not and members need to express their sadness about this group's conclusion. For some students, this may be the first time that they have felt some sense of control over lost relationships; and so this event may have a particular poignancy.

There will be students who have difficulty saying goodbye. They may "forget" that the final group session has occurred. Still others may terminate prematurely by failing to come to the last session or two. These tend to be youngsters who have already experienced serious personal losses and for whom endings can feel overwhelming. If you sense this is happening, try to find these members individually before the last session and talk with them about what they are experiencing. Helping them to understand how important the group is to them and reciprocally they are to the group may encourage them to participate in this critical stage.

Feelings

As you might imagine, both you and your students experience a mix of feelings now, ranging from sadness to confusion to contentment because you've done something meaningful with people who now matter to you. The intensity of these feelings will vary; but if pressed to disclose, probably all could acknowledge them to some degree. Some may be relieved that the group is ending, believing that it has run its natural course. Be prepared for the expression of any combination of these sentiments.

A very important point here is to be self-aware. Most advisors don't do very well in termination because we have our own separation issues. We face the real possibility of inadvertently colluding with our students in ignoring the importance of this stage and not providing enough opportunity for students to acknowledge its meaning and the losses it entails. We have to overcome whatever natural reticence we may feel about losses and separations in order to work in our students' best interests.

Leader Roles

The facilitator now helps students to fully understand the steps they have taken throughout the course of the group's development, to acknowledge the ambivalence they feel about its conclusion, and to help them verbalize these feelings. The advisor thus helps the students to reflect on what the group has meant to them, what they have learned personally from it, and how they will take this self-knowledge with them into new situations.

Leader Strategies

Students need to be able to review the group's history, recalling specific sessions and/or events. They also need to acknowledge how they feel about each other and how they have learned to view other members in different, fuller ways. As the advisor, you can accomplish these goals either through informal discussion and directed feedback given by members to other members and to yourself; or you can present structured activities that accomplish these functions.

Your own self-disclosure may prove especially important now. If you can model your willingness to share your feelings about what leading this group has meant to you, how you feel about having had the chance to know your students closely, as well as how it is difficult for you to see the advisory end, it will make it much easier for them to do the same.

Students also need to be encouraged to think about the future. What will they take with them from this experience? Are there other types of groups they plan to join over the summer or next year? Has the advisory affected their expectations of what can be gained by being a member of a group? Helping students to project ahead now is an important piece of the consolidation work they need to do; and it also helps mitigate against the pain of separation and loss, confirming for them that they will carry a piece of this group with them forever.

Themes

Parallel process dictates that topics students discuss now often reflect themes of loss, dying, or aging. Another possible thread is students' discussion of the future, either their immediate plans or what their long-term goals. They may check in with one another to determine if there will be opportunities to be in groups with any of them (i.e., sports teams, summer camp experiences, home rooms the following year, etc.) Here again, the facilitator can provide invaluable assistance by hearing the students' underlying concerns about the loss of the group experience and by reflecting these back so that they can be addressed directly.

CHARACTERISTICS OF GROUPS
IN THE TERMINATION STAGE

Atmosphere:	Low keyed
Feelings:	Sadness, resignation, confusion
Participation:	Varies from low to high, some may fail to attend
Decision Making:	More leader centered
Membership:	Self-orientation predominates
Influence:	No one particularly influential
Themes:	Loss, death, aging, the future

Ask Yourself

1. How will you address students who fail to attend the final group session(s)?

2. What would you feel comfortable doing to help prepare your advisory for termination?

3. How will you respond to students who may express only one side of their ambivalence about the group's conclusion?

4. Will you feel more comfortable doing structured exercises or letting discussion flow informally?

5. What themes will alert you to the separation needs your students might express?

6. How do you yourself handle separations and losses?

7. What will you feel comfortable sharing with your advisees about the ending of your group?

8. How will you respond to requests by members that you continue the advisory group the next year or in some other way help them to remain together?

9. Can you recall a termination experience in your own life that has affected how you handle separations or losses now?

10. How might this experience impact on your ability to successfully help your students terminate the advisory? How can you reframe your experiences positively both for yourself and for your role as a facilitator?

Stages of Group Development

	Atmosphere	Feelings	Participation	Decision Making	Membership
Preaffiliation	Polite, deferential	Ambivalence	Limited, student to advisor	By one or a few	Individual concerns prevail
Power & Control	Alive, challenging	Assertive	Fight or flight	By a few	Conformity, scapegoating
Intimacy	Warm	Closeness	Student to student	By majority	Focus only on commonalities
Differentiation	Relaxed, open	High level of interest	Student to student	By consensus	Accepting of differences
Termination	More somber	Sadness, ambivalence	Both student to student and student/advisor	By consensus	Recapitulates experience, need to evaluate

Exercises and Activities for Advisories in the Termination Stage

The Fantasy Trip

Goal: To help students to evaluate the advisory group experience.

Objectives: At the conclusion of this activity students will be able to

1.   identify their most meaningful group experience and

2.   explain why it is so meaningful to them.

Activity

Explain to your students that the group will be taking a fantasy trip. To prepare for it, everyone is to help pack a special memory trunk. Each student needs to think for a moment and to recall a favorite memory from the group sessions over the course of the year. They then describe it, and it is "packed" and taken with them as they leave.

This activity can be processed by asking

1.   How did it feel recalling this favorite memory? Sharing it with the group? (Identify)

2.   What do you think made you pick this particular memory? What was it about your particular choice that was important to you? (Analyze)

3.   What are some of the things you do in other situations to help you remember good times you have had? Do you collect souvenirs? If so, what kinds of mementos? Why is it important to remember such experiences? (Generalize)

Symbolic Gifts

Goal: To give students the opportunity to tell one another how they feel about them.

Objective: At the conclusion of this activity students will be able to

1. tell every other group member what they feel about them and

2. describe what every other member feels about them.

Activity

Explain that in this activity we will be giving one another gifts which symbolize our feelings about them or our wishes for them. You should begin by modeling this activity and speaking in turn to each member of the group. For example, you might say, "Irma, I wish that you realize how very intelligent you really are. Sandy, I hope you make the high school basketball team because I know how much you love the sport. Miguel, I hope your parents let you do the summer program you spoke about to study art." Then each student follows suit, making sure to give a positive symbolic gift to every other member.

This activity can be processed by asking

1. What did it feel like thinking of gifts to give to your peers? Receiving gifts from your peers? (Identify)

2. Can you give some examples of how you decided to give the gifts you did? Why do you think you received what you did? (Analyze)

3. The feedback you gave each other today was positive and caring. How does it compare with the kinds of comments students your age often give each other? What makes it hard to be honest and caring with each other? (Generalize)

First Impressions/Last Expressions

Goal: To provide students an opportunity to receive feedback about the kinds of first impressions they make and how these impressions change as others get to know them better,

Objectives: At the end of this activity students will be able to

1.   share first impressions of every other student and compare it with how they feel about them now and

2.   describe how others' first impressions of them changed over time.

Activity

You can do this exercise one of two ways. On the first day of group you can give each student a batch of index cards. Every other student's name is written on cards. Each student then writes his/her first impression of the student on that card. Then you collect these and redistribute them on one of the last days of group. You then ask the students to go back and fill in the other side of each card, describing their feelings about that student now that they have gotten to know him or her.

If you have not distributed the cards initially during the group's beginning, you can still ask students to complete a card for each student. In this case, they will now be writing their first impression of the student on one side and their current feelings on the other.

You again collect the cards and redistribute them, giving each student his or her packet of cards. Allow time for them to read over the impressions other students have had of them, and then encourage each person to share a few impressions with the rest of the group.

This activity can be processed by asking

1.   How did it feel writing down first impressions of every other student? Your current feelings about them? (Identify)

2.   How did it feel learning about the first impressions you made on different students? Why do you think this might be true? How did these first impressions compare with how these students see you today? Why might they have changed? (Analyze)

3.   How do you develop impressions of others in their every day life? How accurate do your impressions turn out to be? Have you ever found that your first impressions were really inaccurate? What can you learn from such an exercise? (Generalize)

Positive Affirmations

Goal: To give students the chance to comment positively about one another

Objectives: At the end of this activity students will be able to

1.   describe one positive feeling they have about every other student and

2.   describe one positive feeling every other member has about them.

Activity

This activity is reminiscent of the Christmas stocking activity but it is particularly meaningful at the end of the year as a termination activity. It can be done in a couple of different ways.

Participants are given a blank envelope to label with their own name and to decorate in any manner they wish. Then each student rips up small pieces of paper and puts a different student's name on each. He/she then writes something positive about everyone and each student leaves with an envelope filled with positive affirmations about themselves.

A variation is to ask students to write their names across a piece of $8^1/_2$ x 11" paper or a piece of poster board. These sheets are then passed around the group and everyone adds a positive comment to the sheet. These are then either folded and put into the envelopes or carried home as posters.

The activity can be processed by asking

1.   How did it feel to write positive comments? Receive positive comments? (Identify)

2.   Why do you think you received the comments you did? (Analyze)

3.   How can you give one another such positive affirmations on a daily basis? (Generalize)

I Want To Thank You For Teaching Me

Goal: To enable students to reflect on what they have learned about themselves in the advisory and the experiences/persons responsible for their learning.

Objectives: At the conclusion of this activity students will be able to

1. describe one thing they have learned about themselves and how they learned it and

2. relate what it has meant to them to learn this fact.

Activity

This is a very simple, straightforward activity which is appropriate for the final session of your advisory group. You will ask each student to reflect on what he or she has learned about themselves as a result of being a member of the advisory. Where possible, the students will also share how they learned this; and if there was a particular member who helped them do so, they will identify that person. Others are invited to comment and ask questions as needed.

This activity can be processed by asking

1. How did it feel thinking about something you learned about yourself by being in this group? (Identify)

2. Why do you believe you were able, or open, to learning this information about yourself? Was it how it was presented, when it was presented, or the person who presented it? (Analyze)

3. Can you think of examples in your day-to-day life in which you also learn more about yourself? (Generalize)

Yarn Toss

Goal: To give students a structured way of sharing how they feel about one another.

Objectives: At the end of this activity students will be able to

1.   share one way another student feels about him or her and

2.   share one way in which he/she feels about another student.

Activity

You begin this activity by explaining that each student will have a turn to pick another group member, to toss the yarn to that person, and to tell something the student has learned about him or her over the course of the year. (For example, Andy throws the ball to Jarad and says, "I've learned that Jarad has a really good sense of humor.") Then Jarad throws it to someone else and shares what he has learned about that student, and so on. You will begin this activity by picking a student and being the first to throw the yarn.

Once everyone has had the ball of yarn thrown to them at least once, the order is reversed, and each person in turn throws the yarn back to the person who had thrown to them, telling something that in turn he or she has learned about that student. At the conclusion of this activity, you should be holding the yarn.

You can process this activity by asking

1.   How did it feel choosing someone to toss the yarn to and sharing something about that person? How did it feel to be chosen by the person who threw to you? (Identify)

2.   How did you choose what to say to the person to whom you threw? Why do you think the other student felt as he/she did about you? (Analyze)

3.   By throwing the yarn to one another and then retrieving it, we've symbolically joined together and then let go. That's what our group is doing now at the end of the school year. How does it feel to say goodbye to our advisory? What makes this easy or hard to do? (Generalize)

Chapter Twelve

$\sim\!\sim\!\sim\!\sim\!\sim\!\sim\!\sim\!\sim\!\sim\!\sim\!\sim\!\sim$

When and How to Intervene: Working With Resistance

Imagine this scenario: You are working with a 7th-grade advisory group. The bell rang a few minutes earlier but you're still missing your student, Rachel. The door opens and she walks in, not looking at you or explaining her lateness in any way. Flopping herself in an empty seat, she immediately makes eye contact with a boy sitting across from her and begins an animated, nonverbal exchange as you attempt to get the group going.

You feel annoyed with her and somewhat anxious because the group seems more interested in her arrival than it does in what you have to say. Several students are attempting to listen in on her exchange with the other student. What's going on here? How does it leave you feeling? How should you handle this group dynamic?

What you may well be experiencing is "resistance" being demonstrated by both the late student and the others in the advisory group who are now focusing their attention on her rather than on the group's process. What comes to mind when you hear the word "resistance"? Do you find yourself involuntarily tensing, imagining students acting out in ways that challenge your authority or threaten to undermine your advisory group? Do you intend to structure your group sessions so closely that resistance never becomes an issue? If so, reading this chapter may offer you an opportunity to reflect on this concept and to positively reframe it.

The simplest definition of resistance is that it is the use of defense. We tend to become resistant when we feel threatened. When a member of an advisory group acts out it is often because a) Something that is being discussed or is occurring in group frightens them; b) an event has occurred outside of group which has made them fearful about the overall safety of the advisory; and/or c) you, the group leader, have made a tactical error in one or more of your interventions which has had a negative impact on your students.

Resistances can be conceptualized as the ways in which our advisory group members show us what is troubling them. It is up to us as facilitators to use our skills to understand what it is our students are feeling and to help them to address these feelings verbally. We have talked about how difficult it can be for young adolescents to know what they are experiencing, let alone express it. Indeed, many of the interventions we discussed in chapter 5 are geared toward helping to build our students' affective skills. Embracing our students' resistant behaviors nondefensively can instruct us in what we need to focus on with our advisees.

Corey and Corey (1997) accept student testing as a necessary means for them to determine if they can trust their group leaders:

> Remember that many of the freedoms a group offers typically do not exist for adolescents in their daily lives. Their teachers may not be interested in their personal views or concerns, the atmosphere of their school may be one of oppression and control, and they may be victims of racist attitudes. Their parents may not hear what they say or appreciate them as young adults. . . . If we accept their testing in a nonjudgmental and nondefensive way and resist giving lectures about how they should be, we progress a long way toward gaining their acceptance. (p. 331)

They encourage us as facilitators to respect a student's wishes not to disclose, but at the same time to acknowledge that he or she is acting defensively in some way and to explore it within the group. Ignoring a resistant behavior, or worse, combatting it, sends a very negative message to all group members that they will not be safe emotionally in this advisory.

While this is more often true of counseling groups than advisories, we may sometimes reflect back a resistant behavior only to hear our student indicate that he or she cannot or is not willing to discuss his/her feelings about it. Depending on the stage of your group and your relationships with your students, you may wish to explore the depth of the resistance by asking him or her to help you understand why it would be difficult to talk about this issue. You are not pushing the student to reveal the painful experience itself, but you are asking a process question that encourages that member to think about why it is hard to share; and you also send a powerful message that you're here, ready, and wanting to listen when the student feels comfortable doing so.

Recall the duality we discussed in chapter 8 between students' desires to draw closer to one another and their fears of the consequences of doing so. Much of resistance stems from this tension and can appropriately be explored in the service of helping both the individual and the entire advisory group move on developmentally. Also, it is important to remember that the group is simply a microcosm of the larger world. The ways in which advisees act here mirror the same issues they present to others in their everyday lives.

Corey and Corey (1997) also identify several common fears that underly resistant behaviors. These include the fears of

- making a fool of oneself
- rejection
- the discovery of personal emptiness
- losing control
- self-disclosure

Given the universality of these fears, it becomes critical that they be addressed as they surface. Remember that one of the greatest curative factors in any type of group is the realization that one is not alone in what he or she is feeling.

Students might demonstrate resistant behaviors in any number of ways. They may choose to limit how much they will communicate in an advisory (such as, by refusing to talk or, conversely, talking incessantly), restrict the topics they will discuss, attempt to manipulate the advisor, act out by coming to sessions late, or be disruptive while in group, and so forth.

Rachel appears to be illustrating this final type. Although part of her may be embarrassed or annoyed at the facilitator for calling her on her behaviors, Rachel knows that anything acted out in group is fair game for discussion. If the advisory atmosphere is a safe one, she may well be willing to share some part of what she is experiencing emotionally and may welcome the facilitator's concerned questions.

Resistance should not be confused with adolescents' general tendency to act on feelings rather than to discuss them. If you have ever watched a sandcrab by the ocean's edge you'll notice that it darts out of its hole, then back, then out again. Adolescents in groups act similarly. In one session they will work together harmoniously. Invariably, in the next session they retreat back into their private places leaving you, the advisor, to ponder why. In working with young adolescents, there tends to be a continous movement back and forth between talking and acting on feelings. To make the situation even more complicated, this seesawing tends to happen across all stages of group development.

Such a "shifting rhythm" is characteristic of groups at this age, and it is important to keep in mind that sessions in which students verbalize insights are no more valuable than others in which they act out what they are feeling. Most facilitators, however, prize the former over the latter and are very gratified when an advisory session addresses serious issues that students discuss collaboratively. The risk is that they may feel disappointed in the next session when students revert to more child-like behaviors.

Addressing Resistance

When a student acts out we may feel personally challenged; and if we're not careful, our response may be to get angry and to criticize that individual. He may then feel insulted and act out even more strongly. What has happened here? How did a difficult situation become worse? When we allow ourselves to respond defensively to students' actions, we lose a valuable opportunity to both forge a stronger relationship with them and to help them examine their own feelings and how these translate into behaviors.

Recall the cognitive model presented in chapter 5 that details the ways in which we experience encounters with others and how we can misinterpret them. Even when we do interpret them reasonably, we can still be vulnerable to both immediate upset responses and underlying negative feelings about ourselves which are somehow triggered by the exchange. In such instances, we are less able to respond to our students' behaviors dispassionately.

Let's rexamine the situation with Rachel. Rachel walks in late, seemingly indifferent. Suppose that you interpret her behavior to mean that she doesn't take the group, or your leadership of it, very seriously. Your response is to feel insulted. But what if, looking deeper, we find that in fact your underlying response is a strong sense of self-doubt about your ability to assume the role of advisor. If that were the case, you might be especially affected by Rachel's actions and more likely to interpret them personally. This leaves you feeling very exposed, and your reaction might be harsh—for example, criticizing her lateness and her subsequent inattentiveness. Your response provokes her to become even more sullen and defiant. A teachable emotional moment is lost as a battle is waged between you and Rachel.

RACHEL'S ACTIONS	YOUR FEELINGS	YOUR REACTIONS	RACHEL'S BEHAVIOR
LATENESS, SIDE CONVERSATION	INSULTED	CRITICIZE RACHEL'S BEHAVIOR	BECOMES MORE SULLEN

A colleague once pointed out that the best antidote to being judgmental is curiosity. Her point has direct application to the effective handling of resistance. What if, instead or responding personally, as in the above example, you used a very simple three-step approach to communicate Rachel as she acts in a way you don't understand. As the facilitator you can

1. surface her behavior,
2. ask Rachel to explain her behavior, and
3. reflect back the underlying concerns you hear being expressed.

You might simply comment on a behavior that a student exhibits; or you may identify the behavior, tell the student that you are puzzled by it, and ask him or her to help you understand it better.

Using the above schematic, such an approach might look like this:

RACHEL'S ACTIONS	YOUR FEELINGS	YOUR REACTIONS	RACHEL'S BEHAVIOR
LATENESS, SIDE CONVERSATION	CURIOSITY	COMMENT THAT RACHEL IS LATE TO GROUP	DISCLOSES THAT A FRIEND HAS BEEN HURT

Rachel comes in, doesn't acknowledge her lateness, and immediately engages Mike in a nonverbal exchange. You say to her, "Rachel, you're late and you seem to need to talk to Mike. What's up?" This puts the ball in Rachel's court and allows her to reflect on her behavior, to think it through for herself, and to decide what she wants to reveal. She tells the group that she's just come from gym class where a friend of hers and Mike's fell during a volleyball game and hurt herself.

By recognizing our own vulnerabilities and consciously trying to respond objectively to a student's behavior—choosing not to take it personally and giving that student the benefit of the doubt—we give our students the opportunity to understand that their behaviors have an impact on us and that it behooves them to understand what they are doing and why. We also want them to know that we're curious about how they are feeling and the ways in which their actions reflect these feelings.

Let's take another example. In another advisory session, Shana tells a lengthy story about an argument she had with a teacher the previous day. While she speaks Malik sits with his arms folded tightly in front of his chest, looking away from her, and at one point rolls his eyes in response to her comments. As the facilitator you can choose to address this behavior or not but, remembering that anything that happens in an advisory session will impact on its members, you will probably not want to ignore it.

If this is a very early session, there are a number of possible explanations for Malik's behavior. You might assume that Malik is still unsure what the advisory is all about and what he will be required to share. On the one hand, he may have no interest in talking as personally as this student is; and his posture and eye-rolling reflect this attitude. He and Shana may have a history together that's unknown to you that explains his response. The reality is that we never know exactly why our students behave as they do, and one of the biggest mistakes we can make as advisors is to assume we understand what we're seeing without checking it out with the students themselves.

As the advisor, you can comment on Malik's reaction to learn what he can tell you and the group: "Malik, you seem to have some feelings about what Shana is saying." Period. If Malik denies this, you can refer to the behavior you have witnessed: "Are you sure? You just rolled your eyes in response to her last comment." See what he says back. Given the fact that the group is in its early childhood, you should be prepared to model a response. For example, you might note: "This is still a new group, and we're just getting used to the idea that this might be a safe place to share personal experiences. How do you feel about this possibility, Malik?" Again, if you're accurate in your assumption about his underlying feelings, the odds are that Malik will somehow acknowledge this. If you are wrong, he will definitely let you know that, too. You can then ask him to help you better understand what he is feeling.

If the advisory has been meeting for a while and is in the power and control phase or beyond, the group can provide assistance. You can direct your follow up question to the group: "Shana is talking personally and Malik seems to have a response to what she's saying. Any ideas about what might be happening?" Invited to offer their responses, other students may be able to shed light on what is happening and to assist both students. As the group develops, your students will be able to respond without being prompted. If they are unable or unwilling to do so now, you might use the experience to inform Malik about the impact of his behavior on Shana by asking her to comment on his reactions or you might make a general comment about the group as a whole: "We may not all always be in the same place. Some of us may feel more ready to talk personally than others. The important thing is for all of you to feel safe participating when you are ready to do so."

Handling Common Forms of Resistance at Different Stages of Development

Building on our discussion of resistance and our knowledge of how groups develop over time, the following is a series of typical behaviors that advisors may encounter. Each example is followed by suggestions for addressing this behavior in the various stages of group development.

Silence

Preaffiliation

Ask easy, inclusive questions that include everyone. If a student asks not to participate, allow this without question. (This concern often surfaces during the group's first session as its members establish their ground rules and request that students not be pushed to share if they don't want to.)

Power and Control

Ask the quiet member to comment on a point made by another group member. If they are unwilling or unable to do so, explore the depth of resistance by asking them how it would feel for them to comment. If they cannot respond to this question, go on to someone else.

Intimacy

Allow the student to continue being silent, but be prepared for others to respond to him or her negatively as they feel they are taking risks that the silent members are not. Help the distressed student(s) articulate how they feel about silent members' behaviors, then invite those students to respond. As intimacy moves more into its disenchantment phase, you might wish to ask each student how they are feeling during this session or in response to a specific group incident. Do this in as structured a manner as you would have during Preaffiliation to help reengage students. Do not allow silence now.

Differentiation

No intervention will be required of you. Students can tolerate one anothers' silences, which tend to be more comfortable now. They can also ask one another what is wrong if they sense that the silence indicates a problem.

Termination

Send the silent student(s) an "I" mesage such as, "I notice you're very quiet today. I'm especially aware of this since we're approaching the group's ending, and I wonder if your silence has anything to do with that?" Take the opportunity to then generalize to all other members of the group, who are themselves experiencing ambivalence about the group's closure.

Side Conversations and/or Unwillingness to Join the Group

Preaffiliation

Ask the group to establish their own norms for participation as part of their ground rules. Will they want everyone to sit together? Why or why not? What will the impact be if students opt not to? Do they insist on showing respect for one another as each person speaks? If so, what will be expected? How should side conversations be handled? It is critical that advisory students "buy into" the need for group cohesiveness and mutual respect. Once they have done so, you as the facilitator can always refer back to the ground rules when addressing problematic behaviors

Power and Control

If one student is talking to another while the rest of the group is trying to have a discussion, ask the listener what the speaker has said to him or her. Surprisingly, this often works and the speaker will share the content of the side conversation in a noncritical way. This is undoubtedly because side conversations often signal students' ambivalence about being a member of the group. They want to participate but are nervous about it. Talking with one member somewhat satisfies both needs. The listener may want to participate in the total discussion more than his/her partner and may share with the total group as a way of reentering it.

One advisor faced a situation in which the boys in her group seemed to be uncomfortable when the girls spoke personally, and they responded by talking to one another and interrupting the overall discussion. She says,

> I am constantly torn about how to deal with these behaviors. At times I become the disciplinarian because the distractions are beyond a reasonable limit, or I am begging the group to follow the rules they themselves developed to get everyone back on track.

One of the facilitator's most important roles during this phase is to help students understand the purpose of their behaviors. You might make a general statement that a side conversation or listening to what the group is saying while sitting away from it, often allows students to participate on their own terms and at a distance that feels safe to them. On the other hand, our goal in an advisory is to increase everyone's sense of safety so that all can talk together comfortably.

Intimacy

Side conversations at this point may indicate students' uncertainty about whether they can share very personal information in advisory. You can surface the behavior with the students involved in the subgroup and ask them to help the rest of you understand why they are having a private conversation. You can also invite the other students to share how they feel about two or more students breaking away in this manner.

As intimacy dissipates, ask each student how they are feeling at this point and what might be blocking them from speaking freely to the group as a whole. Recall that in Disenchantment issues similar to those of Power and Control may emerge, including the development of cliques. This dynamic reflects real group needs which you must address, specifically the need to back away from the intimacy created in the previous stage in order to regroup for real intimacy in the Differentiation stage.

Differentiation

This rarely, if ever, is an issue now. If it occurs, it probably represents some regression to preintimacy. Wait to see how the other students address it. If they do not and if it doesn't seem to be affecting the group negatively, let it go. If this behavior seems to continue with negative effect, address it as you would in Power and Control.

Termination

The advisor should direct questions to individual group members about how they are feeling as the group draws to a conclusion and comment on how they appear to be retreating from the group by having these side conversations. Remember, that when this occurs now it is usually the students' attempts to handle their own separation issues and to minimize the experience in a way that makes termination less uncomfortable. You need to surface this to ensure that students allow themselves and others the opportunity they need to evaluate the advisory experience and say goodbye to one another.

Scapegoating

Preaffiliation

Scapegoating is unlikely to occur during this first phase although you may see foreshadowings of it. Again, your emphasis is on helping students to establish groundrules that are protective and to which you can refer if and when scapegoating does occur later.

Power and Control

It will be now that most scapegoating occurs. Remember that both the scapegoat and his/her persecutors play roles in this dynamic. Try not to take sides or to protect the "victim," who often either consciously or unconsciously colludes in creating this role. Instead, comment on what you see happening and invite those involved to reflect on why they believe this is happening and how they feel about it. In one group, members unmercifully teased a boy who was overweight, disheveled, and had an unpleasant body odor. When the advisor asked him to tell the others how their comments affected him, he was able to do so very assertively and effectively. To virtually everyone's surprise, they listened to him and a true dialogue developed. While he was always more on the periphery of the group than its center, the scapegoating ceased after this session.

You must remember that the group now tries hard to pull its members into conformity out of its own security needs. A scapegoat often represents either qualities others don't like in themselves or someone who threatens the group's solidarity. In either event, the behavior can and must be addressed directly and dispassionately now.

Intimacy

Scapegoating rarely occurs now. If at all, it may happen in the earliest minutes as the group is tentatively exploring how much they can share that is personal and one member is out of step with the majority. Either that person is readier to share than the others are or they are markedly less so. Either way, if their behavior is perceived as a threat to the overall group, other students may call them on it. Remember that your task is to ensure that all students feel protected from sharing more than they may be comfortable doing.

Toward the end of this phase, power and control issues like scapegoating may easily reoccur. Even more than during the second phase, though, you as the advisor want to make sure that both the scapegoat and those attacking him individually verbalize the cause of their disappointment and anger. From these comments you may discern that the scapegoating reflects the group's disappointment at having moved out of the intimacy stage and you can explore this possibility with your students.

Differentiation
Scapegoating shouldn't be an issue now. If for some reason it does occur, the scapegoat should be asked to give feedback to his/her victimizers and to those witnessing the problem about the impact of their attacks on him or her. You should facilitate this exchange, and you might want to ask your students how they feel the problem should be resolved.

Termination
Scapegoating in this final stage is a regressive behavior, and you need to label it as such. You might comment that it is surprising to see such an old behavior resurface after the group had ostensibly resolved it, and ask them why they think this has happened. Understanding that such regressive behaviors often signal students' (unconscious) wishes to extend the group by demonstrating their need for it, the leader might then enter into a discussion about how the students are feeling about the group's ending.

Dominating
Preaffliation
Be directive and closely monitor your students' sharing. If necessary, go around the circle and ask each member in turn what they have to say. Thank the dominating person for his or her contributions, but say to the group that we want to make sure that everyone has a chance to express themselves. At this point, others may be willing to allow one member to do the talking for them; but you want to work

hard at not to allowing this to happen lest it send an erroneous message precluding the opportunity for everyone's full participation.

Power and Control

You need to observe the dominating behavior closely to determine its impact on the group's atmosphere and participation levels. If others continue to allow this one student to dominate, you may wish to comment on this, even humorously ("How nice of all of you to let Frank do all the talking for you! Why are you being so generous? What would happen if more of you were to start talking?"). Your group may not be able to respond in full, but they will have heard your observation and the norm you are hoping the advisory will establish.

Intimacy

One or more members may also dominate now, but they will do so in the form of sharing more personal information than you would wish. Again, your job is to protect all group members by ensuring that students exhibit appropriate personal boundaries (as opposed to the truly at-risk student protrayed in chapter 13, who often shares inappropriately in advisory, particularly during the Intimacy phase and sometimes even earlier). Your immediate response in this session will be to identify that student's underlying feelings, allow him or her a chance to elaborate on them, and then to quickly and firmly generalize to other students to ensure that the optimal balance is maintained.

If a student dominates toward the end of intimacy, it is probably to express the group's disappointment over their loss of closeness. You will need to be directive, acknowledging that student's feelings (whatever they are) and also going around to every other student to see how they are also feeling.

Differentiation

Again, dominating is very rare now. Given that it is often fueled by anxiety and that the group has worked through a number of interpersonal issues by this stage, the atmosphere tends to be comfortable enough that the behavior is no longer functional. For the most part, students will be able to handle any problematic behaviors that emerge now on their own.

Termination

Should dominating reemerge now you will wish to listen closely to the subtext of this student's comments to discern whether or not they relate to loss or termination, and they probably will. If they do, you will identify these feelings, give the student full opportunity to express them, and then generalize to the others who are also experiencing the same feelings.

As you become more comfortable and skilled in recognizing resistances, embracing them, and allowing them to help you understand what your advisory's issues are, you will find that they no longer cause you to feel anxious. Remember that your task as an advisor/facilitator is to help your students become more "group wise." The more you can share with them about what you are observing, how these behaviors make you feel, and why you believe they are happening, the faster and more readily your group members will be able to assume these process and leadership functions themselves. Don't be afraid to be wrong. Your students will let you know that you have made a mistake, will forgive you for it, and you'll all survive. What advisory students are much less likely to forgive or forget is the facilitator who doesn't care enough to struggle to understand their behaviors when they cannot find the words to express themselves verbally.

Test Yourself

Below are several vignettes. How would you handle each situation, given the stage of development of your advisory?

1. A student in your advisory shares a very personal and serious problem. The other group members appear to be clearly uncomfortable with this revelation and try to change the subject (late Intimacy moving into Disenchantment).

    Possible Response: You may be experiencing parallel process here. A student talks about something personally difficult while the group is transitioning into a phase that feels collectively disappointing. The timing of this revelation is not inappropriate, as it would have been much earlier in the group's life, so it's not likely that the other students are responding negatively because the personal sharing feels premature to them. It may be that the problem is either so serious that they know intuitively they shouldn't be a part of its solution and/or that they are not together enough as a group to help problem solve at the moment.

    As the facilitator you need to give the message that the

problem is real, deserves attention, and that you will speak with that student privately. You then need to take the necessary measures with the student and the appropriate staff person to make sure the problem is addressed. This sends a message to both the student and the group that the student has been heard and that the group can relieve themselves of the responsibility for addressing a problem of such a serious nature.

2.   You have played some games with your students which they have loved. They don't seem to be very willing to discuss topics of any real seriousness. They ask to continue playing other games during the advisory period (Power and Control).

Possible Response: You have a couple of choices here. First, you can simply observe to your students what you are experiencing and ask them what they feel is going on. What makes them want to only play games? What would happen if they were to talk about real-life situations in advisory? How would this feel? If necessary, you can remind them again about the advisory's purpose; but this is touchy because they may hear your comment as scolding, and it may prove counterproductive. Another way to go is to introduce more serious issues or demanding tasks via game-like activities. For instance, "The Ungame" is a game that asks students to reflect personally by using cards with questions on them. Students invariably love this game, and it helps them to look a little deeper with virtually no discomfort.

3.   One male student refuses to sit in the circle or to join in any advisory discussions. The other students now ignore him; and when you try to engage him, they suggest that you just leave him alone (Power and Control moving into early Intimacy).

Possible Response: One way to engage such a student is to ask him to comment on points other students make, rather than ask him how he feels about a subject himself. This often works to break the ice. Another, more direct, way of dealing with such a situation is to ask students why they would have you ignore him; then ask the student what he thinks about the reaction others are having to his distancing. Ask him why he thinks the others might be so annoyed by his behavior, and then ask the same question of the entire group. If you feel comfortable doing so, you might directly ask the student how he would like you and the other students to respond to him. I would personally be loathe to "just leave him alone," and I would ask the group to struggle with this with me. We can allow students to "pass" periodically when they need to, but we obviously cannot allow one member to isolate him or herself over a number of sessions.

4.   A student loudly proclaims that the advisory group is "boring" and that he'd rather be at his club meeting (Power and Control).

Possible Response: I would probably simply listen actively and paraphrase first, hoping to encourage the student to reveal more about why he would rather not be part of the group today. Given the stage of development, you can also acknowledge the fact that this student feels "powerless" over where he is assigned this period and that this is a frustrating experience. ("What's it like to not be able to choose the activity you're in this period? How about the rest of you, how do you feel about it? Since we are all here, how can we work together to make this session interesting rather than boring?") Often this helps engage the student and his peers. You can also simply acknowledge the comment, commiserate with the student, and go on to the next activity, hoping that the process will naturally interest and involve him. This gives the message that you aren't particularly concerned that he's bored, you expect it to be a temporary reaction, and you're ready to focus elsewhere.

5.   In your last group session, your group members had engaged in an animated discussion of the qualities they looked for in a boyfriend or girlfriend. Today they are very quiet and withdrawn (Disenchantment phase of Intimacy).

Possible Response: Whenever you experience a pronounced atmospheric shift, you are well advised to comment on it. ("In our last session you couldn't say enough. Today you're very quiet. Any idea of what might be going on?") They probably will not be able to answer you collectively, but you will have identified the most potent, immediate dynamic. At this point, I would ask each member in turn how they are feeling today and see what surfaces. The conversation of the previous session is another example of parallel process. Your students were talking about what they want in a potentially intimate relationship during the group's intimacy phase. Now the group's reality has shifted, and they feel let down. Give them a chance to tell you so individually.

6.   Your advisory group is ending next week. Two students who never miss group are absent from today's session, although they are not absent from school. The group seems especially muted and unwilling to speak (Termination).

Possible Response: Whether or not students can acknowledge this, they keenly feel one another's absences in group and never more so than during its termination phase. Absences at this stage are almost like a betrayal of the group and thus make it harder for members to put closure on the group experience. Something feels incomplete to those who are present. You will want to ask them about how they are feeling, observing to them that they seem very muted. Depending on what they can tell you, you may also point out that you're very aware that these students are absent; and ask them for their reactions to this, sharing why you personally feel disappointed that they are not present. Then you can do a structured termination exercise, if necessary, or initiate a discussion of how students feel about the group's coming to a close.

7.   Your advisory group, usually alive and talkative, is quiet today. Your efforts to generate discussion fail. Finally, one student tells you that another in the group has broken confidentiality; and as a result, she herself doesn't feel like talking in group anymore (Power and Control).

Possible Response: This is a big one and a situation which comes up very commonly in groups like advisories. It must be dealt with immediately and decisively. If the student is not present, you should try to table discussion until the next session when the group can directly talk to him or her. If the student is present, you gather as much information as you can from those students willing to share what they know, then ask him or her to comment on what is being said and to either confirm or deny it. If some members are convinced of the broken confidentiality but the student denies that he or she has done so, you will need to present this as a group problem and ask your students how they think they can resolve it. Ultimately—and you can point this out—this breach of trust will seriously impact what members feel they can talk about. Ask the group how they feel about this. How close would they like to become in this advisory group? What do we do when a basic ground rule like this one has been broken?

Often the intensity of group pressure is strong enough to bring the student in line and prevent further leaks. Sometimes, however, the damage is pronounced; and, in fact, the group really doesn't feel comfortable talking personally. In this case, the sessions ultimately begin to feel stale and boring. If this happens, you can ask them to again talk about why, redirecting them back to this session in which their trust was broken, and again encouraging them to struggle with whether or not they are willing to try to trust one another at this point.

8.   Two girls in your group have formed a subgroup. They talk to each other several times during each sesion, distracting other students from speaking and listening to each other (Preaffiliation).

   Possible Response: Remember that subgrouping and side conversations are often a way students express their ambivalence about being in the advisory. You can ask them to share what they are talking about with the group as a whole, ask the listening member of the pair to tell you what the other has just said to her, or temporarily ignore them and assume that in short order the behavior will stop. If it doesn't and it is having an impact on the overall group, you can tell the girls how the behavior is making you feel. Since it's probably too early to ask other members to be this direct. You can then ask the other members how they are feeling about it. Even if they don't support your view, you will have served notice that the behavior is occurring and that it is undesirable.

9.   One student has been consistently silent in all your advisory sessions. Another student, who has just confided a family problem to the group, attacks her silent peer saying that if other people are going to talk personally, he has to also (late Power and Control/early Intimacy).

   Possible Response: Your response will be dictated by how the silent member responds to the student confronting him. If he makes no response, you can ask him how he feels about being told he needs to talk. You can also direct the same question to the group as a whole. What are members' rights to be silent? Is there a point at which one student's silence affects the rest of the group? How should we handle this? The truth is we cannot force anyone to speak if he or she doesn't want to. Thus, we can also, and probably more helpfully, direct our questions to the student who is upset about the silence. What exactly concerns her about talking personally when someone else doesn't. Try to tease this out, then ask other students to share their points of view. See if you can help them to surface the fears about trust and vulnerability that underly this exchange.

10. One student tends to dominate group discussions and has now done so for several sessions. The other students have tolerated it

but have gradually become quieter and less engaged themselves. (Preaffiliation moving into Power and Control).

Possible Response: You have probably tried several times to direct conversation away from this individual to other students, inviting their comments or reactions to things he or she has said. If this modeling has failed to encourage them to take on the "dominator" themselves, you would probably be wisest to ask them what is going on, observing that they seem to be getting quieter and quieter in group. You might also comment that the only person who seems to talk is _____. You might ask them what would happen if _____ weren't the only one talking. What would the group be like? If this fails, you might ask each member individually how they are feeling today and what they feel like talking about. Generally, drawing attention to a dynamic such as dominating frees the logjam and encourages other students to react to it.

Handling the Situation Differently

Think back to a problem you had with a student, colleague, friend, or family member in which something they said or did upset you enough that you responded in an unhelpful way. Go through this schematic twice—once recalling the actual experience and again as you would do it now if you had another opportunity. As you do, try to be cognizant of your own "buttons," those underlying feelings you may struggle with that leave you vulnerable to responding defensively.

OTHER'S BEHAVIOR	YOUR FEELING	YOUR RESPONSE	THEIR BEHAVIORAL REACTION TO YOU

Can you discern how your immediate interpretation and the subsequent feeling it generated, led you to respond to your own concerns rather than to help the other individual to examine their behavior and explain it? How does your reasoned response to this same scenario today differ from what you did initially? How do you think it would have changed the outcome of this exchange? Remember that in reflecting back a behavior that disturbs us, it is usually very helpful to do so by sending an "I" message and then to listen actively to their response.

Chapter Thirteen

~~~~~~~~~~~~~~~~~~~~~~~~

The At-Risk Student

O nce when I was a psychotherapist in private practice, I was asked by a colleague to see an adolescent female client who had great difficulty expressing anger. She was physically slight and unassuming in her manner. She wore shorts to our first meeting. On her head was a visor cap with a dark plastic rim which made it difficult to see her face. In that first session, she talked very softly, always looking down at her lap. I strained to hear what she had to say. Midway through our session, I realized that I felt very physically uncomfortable. In fact, my efforts to make eye contact with her had left me doubled over and peering upward at her.

Three days later I received a phone call from a young woman whose name and voice I didn't recognize. She quickly revealed that she was another personality of the young woman who had come to see me. Ultimately, with a supervisor's help, I was able to understand that she probably suffered from what is called a dissociative personality disorder and when under severe stress, this other persona emerged. I was new to the field and not at all skilled enough to treat her, so I referred her to an inpatient facility for adolescents.

I mention this case because one of the first cues I had that something was wrong was her inability to make eye contact when she spoke. While this is a very extreme example, in fact there may be times when students in your advisory present symptoms that clearly suggest they need far more intensive attention than you or your group are prepared to offer. The process observational skills you develop will help you to know these children; and you must trust your instincts when you see, hear, or feel that one of your students is in emotional distress.

Are there students whose behaviors trouble you now? What behaviors do they exhibit that are problematic? If it were up to you, living in a perfect world with unlimited financial resources available to your school, would you recommend that these students be given special attention of some sort? If so, what type?

As middle and high school teachers, you are on the front lines of defense in recognizing students' problems. You see them acted out daily in the classroom, the cafeteria, and the playground. You probably worry most about those children who appear capable of violence against others or themselves; those who are socially isolated, seemingly depressed, or fearful; or students who cannot seem to act in their own best interests.

In this chapter we will discuss who the at-risk child is, what contributes to risk proneness versus resiliency, and how we can identify children at risk for specific behaviors and address them helpfully. We will specifically consider children who manifest signs of post traumatic stress disorder, which may in turn signal physical or sexual abuse or exposure to violence or unforseen catastrophes. This condition can trigger serious depression and anxiety and leave youngsters prone to substance abuse, aggression, or sexual acting out.

Understanding the At-Risk Child

One researcher whose work has been in the forefront of efforts to understand the at-risk child is Richard Jessor (Jessor, Donovan, and Costa, 1991). He believes that there is a complex interplay of factors, including personality, perceptions of the environment, and behaviors, that makes youngsters more prone to acting out; and that if adolescents are at risk for one behavior, they are at risk for others as well.

Personality wise, we tend to think of at-risk students as those who exhibit poor self-esteem, do not value their unique qualities, and may exhibit behaviors which include:

- fear of new experiences/doubt that they can handle them
- devastation by failure
- boastfulness to overcompensate for these fears
- demand for constant support and encouragement OR the opposite, difficulty in seeking it
- unwillingness to assume responsibility for their behaviors
- passivity and depression
- reactivity rather than proactivity
- being a follower rather than a leader
- isolation
- excessive criticism of others
- difficulty living in the moment

At-risk children often accurately perceive that they do not enjoy the same opportunities for quality education and employment, or racial equity and justice. Instead, they suffer from abuse, neglect, interparental conflict, and poor parenting, whatever their socioeconomic status. As a result, they may exhibit what Garbarino (1996) has termed "terminal hopelessness," which saps their motivation to act healthfully because they don't see any kind of positive future for themselves.

Kellam and Brown (1982) studied children longitudinally from 1st grade through middle school and observe a mixture of shyness and aggression which they believe foreshadows later behavioral problems, particularly substance abuse and dropping out of school. They contend that it is entirely possible to sit in on a 1st grade class for a matter of hours and predict those children who will leave school prematurely.

A child is less prone to at-risk behaviors the more he or she is independent, values achievement, feels able to meet personal expectations, is comfortable with social conventions, is engaged in school and with peers, and believes that family and friends would be disappointed by severe acting-out behaviors. Furthermore, children and adolescents can become more resilient when they enjoy social support, the presence of a caring, supportive adult, parent or otherwise. Clearly, the school has a vital role to play in developing resilience and in addressing the needs of even those children at high risk.

At-Risk Students and the Role of Advisories

Although advisories are not therapeutic groups, as we have already stated, there are those who believe that they have a role to play in helping at-risk children. Indeed, it is frequently those students who are most disaffected who will show the greatest gains from participating in advisories because they have so much to say. Once these youngsters are confident they are being heard, they tend to become more engaged in school and to try harder in their classes. Schools with strong advisory programs are well positioned to also provide individual guidance which may be needed by students with personal problems.

The advisory group, of course, provides yet another milieu in which we observe our students, hopefully more closely than elsewhere; and it is here that students often reveal problems that are deeper rooted and may require referrals for more intensive assistance. In one junior high school located in an impoverished, drug-ridden area, for example, it became apparent that a disproportionate number of students had suffered the deaths of parents from AIDS. School counselors decided to begin special bereavement groups for these children; and at one point, three groups were running simultaneously to try to accommodate all who were grieving. Most of the referrals to these groups were made by advisors who had learned about the parents' deaths in their groups.

This "tiered" approach can be tremendously helpful to children. A violence prevention program, which originated in New York City a few years ago, implemented a three-level intervention. All children participated in school-wide assemblies and poster contests designed to spark their critical thinking about ways to prevent violence. On the second level, a 15-week course was offered to selected classes which taught them ways to predict violence and to protect themselves against it. Finally, those children who revealed personal experiences as victims or victimizers during that course were referred for an additional 15 weeks of group counseling. In this way, helpful services were effectively targeted to those who most needed them.

Advisories typify a "universal" approach to prevention, one targeted at the entire school population, because it is considered to be good for every student with a minimal risk to their well-being. The bereavement and violence groups characterize a second prevention approach which is "selective," targeting students who are considered to be at risk of developing acting out problems like depression, suicide, substance abuse, sexual promiscuity, delinquency, and so forth.

When Can We Help as Advisors

So again we ask: Who is the at-risk child? Is he or she always easy to spot? How do we differentiate between troubling behaviors which may be successfully addressed in advisories versus those who can benefit from the groups but also need additional counseling. What about other youngsters whose problems are so serious that advisories may not only be unhelpful but their presence may negatively affect the quality of the advisory experience for all involved? It is not always easy to make these distinctions. Dreikurs (1972) notes

> The resistance of the child may develop to such a degree
> that he may seem to be "abnormal." However, one must be
> careful about what one considers pathological or abnormal
> in a child. As a rule, the child's reactions are not abnormal,
> even if they are extreme and seem out of the ordinary, be-

cause they are generally sensible and adequate response to
the situation as the child sees it. (p. 117)

For example, we have all been witness to the national tragedy of
students who inflict violence against their peers or teachers in seemingly random outbursts. Often these are adolescents who feel socially isolated and have been victimized by others for extended periods of time. Indeed, one study revealed that 80 % of middle school
students admitted bullying behaviors in the past 30 days in the form
of teasing, name calling, threatening, social ridiculing, and sometimes physical assaults. As incidents of bullying increased so did reports of misconduct and anger, while conversely, prosocial skills di-
minished. In fact, bullies themselves are often depressed, lack the
necessary skills to resolve conflicts peacefully, feel disenfranchised
at school, and believe that violence is their only solution. Group
approaches such as advisories can positively modify such attitudes
and, theoretically, the behaviors themselves. Thus, at what point do
we make the decision that a known bully is less a candidate for an
advisory group than for counseling?

We might also ask if it is possible to run special advisory groups
for those who might also benefit from more intensive counseling. In
one school, the psychologist volunteered to run a special advisory
group for students with conduct disorders. He invited all advisors to
refer those students who were most disruptive in their groups to him.
They did so and initially these youngsters, all male, felt stigmatized
by their assignment to this group. However, the psychologist was an
exceptionally compassionate and skilled worker whose concern for
these students was obvious. They quickly blossomed under his attention and grew to identify strongly as his "boys." In this instance,
even youngsters with serious behavioral problems were good advisory candidates.

Much has to do with the skills and predisposition of the advisor,
coupled with the kinds of supports available to help them address
their students' needs. First of all, training and supervision are essential;
and imbued in staff development must be opportunities for advisors to
talk about the problems they are encountering, why they feel troubling, and how they have attempted to address them on their own.

As we have already discussed, each of us has our "buttons" that
can be pushed and which cause us considerable discomfort. While
one of us may find it especially difficult to deal with a student who is
depressed, another may shirk from one who is overtly hostile. Still

another may have difficulty relating to students who are especially clinging. The list goes on. In chapter 12 we talked about our students' behaviors as the way in which they may "show" us their problems. Dreikurs, Grunwald, and Pepper (1971) describe different motivations for student misbehaviors, suggesting that we can understand a great deal about why our students are acting out by assessing our own reactions to what our students do.

We would probably all agree that many of our students demonstrate the need for attention, both in the classroom and in the advisory group. While irritating, this is hardly cause for panic; and there are a number of effective means at our disposal for addressing the students' underlying concerns. Students who engage in power struggles with us or with their peers impact the group's process, sometimes fairly negatively. However, as we have seen, much of this is expectable and is associated with the stage of the group's development; and you as the advisor can allow the student the time and space needed to work through their authority issues safely.

Students whose behaviors leave us feeling threatened or despairing, however, are another matter. Although they may still be very viable candidates for advisory group membership, their behaviors strongly suggest the need for additional services. Children who act vengefully are ones who have been badly, badly hurt and apparently feel they have no other recourse than to hurt back. They may well not feel any remorse for their decisions.

One advisor describes such a youngster whose behavior in a particular advisory session, coupled with repeated classroom incidents, left her very concerned:

> The students wanted to talk about sex and relationships. The discussion eventually broadened to include some of their own sexual experiences, which revealed that a few of the boys were sexually active while the girls generally were not.
>
> One student announced that he wanted to have sex with me. I felt violated. I no longer felt safe with him and the other students were very upset with him, too. He announced that he was not sorry for what he had said to me. I took it upon myself to refer him to the guidance counselor because I felt that this behavior, coupled with home problems he had shared, suggested he had a need for more intensive help than I, or the group, could give.

Far from feeling flattered or touched by this child's behavior, this facilitator felt threatened by it. Was the student's goal the need to achieve power? Was it vengeful in some way? It's difficult to say, but the advisor knew instinctively that a more comprehensive intervention was needed.

The child who fills us with despair is one who has given up. Initially a student who may have acted passively, conveying the message that he/she felt deficient in some way, has now withdrawn much more completely and threatens to be lost to us. Such students demand our immediate action. There is a clinical adage that says that often when working with others in a counseling setting one finds that he/she "holds" their client's feelings. In other words, if a student is feeling very depressed in an advisory session, we may become aware of feeling this sadness ourselves. We need to be exceptionally attuned to our responses to what our students tell us (content), because again, on a process level, we are responding to their feelings. When we become aware of feeling helpless, it is a clear sign this student needs more help and so do we.

In one case, a student expressed his negative self-feelings very openly. In response to an advisory activity in which students responded to a cue card which asked them to complete the sentence "I am . . . ," he wrote, "I am someone who hates myself." The advisor became understandably concerned about this student. She knew that he was definitely asking for help, and she paid especially close attention to what he said in group from that point on in order to determine if a counseling referral was warranted. Ultimately, while continuing to work with him in her advisory, she also referred him to the guidance counselor.

This example underscores a second essential need—an on-site social services infrastructure that can address the problems of seriously at-risk students. It is unreasonable to ask teachers to assume advisory roles if they don't have the assurance that the school's services will be adequate to address those problems revealed through their advisees' personal sharing. On the other hand, teacher-advisors can become very able partners with school-based clinicians, learning to reframe a student's behaviors more perceptively as that child's way of demonstrating that he or she is in need of help and making the appropriate referrals more readily than they might based only on classroom observations.

School-based clinicians can well use the help, too. Commonly, personal problems are referred to the guidance counselor. Given the numbers of students for whom these workers are responsible, as well as the scope of their work (that is, high school maticulation), it is not resonable to expect that they will be able to provide the type of interventions at-risk students need. The school psychologist is a resource for testing and, in some instances, actual counseling. School social workers are also obviously an excellent resource. In some schools, however, they are hired to work only with children with special education needs. Many schools have secured grant money which allow them to provide substance abuse counseling for students. Other schools may have social workers and counselors outstationed on their premises, and these professionals are potentially excellent adjuncts to school staff.

Whatever the staffing solutions, skilled individuals must be available to work with those students whose needs exceed the advisory's potential. It is essential that the administration provide in-service training opportunities through which these professionals can both educate other staff about the nature of the services they offer and about when and how to make referrals to them.

Recognizing Different Types of Emotional Problems
Post-Traumatic Stress Disorder

Post-traumatic stress disorder (PTSD) is diagnosed when one has undergone an event which threatens one's own or another's life or "physical integrity" and experiences helplessness or fear as a result. In the United States, it is estimated that anywhere from 15 to 43 % of children and adolescents have experienced at least one trauma. As many as 15 % of girls and 6 % of boys meet the diagnostic criteria for PTSD. Furthermore, the rates are far higher among children in at-risk populations—that is, 93 % of sexually abused children will be PTSD sufferers.

Children of middle school and high school age are likely to manifest symptoms which include nightmares and "trauma reenactment" in which they replay elements of the incident in their everyday lives. Children may do this through play. Adolescents are more likely to do this via impulsive and aggressive actions. These youngsters may also become very depressed; self-medicate for depression and anxiety by using drugs; experience panic disorder, separation anxiety, attention-deficit/hyperactivity disorder, and conduct disorders.

Sexual Abuse

One specific form of PTSD is sexual abuse. Children who have suffered this type of assault may manifest symptoms such as the aforementioned fear, anxiety, depression, and anger. They may also act in other overtly, self-destructive ways such as using drugs; and they may choose to isolate themselves, demonstrating real problems with trusting peers or adults. Their school performance may also suffer.

Another characteristic often observed among sexual abuse victims is sexual precocity and inappropriate language and behavior. Staff, particularly at the middle school level, must know that most very young adolescents are sexually inexperienced. One study found that 80 % of girls and 70 % of boys under the age of 15 have not had intercourse. Although there are increasing numbers of youngsters who are technically "virgins" but are engaging in oral sex, it is still a red flag in an advisory session when a middle school child clearly demonstrates a sophisticated understanding of sexual acts or pronounced seductiveness, particularly in combination with any of the above behaviors.

One of the greatest problems for youngsters who have been sexually abused is that 90 % of them know their victimizers, who are actually relatives about 30 % of the time. The implications of trust violation are staggering and will likely be reflected in the student's difficulties establishing close relationships with others. Some young victims, especially males, may act out by behaving cruelly to others or by running away. Both sexes are vulnerable to severe depression which can lead to suicide attempts.

Community Violence

This term relates to violence committed by nonfamily members and includes incidents such as shootings, stabbings, and beatings that an individual either suffers him- or herself or witnesses. Althyough it is disproportionately a problem for youngsters of color in urban areas of lower socioeconomic status, recent incidents clearly demonstrate that community violence is not limited to these populations. A national survey of children ages 10 to 16 revealed that over one third reported being victims of violence and larger numbers still in urban areas had witnessed it. Such individuals may also suffer nightmares and be troubled during daytime hours by intrusive and disturbing memories of the violent episode. Like victims of sexual abuse, they may startle easily or become depressed, angry, distrustful, fearful, alienated, or feel betrayed. Their parents and other family members may also feel guilty that they did not do enough to protect the child, and some will respond by becoming overprotective or even punitive to their child if he or she acts out in ways related to the trauma.

Depression

It is clear that trauma can cause depression in youngsters. The symptoms of clinical depression in children and adolescents include

- persistent sadness or feeling of emptiness
- a sense of hopelessness, helpessness, worthlessness, pesimism, or guilt
- substance abuse in an effort to self-medicate for these feelings
- fatigue
- loss of interest in daily activities
- eating or sleeping disturbances
- irritabiity
- increased emotionality, anxiety, and panic attacks
- difficulty concentrating, remembering, or making decisions
- thoughts of suicide

Suicidal Ideation

The ultimate fear for depressed individuals is that they may become suicidal. By now, most of us probably are conversant with the danger signs but they bear repeating here. These can include talking about suicide, being preoccupied with death, expressing the viewpoint that death might be preferable to living, a sudden strong mood swing from sadness to happiness for no apparent reason, or a loss of interest in things previously of importance. A person contemplating suicide may begin saying goodbye to others, albeit in indirect or very subtle ways. This can include visiting or calling others unexpectedly, giving away possessions, or making arrangements which put one's affairs in order.

If an advisor fears that a student may be suicidal, he or she must address it directly. (If the subject comes up in group, it should be addressed there immediately, with an individual follow up. If the student approaches the advisor privately, it is handled purely on a one-to-one basis.)

The advisor must do an immediate risk assessment by asking the youngster if he or she has considered committing suicide. If he/she says no, you can discuss the symptoms you've observed which have made you concerned. Explore the student's receptivity to speaking privately with a counselor.

If the student acknowledges that he/she has considered suicide, you need to ask how he/she would attempt it. If the response seems vague, you can probably breathe easier knowing that the risk does not appear to be imminent. You must follow through with a referral, however, and let the prinicipal know. On the other hand, if the student can tell you in some detail about when and how he/she would attempt it, the risk is much more immediate. This student must be referred to an appropriate counselor and the parents contacted immediately. Under no circumstances should this child be allowed to stay on his or her own. Safety is the primary goal now. Remember, suicide is the second leading cause of death among adolescents.

So we see that advisories can play a role in working with at-risk children. In some instances, they may provide the opportunity to help students sound out problems and to seek for help from their peers and their advisor. In other instances, advisories can be modified to be run by professionals with clinical training in a format that more closely resembles a counseling group. Finally, advisories provide an excellent medium in which to identify those students whose problems are serious enough to justify individual counseling.

Chapter Fourteen

~~~~~~~~~~~~~~~~~~~~~~~~~~~~~~~~~~

What Teachers Gain from the Advisory Experience

C lasses at my university were suspended on September 11, 2001. Given my particular teaching schedule, it wasn't until two days later that I met with my students. I had forced myself to prepare the lessons, although I was so depressed that it was nearly impossible to concentrate. When I walked into my classrooms that day and the next and looked at my students' faces, I knew that teaching as though nothing had happened was an impossibility. I had to devote these sessions to groupwork in which they could talk about what they were feeling most intensely.

It was a challenge. Like teachers everywhere, I had just met these students. I didn't yet know most of their names, and we certainly hadn't built up the kind of intimacy one would associate with asking them (30 per class!) to reveal their greatest fears and yet we managed. In effect my classes became impromptu advisories, and my students seemed grateful for the chance to talk. Many of my colleagues had similar experiences, although others said they had not felt confident about approaching their students so affectively. In this instance, my facilitation training and my belief that classes are in fact groups, served me and my students well.

One question frequently asked about implementing advisories is what do teachers get out of doing them? Surely they have enough responsibilities already to dissuade them from trying out yet another initiative. The truth is, though, that teachers can gain a great deal personally and professionally from assuming the role of advisor. As with my recent experience, one teacher participating in a 30 hour group facilitation course for prospective advisors commented that the techniques she was learning were not only helpful in running her advisory but she was finding them to be very useful in her classroom, as well. Ziegler and Mulhall (1994) note this as they say, "the possibility exists for relationships of trust and confidence which develop in the advisory group to extend to other settings in the school, including the academic classroom" (p. 43).

Let's take a typical potential classroom incident. Consider this scenario: Janie and Eddie are sitting in the first row in your history class, chatting and alert. Suddenly Eddie bends closer to Janie, examines her face for a moment, and then announces in a voice loud enough to be heard several rows back, "Nice zit, Janie." Janie withdraws immediately, her face clouding over, head bent down. She neither hears what you teach nor does she participate in any class discussion from that moment on.

Janie has experienced a "developmental override," during which her need to feel comfortable with her physical appearance, attractive to members of the opposite sex, and accepted by her peers overall has been temporarily torpedoed by Eddie's unkind remark. As her teacher, you are an unhappy witness to this exchange; and you probably feel frustrated both by knowing Janie will not learn this day's material and because you are possibly unsure how to handle their encounter.

Such an occurrence in the classroom actually represents a "teachable, emotional moment," when an instructor might temporarily abandon his or her lecture and attend to what Eddie has said and how it has made Janie feel. The question is how to do this respectfully without further embarrassing Janie, belittling Eddie, or creating discomfort for the class as a whole. In short, how can we demonstrate caring to our students in a consistent manner that both protects them and encourages them to be protective of others?

If you have honed your facilitational skills as an advisor and both you and your students have become stronger process observers, you may well find that you are well prepared to handle incidents such as this in your classroom. For one thing, if these students are your advisees, you know them, have developed a rapport with them, and you trust one another. For another, your other students are in the same position and have developed feedback and other communication skills to help if needed. You may find that you are willing and able to stop your lesson to attend to this interaction between Janie and Eddie, possibly even finding a way to integrate what you do into your classroom teaching. It will all be part of creating the kind of supportive classroom environment to which you are dedicated.

As was noted in the introductory chapter, all too often students question whether teachers and schools have their best interests at heart; and if they believe their teachers don't care, it can have a deleterious effect on their motivation. What if our experiences as advisors mitigated this possibility?

Teacher-advisors often develop closer relationships with students, which in turn may increase their motivation to guide and to listen to their students. The classroom environment may improve measurably as students also develop closer relationships with others they may not typically socialize with and learn from one another, making the teacher's job easier and ultimately more enjoyable.

Teachers facilitate this process in a way that creates a clear connection between what students are discovering about themselves in the classroom and what transpires in their everyday lives. As Kottler (2001) observes, "The teacher moves the discussion from one level of engagement to quite another that involves the students' own experiences, feelings, and values. One could say that this is what all good teaching is about" (p. 8). In such a classroom, students are really involved in a metacognitive process in which they move beyond learning facts to considering why things happen as they do and how they feel about what's going on.

It may be true that in certain respects you may feel that the role you play as advisor is less formal than that of teacher. One advisor articulates this role when he writes,

> As an advisor I have learned that I can take control and also step back, that I can take responsibility, and yet not take everything to be my responsibility. I have learned that I can be human and real with my students. . . . different than my connection to them as a teacher.

Might not this connection be strengthened? Isn't it true that we teach more effectively the better we understand our students' learning needs and design "instructional and relationship strategies" to meet them? Indeed, as teachers, we use our process skills and innate understanding of group dynamics in the classroom all the time, even when we may not be conscious of doing so and whether we have ever run an advisory group or not. Our willingness to assume a facilitative rather than authoritative role can be very liberating as we learn that our students can and will learn to make sound decisions when given greater autonomy in the learning process.

One teacher shared the following experience in his 5th grade class, which illustrates this process and also demonstrates concretely how the lines between advisory and classroom learning may blur. Out of necessity, he had split his class into two advisory groups and ran them both himself. The students had formed identifications with their advisory groups within the total class. He recalls,

> One of the most remarkable moments in the advisory program actually occurred during class. The students were working hard on a math task. There was one child who was a member of the first (advisory) group. He just could not get a particular answer. As usual, when he was stuck he shut down. He refused to comunicate with anyone, including the teacher. Some of the other students tried to give him hints. The young man refused to use the help, even when he finally understood what they were trying to tell him.
>
> Some students in the other advisory group started to laugh at him because the answer was now so simple to get. This student customarily refuses to do his work when faced with something he doesn't understand. This time he not only refused, but he started to cry. The class gathered around him, and one of the young ladies from the second group asked for an advisory session. It was seconded by another young man from the first group. They surrounded the student who was struggling with the math problem.
>
> One student began to speak words of comfort to the crying student. Everyone went around the room expressing what they thought this student's strong points were. They told him why they thought he was such a valuable addition to the classroom, but most of all they told him why they felt he was not stupid. Other students began to cry, and there was much embracing and hugging from the individual students. It was a heart-wrenching moment. The students definitely felt close, and a bond developed between the student that was strugglng and the rest of the class.
>
> This incident has led to other positive results. The struggling student no longer shuts down when faced with things he does not understand. He knows that the class wants him to succeed and he does take their hints and cues. I felt that this was our most important and successful "group" session of the year.

We have discussed how the same type of constructivist, student-centered approach that is the cornerstone of the advisory group can be demonstrated in the classroom by a teacher who is willing to act more as a facilitator than as the expert. This approach creates a group-oriented classroom environment that not only works for the general student population but seems particulary well suited for academically at-risk students, as well.

The facilitative teacher plays a number of critical roles for students in the classroom just as the advisory facilitator would. These include instilling a belief in these students that they can achieve; emphasizing correct standards of behavior that promote mutual respect among students; requiring students to develop class rules and to support them; identifying improper behaviors as they occur and discussing with the students why they are unacceptable; being consistent; demonstrating an awareness of and caring for individual students while simultaneously addressing the class as a whole; being open about one's personal values, beliefs, and experiences when helpful to the class; openly admitting mistakes; being willing to talk to students about their problems; listening to students actively; and allowing freedom of movement.

Can the facilitational techniques used in advisories also improve teachers' classroom management skills? What about those students at risk for acting out violently? Many students feel that an aggressive response to provocation is the only acceptable way of maintaining others' respect. When they go off on teachers, it is often because they feel they have been disrespected and have no other recourse.

There are a number of approaches to working with these students. First school staff need to give students the message that they are really listening to their concerns. Secondly, programs such as advisories can be initiated which are dedicated to improving understanding and communication between staff and students. Third, schools can teach the fundamentals of interpersonal skills to students. Again, the advisory is an excellent forum in which to accomplish all of these goals, which can then be continuously reinforced in the classroom.

Facilitative teaching is essential at every level of learning. Although our focus here is predominantly on middle and high school students, the value of encouraging student exchanges with one another that provoke a deeper exploration of values extends to college courses as well. I recently taught a health methods course in which students consistently cited their opportunities to work in small, problem-solving groups as the most helpful facet of the course. And a university colleague once commented that the compliment she most treasured over the course of her career came from a student who said, "I can't figure out how you taught us so much by always asking us what we thought."

Conclusion

So, what do we gain from this extraordinary experience of becoming the designated caring adult for several young people? Is the effort worth the time, energy, and consistency it requires? Can we afford to delve more deeply into our students' personal lives, possibly learning that to which we don't know how to respond and that which makes us feel more deeply than we might have desired?

Recently I heard a member of the clergy give a sermon about love and she made the point that loving is risky because we open ourselves up to the possibility of misunderstanding, even rejection. As advisors, we open ourselves to caring deeply about students in ways that exceed what we generally experience in our classroom relationships. We open ourselves to learning more about these children, knowing that sometimes we can help them but at other times we may fail. We open ourselves to self-exploration, which can be both painful and exhilarating.

But most importantly, by taking these chances, we increase our abilities to effect positive change in the lives of our students. As one advisor wrote,

> Change is a powerful instrument that we need to continue to give these children HOPE so they don't hurt someone else because of the haves and have-nots in their lives. I hope I see the day when my son will not be judged because he is black, or be judged by the area in which he lives, or by the friends he keeps because they are white, blue or green.
>
> Most importantly I hope that advisory will show the unique differences we all possess which make us special. Until then I pray that every parent's child comes home and slips into bed safely, and I pray that the children I advise make it to a ripe old age before the concrete playgrounds on which they play consume their innocence.

You who choose to become advisors owe it to yourselves not to minimize your potential importance to your students nor its impact on you. Rather, you must understand that you are helping to provide students the chance to know and to be known, the chance to feel genuinely safe.

Does the advisory have an impact on youngsters? Here is what a 7th grader had to say, "Thank you for this group. It made me feel good about myself."

Chapter Fifteen
~~~~~~~~~~~~~~~~~~~~~~~~~~

In Their Own Words:
Reflections on the
Advisory Experience

B ack in 1995 I consulted with staff at Joan of Arc Middle School
in New York City as they initiated their advisory program and
underwent staff development to prepare them as facilitators.
After meeting with their "family groups" (so named because they
attempted to simulate the best a family has to offer its children) several times weekly for a year, four of them agreed to reflect on their
experiences as advisors. Although it has been some time since they
wrote these pieces, the staff's spirit and integrity and the passion
they brought to their group facilitation is as clear today as it was
then. All would agree that their advisories positively affected their
students' lives. Here are their stories.

Jonathan Gamarra, 7th-Grade Math Teacher

As I told my "family group members" of 15 (9 females and 6
males) to arrange their desks into a circle, I must admit I did not
know what to expect. You could feel the tension and silence in the
air once we were all seated. I explained to them first what this family
group was all about. Second, I proposed the following rules to them:
no put downs, confidentiality, and attentive listening. With a degree
in engineering and now teaching math to junior high schoolers, I
doubted my ability as an efficient and effective facilitator.

Every morning the students eagerly waited for our group sharing
to begin. I felt that all their input was important. The only problem I
had up to this point was Darron. He was the most timid person in the
group. Every time it was his turn to speak he would decline, which

irritated the others because they felt this was unfair to them. They were sharing but he wasn't.

Another problem was Raymond, who usually came late to school, bringing his arrogance and rudeness with him. Any individual could see the fear he instilled among the other group members. Raymond intimidated students who were much bigger and taller than he was; he had power and control over the others. He would always brag about the gang he was in, and I suggested we talk about the dangers gangs can cause in neighborhoods.

I asked why people joined gangs and heard responses ranging from peer pressure to the desire to be loved. Why would a teenager want to join a gang to feel loved, I asked. Shaniece shouted out: "There's no love for us at home!" After she said this the room was silent. I could see the emptiness in their eyes. Everyone in our family group could relate to what Shaniece said. At this point, we grew a step closer to one another. Almost automatically we each started sharing reasons why we did not feel loved. There was a sense of relief and security amongst ourselves after we expressed our sadness to one another.

None of this seemed to phase Raymond at all. He was apathetic since he had been abandoned by his parents. Raymond is very bright. Why was this happening to him? Who was really there to love him? In Raymond's mind there was no family love, hence he formed his own gang. This gave him a sense of accomplishment, pride, respect, and security. Although I knew the group disagreed with Raymond, they didn't want to comment out of fear of him.

One day the group discussed an incident in a nearby city in which a white police officer had shot and killed a 16-year-old African American male. The youngster was clinging to life with a bullet in his head. Raymond angrily stated: "The police shot him in the head because he's black!" Everyone else agreed. This led to a discussion about how discrimination affects them. They claim to experience it daily. One student described what happens when he and friends enter a convenience store on his block: "When we enter the store we are watched and if we touch something we're asked if we're going to buy it. White customers aren't treated like that."

Another topic, although much lighter, showed us how one group member could be brave enough to stand by his convictions. Edward, a transfer student, was the newest member of our group. The other students soon realized that Edward was a very unique individual, not influenced at all by the opinions of the other family group members.

We once discussed what each student would do if he/she found a person's wallet containing $500. Edward was the only person who said he would return it to its owner. The others teased him about being foolish, but he calmly defended himself by asking, "What if it was your money?" This was the first of many moments when Edward impacted the group.

Although we met formally as a group only once a day, I felt that we watched out for each other all the time. One day, two female members of my group approached me with their personal problems. They were both certain they were pregnant although they had not yet had tests. After considering the pros and cons, one girl decided to have an abortion. The other girl's test results were negative. Later in group we talked about the risks involved of becoming sexually active—pregnancy, contracting STDs, and so forth. Most of all, we discussed the difficulties in handling the physical and emotional demands sexual relationships entail.

After all these events took place, I realized how important our family group was to each of us. It was a place where we could share our feelings, express our emotions, find some consolation, and talk over our experiences with each other. This made the students feel very important as young people growing up in an urban environment. As the school year came to an end, I asked them how our "family group" had affected their lives. Most responded very positively, saying they wanted to continue the following year. As they expressed how they felt during the school year about their advisory, I felt a sense of relief because I believed I had made a difference in their lives as a facilitator; and we had made a difference to each other.

We as facilitators must remember certain points such as patience, understanding, fairness, and caring. If you incorporate these points into your advisory sessions, the end result will be a fulfilling experience for you as well as for your students.

Rosalie Scaglione, Guidance Counselor

I have been a guidance counselor for the past 3 years. Before this I taught remedial reading, mathematics, and English classes in elementary school and junior high school. I had also worked in a remedial reading class with small groups of 10 to 12 students and conducted a weekly advisory for 9th graders.

As a family group advisor, I was assigned to work with a group of fiftheen 7th graders. I was nervous as I approached the day of our first meeting; and as I look back on it, so were they. We sat stiffly in chairs which had been arranged in a circle and everyone looked at me to start the ball rolling. I introduced myself to the group and told them a little about me. I then asked the students to introduce themselves to each other and to me. I asked them questions about their families, hobbies, favorite foods, and things they enjoyed doing for fun.

Because of my varied experiences in small group work, I felt a family group setting was something for which I was well prepared. However, I was concerned I might have difficulty switching from a teaching to a guidance to an advisory mode—and I was right! As a teacher, it is necessary to establish a disciplinary code—usually with the help of the students—and then to enforce that code in a fair manner. This means that students look to the adult in the group as the person who ensures that discussions run smoothly and that discipline is maintained.

In a small group teaching experience, the students still look to the teacher as the person who guides them in discussions and maintains order. The family group experience involved a more indistinct role separation. The facilitator is still responsible for maintaining order and initiating discussions (when needed), but the group members are expected to take a more active role in terms of discussion, inclusion of all members' opinions, and discipline within the group.

When one has been as strong a teacher as I was, it was difficult to watch group members flounder at times while working things out—determining which topics should be discussed, how to include members who are reluctant to speak, and what to say to group members who work against the process. However, this separation must be made if the group is to make progress. One person cannot be in charge while the others sit back and relax. The effort to make the group viable must be made with contributions from all members—not the same ones each day. Encouragement to particpate must come from the members, not the group leader.

I wasn't alone in my struggle to wear a different type of cap. The group members with whom I was assigned to work had the same type of difficulties I was having—they had put most of the adults in the school into a "teacher" mode and it was hard for them to look at us (and me!) in any other way.

I talked to them about the concept of a family and how we were trying something new at our school. I introduced the Magic Circle, which was a guideline I used for group behavior. The Magic Circle is a list of rules that are meant to guide the actions of the members.

These include

- All members have the right to speak on a particular issue.
- All members respect the space of others.
- There is no foul language.
- No one is allowed to gossip or "put down" another student.
- All members listen to someone who is speaking without interrrupting that person to make a comment.
- A member of the group may pass if he or she does not wish to comment on a particular issue.

Our first meeting broke some of the ice, but it certainly didn't melt the iceberg. During the next few sessions we talked about famiies and what things made our families different from anyone else's. Again, I was met with an invisible wall of silence from about half the group members. We talked about traditions, and I told them about some of my family's—Sunday dinners, holiday celebrations, birthdays, and other special occasions. A few of them participated in the discussion, others nodded, and some whispered to their neighbors. But in general, they just weren't used to sharing any part of themselves with strangers, even if the strangers included students with whom they had spent the entire year in 6th grade.

Over the first weekend, I thought about how my family nurtured and cared for the spirit—and usually it was around the kitchen table. Traditionally, Italian homes are known for their busy kitchens; and when I was growing up, the kitchen was the largest and noisiest room in the house. It was the center of activity, in addition to being the place where we ate most of our meals. So I decided to take some of that spirit of nurturing into my family group at school, and thus began the Monday morning tradition of having breakfast together.

Each week I brought some type of breakfast food to the group. We've had muffins, cereals, banana bread, donuts, bagels, and cereal treats. Some of the group members contributed fruits or juices, but the responsibility for most of the breakfast food was mine. It became a good way to start the week and loosen tongues.

During one session, we talked about taking chances and trying new things. Many of them were fearful of risk taking because it comes with the possibility of failure. In the vein of this discussion, I brought some unfamiliar fruits (kiwi, star fruit, and pomegranates) to a session and "dared" the members to taste them.

It was fascinating to see the looks on their faces as they tasted things they had never tried before. The students were so proud of taking the chance of eating something they weren't sure they'd like. I explained there is no "sin" in not liking something. The "sin" is in refusing to give oneself the opportunity to like it.

I attempted many different strategies in working with the group, one of which was a direct attempt to throw the leadership from myself to other members. We made a long list of the things we'd like to discuss in groups—the first being *s-e-x.* However, we decided to shelve that subject because many in the group felt uncomfortable.

I talked to the group leader who works with the other half of this particular class. He is their homeroom and subject teacher. We came up with the idea of "For Women Only" and "For Men Only" groups one day each month. On these days, all of the boys report to him and all of the girls to me. It is a good way for both sexes to ask questions about hygiene, sex, pregnancy, and their bodily changes without feeling inhibited. At some point we will mix the groups up, but the separation seems to be functioning quite well for now.

We worked our way down our list of topics, but usually one led naturally to another during our discussions. We created a family group memory book in which we have recorded some of our more memorable events—birthday celebrations, Thanksgiving dinner, and our Christmas trip to Rockefeller Center and to the ice skating rink in Central Park. I feel the latter two events pulled our group together.

For the Thanksgiving dinner, I asked one of the quieter group members to take charge as chairperson. I chose her because she usually sat apart from the group and seldom participated in any discussions. I wanted the others to see that she had some strong leadership qualities, even though she was not choosing to exericise them in family group. It was a marvelous experience, and it was really the turning point in terms of bonding. Members came in, sat down, waited to be served, complimented people on the dishes they contributed to the dinner, and were well mannered overall. I think the most impressive gesture of all was when the chairperson asked some group members to invite adults who had no family groups of their own to join our dinner. I feel that group members who had once viewed the chairperson with detachment now saw her in a different light; and she seemed to see herself differently, too. She began joining the circle rather than sitting to the side.

During one session, I asked the group members to give me their opinions about family group. Most of them felt it was great to have a place to talk about the things that were on their minds. Some felt that I should have the group all day long and teach every subject. Only one person thought family group time was not fun. He had trouble sitting still and felt the group was too confining. When it came to suggestions for improvement, many felt we should have a period at the beginning and a period at the end of the day for family group. I can see that many friendships have been formed, and that's a real positive.

However, I also see a dependence on me as the group leader that I know is not beneficial. There is, in fact, a small group of members who come by almost every period to tell me where they will be or where they are heading. I explain that they do not have to check in at the beginning of every period, but the practice has been hard to break.

On several occasions I have become discouraged because the group seemed to be coming "unglued." Some group members would come in late and disturb the group with loud talk or disruptive actions. Others would break off to form smaller groups within the advisory when they didn't want to talk about a particular topic. They didn't want to share their feelings. Still, at other times I have sensed a "backstabbing" feeling when someone had done something wrong in group or in class.

On a few other occasions, members have said hurtful things to each other which they knew would cause ruffled feelings. It's almost as if they searched for something to say which would cause another to respond inappropriately or feel badly. I knew this happens from time to time, but I saw the good things that have been part of the group being taken for granted. I sensed a selfish attitude on the part of some members.

One incident which illustrates this concern happened just before Easter when three of my group members were celebrating birthdays. I has purchased birthday gifts for each celebrant, ordered pizza, and filled Easter baskets for everyone. The morning of the party we met in group and some students asked if they could bring friends. I told them no because I couldn't buy pizza for so many. One student said, "You're earning enough money." Having spent almost $50 on that day alone, I replied that since I earned the money I could decide how I spent it.

That type of response was not particularly in character for me, but I really felt I was being taken advantage of. The group was very quiet and then it was time for them to go to their next period class. I quietly asked if there were people who would rather go to lunch than come to the party, but everyone said they would be back.

Although it was a lovely gathering, something was missing; and I think I was becoming resentful of the "gimme" attitude which had come to light. After the party, several students remained for cleanup (without being asked) and for this I was grateful. However, the following period I asked them to go on to class as I had students coming in for counseling; and one little girl pulled away from me. She said some very nasty things and shouted at the top of her lungs that she hated this "stink" room and that she hated the "stink" teacher.

I told her she needed to find herself another group because she was not welcome to return until she apologized. The next few sessions she wandered around looking to join another group, finally ending up in the principal's office explaining her predicament. I sent someone after her and then explained to the group why I had reacted to this member's outburst in this way. I asked that the students talk about her participation in the group, and said I would abide by what ever they decided. They did confront her about her disrespect and her attitude. In the end, we took a vote and decided she should remain in the group. I voted for her to remain and so did she.

Perhaps this was all in preparation for the end of the year and our parting, but at this particular time I was having difficulties sorting out my feelings about some of the group members. While I fought with my own feelings, I knew the experience had been a good one for the students. They really felt they could talk to me about almost anything that was on their minds. In fact, one of the boys has been traumatized by his first brush with the law and the court system. After his second court appearance, he told me he was desperately unhappy and not sleeping. He cried as he talked about the pain of going to court, disappointing his parents, and feeling like a failure. I knew he would not have revealed any of these emotions to another adult in the school.

So, while I felt discouraged at times, I can also see how family group had been a worthwhile experience for these students. It was a way of connecting to an adult other than a teacher in a school situation. It had also provided a strength to resist some of the temptations which present themselves to students in the school environment.

Much can be learned from the family group experience. People must be trained and supported in their endeavors to work in a situation which may be uncomfortable for them. Parameters should be set by administration. While "glitches" need to be worked out, everyone must be patient and accepting of ideas and criticism which will make this a more viable practice.

Karen Stevens, Special Education Teacher

September 7, 85 degrees, the first day of school for teachers. I sat, jammed into a desk and dripping, listening to the facilitators explain the implementation of a new program called "family group." "Great," I thought to myself, "another subject I've got to plan and teach." OK, I was whining already, only one day into the school year.

I teach special education. This year I was assigned a MIS III class of language and speech-impaired students. That meant reading and math levels no higher than 3rd grade in a class of 11- to 14-year-old children. My class is self-contained, so I teach 5 subjects. I did not welcome another curriculum to develop and teach.

Orientation progressed with intensive workshops about running a family group. I began to feel less resistant. I had participated in many of the same exercises being demonstrated for us in other situations like acting classes and group therapy. The goals were similar: learning to trust, to express feelings, and to listen. By developing these skills one can become a happier, more effective person. Perhaps family group would help my class become a more cohesive learning unit. Trust, honesty, compassion, and risk taking are values always in need of support; perhaps they would solidify for my class through the vehicle of family group.

Each class I've taught during my 9 years at this school has been unique. Every student walks into class carrying a full plate of similar problems—below-grade reading and math skills, poor self-image, anger at and fear of the war zone of inner city violence, as well as disintegrating families and communities. They also walk in with humor, curiosity, and hope for a future that includes a good job, a nice home, and a happy family. Their chances of achieving these goals may be lower than most other children but the hope is there. Perhaps family group could nurture this hope by increasing life-coping skills like effective communication and problem solving. This was my hope—that by providing a time and place where students could relax, trust, express themselves, and listen, they could survive puberty more effectively and with less damage.

Oy, such a windmill! Could their curiosity counteract troubled nights of family violence and nightmares? Could their small acts of camraderie and kindness cancel out the effects of street life where "do unto others before they do unto you" is the rule? The courage I've grown to admire in my students over the years, the fact that they have shown up at school with a smile and a desire to be part of the class, has given me the incentive to give family group my best effort.

The first day of class, I introduced the idea of family group and repeated the rules outlined during orientation. The students seemed amenable to the idea. I began by running a "getting to know you" exercise even though most of the students knew each other from grade school. I shared about my summer, my family, and what I wanted to happen in class. I asked why each child thought they were in special education. I asked what each child wanted to accomplish in school this year. We took turns around the circle of 9 children, the paraprofessional, and me. Almost every student had experienced a "nice" summer and hoped they would "learn" in school this year. OK . . . the answers were general, but at least positive.

As to why they thought they were in special education, most of the students were aware that their reading and math scores were low. Vincent, a student who turned out to be misplaced in this class setting, replied he was in special education because of his behavior. He was eventually placed in a SI VII class for severely emotionally disturbed, acting-out students. I ask the reason students think they are in special education every year so I can begin to inculcate into every subject, everyday, the fact that special education does not mean dumb and therefore hopeless. Special education means students learn differently and have weaknesses that can be strengthened. I constantly point out to the rest of the class whenever a child figures out a new way to solve a problem or behaves in a way that proves how bright and clever he/she is in his/her own special way.

Even with my enthusiasm and positive reinforcement, family group began to fall apart. In spite of reminders about rules, explanations about the need for teamwork, pleading, and finally threats of phone calls to home, the students increased their disruptive behavior, teasing, "dissing," poking and intruding on each other's persons and property. Vincent, as yet unmedicated, made faces or performed handstands while others were speaking, and physically threatened the other students until Mrs. Smith, my paraprofessional, escorted him out of class for a stroll in the halls. Frank would storm away from the group if he was in the least challenged or teased, even though he often was the first to insult or verbally attack another with a mean, angry comment. Kwami would start cursing if Shaunte teased him about his uncontrollable drooling.

I became frustrated and angry that these children refused to enjoy a half hour of talking and sharing. Why? Perhaps the idea was a new change. Perhaps my students couldn't deal with talking about their feelings and fears. Were they using the same distracting behavior used to avoid math and science? Why not? Educated and enlightened adults, including myself, often enough were unwilling to share and reveal when given the opportunity in a safe and anonymous situation.

I thought back to acting classes, therapy sessions, and motivational workshops I had attended. All of these groups involved risk. With trust being such an immense issue in my life, revealing secrets and fear to mere acquaintances in a group, no matter what the purpose, was frightening to me. I had always handled my nasty stuff alone. Now I've learned I can't handle everything by myself. It took many years and much work. How did I have the audacity to think my students were ready to embrace such uncharted territory immediately and unconditionally? I was expecting 12- to 14-year old children with inadequate coping skills, including bragadaccio, manipulation, withdrawal, and physical and verbal acting out, to jump on my wagon train to mental health. Right!

I needed help. Two staff developers suggested behavior modification, which I initially resisted. No! Pavlov had no place in my family group. They patiently pointed out that family group was not going to evolve into anything unless students kept their seats, respected each others' boundaries, listened, and contributed. I had to admit they were absolutely right. The loudest students, the most acting out students, were getting all the attention in spite of my efforts to see everyone participate. The girls had withdrawn and Kwami had also, except for outbursts of filthy language when someone teased him.

I agreed to give behavior modification a chance, as well as using a talking stick. Members of the group were allowed to talk only when holding the object. In our group it was a pillow to prevent injury just in case the talker got a little carried away.

I returned to family group with this information. I decided to discuss the problem with the group and develop a plan with them. This way, the students would feel empowered and accept the resulting actions more readily. We made a chart with everyone's names on it. We decided that each day a child could earn two points—one for behavior and one for contributing. If a child earned 7 out of 10 possible points in a week, he or she would receive a prize. These included special pencils, free time, something to eat, and so forth. The rules remained consistent: Students must remain in their seats, bring only themselves to group, let the person holding the talking pillow speak without interruption, keep their hands and feet to themselves, and no put downs.

I was very pleasantly surprised. The group became more focused; and even when Vincent and James, another severely disturbed boy misplaced in this class setting acted out, the other students remained focused on their 10-point goal. The behavior modification approach worked. The students gave themselves the points they believed they deserved and were harder on themselves than I would have been. They were quick to point out specific behaviors that warranted point losses and actually showed a real sense of justice. Eventually the points and chart became unnecessary. We were not without slips and back-slides, especially at the end of the year when parting caused anxieties the children found hard to handle, but overall the group did well.

Activities for family group did not vary that much. The children wanted to talk and to be listened to. About once a month we ate breakfast together with everyone contributing something. Sometimes I read a book, to elicit discussion of a planned topic. Sometimes I read a book, just to ease the students into the day. Journal writing was not a big hit because most of the students had inadequate writing skills.

What about the original goals of learning to trust, feeling safe enough to express feelings, and listening? Did the students develop coping skills like effective communication and problem-solving strategies? I'll let you be the judge. Here are a few changes I noticed:

- All the students became more comfortable when expressing or receiving positive feedback.
- Although slightly decreased, putdowns remained a problem but some students became noticeably kinder and less critical.
- Many students opened up and shared very personal concerns with the group.
- Trust increased and students began to discuss concerns about family, death, sex, and daily fears.

In large part because of family group, Class 403A really did become a family. When children from other classes were placed in our room for one reason or another, I noticed that a stronger feeling of protection for each other had developed; and even students who were teased normally were defended against any slight by an outsider. If a student was rudely interrupted, other students would say, "Let him speak!" or "Let her finish!" Again, this would not happen everytime, but more often than at the beginning of the year. Behaviors did change, not in giant, dramatic steps, but enough to build a cohesiveness I thought significant enough to make family group worthwhile.

Where will next year take me and my young fellow travelers? I will be teaching most of them again. Our staff has decided to cut family group sessions down to three days a week next year. I look forward to building on a relationship already strengthened and enriched by family group.

Richard Pashley, 8th-Grade English Teacher

The crash was startling. I knew at once what had happened. Fearing the worst, I bent over to pick up the fallen, framed picture laying on its belly. Upon turning it over, I saw that while the art work was intact, the glass had cracked: The bodyguard had taken the bullet and was mortally wounded. A series of errors in judgment had led to the catastrophe.

The artist, Jeff, had lain the painting on my desk for safekeeping. He was going to take his creation home at the end of the day to hang in his room. Ironically, we had just talked about how important it was to him; and I had reminded him that I had seen the painting's inception in his journal writing. Several people, including the principal, had asked Jeff if they could hang the painting; but he had refused all offers. It mattered a lot to him.

Fortunately, he was out of the room on an errand when the accident happened. Needing room to write, I had removed the painting from my desk and had placed it on a student's desk. As Tamara walked by, her coat caught the edge of the painting, causing it to fall. "How could you do that!" I yelled at her. After that, all was stunned silence as each member of the family group slowly grasped the seriousness of what had happened and waited tensely for Jeff to return.

When he finally did, we told him what had happened; and predictably he reacted with disbelief and suppressed rage, bolting from the room. Just as predictably, he returned in a few minutes. After several uncomfortable moments of tense silence, I spoke up sugesting that we use what had happened as a topic for family group discussion.

Reluctantly at first, but with more involvement after I had broken the icy silence, several group members tried to comfort Jeff, one actually getting up and talking to him privately. I asked what bothered him most, to which he replied, "I really cared abut that picture. I wouldn't even let the principal hang it in her office. I wanted to hang it in my room at home."

I told the group that I wanted to take some of the blame for the incident, but they said no, that we were all human, and that it was just a horrible accident. I then asked the group what they thought we should do, and I told them I was willing to pay for a new frame. One individual suggested that since it could have been any one of us who knocked the picture off the desk, that we all share the cost of replacing the frame. That became the consensus and Jeff, relieved that the actual artwork had sustained no damage, started to calm down.

At that point I realized that Tamara had her head down on her desk and was crying. Someone said that I had been too harsh with her, and I got up to comfort her. Although I apologized, it was Jeff who achieved closure by coming back to my room after math class the next period to tell me that he had made Tamara laugh. Had it not been for the healing process made possible by the family group session, both Jeff and Tamara would have gone through the day with an unresolved confict, which might well have escalated into a major incident.

This is what our family group does best: We support each other, rising to the occasion of confronting crises as need be. Our normal emotional temperature is much lower. In fact, a casual onlooker might see us as just a group of relaxed individuals who enjoy each others' company and are grateful to be able to relax a bit before starting the rigors of a typical academic school day.

Indeed, many group members have said that they are rushed in the morning as they struggle to cope with the many stresses at home. Consequently, they really look forward to the family group time as a means of sitting back, taking a deep breath, and regrouping, so that they can then calmly step, rather than hurl headlong, into the school day.

I must confess that I, too, appreciate the chance to unwind. I find that family group invariably calms me down and helps improve my mood, no matter what personal problems I may be facing, and allows me to be more focused for the rest of the day.

Our group has dealt with tough issues, from suicide to AIDS awareness. The fact that we have confronted such issues successfully has hinged upon our strict adherence to our four underlying rules: no putdowns; attentive listening; the right to pass; and, most importantly, confidentiality. Without these principles, our discussions would have been nowhere as searingly honest, compelling, and involving as they were.

The AIDS piece was a gamble, but one very much worth taking, because I felt that a group of teenagers needed to confront that particular issue. Fortunately, the discussion, protracted over several days, was frank, moving, and ultimately cautionary enough that I think everyone became more aware of how vulnerable we all are—an especially apt lesson for teens.

Incidentally, my student teacher was with the group at the time of that discussion; and his input was invaluable because he was closer in age than I to the students. His telling them about a friend whom he had helped and whom he had ultimately watched die from AIDS packed more of an emotional wallop than anything I could have said.

In fact Carlos, my student teacher, became so much an integral part of the group that his departure at Christmas time was extremely traumatic. We had a farewell party during which many group members were in tears as they told him what his being part of the group had meant to them. Such a moment was telling proof of how close-knit a group we had become.

We have had our lighter moments, of course. These have included our weekly breakfasts, two of which have been excursions to McDonalds, as well as birthay celebrations for each group member. I feel that these social activities, which we all thoroughly enjoyed, helped to cement us together so that we had the cohesiveness to tackle meaty issues and debates without having them degenerate into arguments.

If a solid foundation is established, then controversial issues involving differences of opinion can be handled without anyone taking what someone else says as a personal attack. We like each other and have enough confidence in that fact to risk expressing opinions which, in a less tightly-knit group, might cause problems. Because we trust, care for, and respect each other as individuals, we can agree to disagree.

Just as we had to adjust to Carlos's departure from the group, we had to accommodate another change when a new student was added to my class. While there was no overt resistance to his joining us, I sensed that Noah was apart from, rather than a part of, the group.

For about 2 weeks nothing changed but then, under the most unlikely of circumstances, he became one of us. We had been talking about suicide, a discussion which I would rank as one of our least successful explorations of a serious topic. It's easy to tell when sparks are flying; and they just were not, until I posed one final question.

I asked the group, "What are some things that make you sad; not suicidal, but just depressed?" As we shared stories, I made a point of asking Noah for his thoughts on the matter. He seemed startled at first; but quickly rose to the occasion, telling us about how upset he had been when his pet hamster had died.

There was nothing unusual: The hamster was dead and he buried it in the backyard using a garden trowel. However, his gentle telling of the story, so self-effacing, loving, and sincere, bespoke his gentle nature; and he had everyone's undivided attention.

The defining moment came when, in the midst of this solemn tale, he mentioned the animal's name, "Cuchi-boom-boom." The effect was as if he had pricked a balloon with a pin. Everyone burst out laughing. He had no idea what the name meant or why he had chosen it; but at that moment, really quite a magical one, our group truly had increased by one. He had made us laugh, and we made him our own.

I love my group. They help me as much as I help them or perhaps more accurately, we help each other. I worry about our inevitable disbanding in June. For me, the experience has not been about structure, or group dynamics, or elaborate plans, but rather about a group of people who genuinely like each other and whose chemistry allows for a relaxed, familiar, and familial linkage.

It is far removed from traditional teaching or learning, yet I cannot remember an experience from which I have learned so much about or given so much of myself. It has also taught me how to relate to others. We are there for each other, through the laughter, the tears, or the more typical neutral times when we just sit like comfortable, old friends talking about nothing and everything. I find the whole experience extremely calming, as do the students. I feel very strongly that our daily morning time together helps us to cope more confidently and successfully with the stresses of life, both in school and in the world outside. Rest in peace, Cuchi-boom-boom, and long live the family group.

References

~~~~~~~~~~~~~~~~~~~~~~~

Adams, C. R., & Singh, K. (1998). Direct and indirect effects of school learning variables on the academic achievement of African American 10th graders. *Journal of Negro Education, 67*(1), 48–66.

Alder, N. I., & Moulton, M. R. (1998). Caring relationships: Perspectives from middle school students. *Research in Middle Level Education Quarterly, 21*(3), 15–32.

Allen, L. (1997). *Report to the W. T. Grant Foundation on the Evaluation of the Advisory Program at Junior High School 22.* New York: New York University.

American Academy of Child and Adolescent Psychiatry (1999). *Your adolescent: Emotional, behavioral and cognitive development from early adoescence through the teen years.* New York: HarperCollins.

Anderson, L. F., & Robertson, S. E. (1985). Group facilitation: Functions and skills. *Small Group Behavior, 16*(2), 139–156.

Anfara, V., & Brown, K. (2000). In their own words: Have our middle schools responded to the needs of young adolescents? *Research in Middle Level Education Annual, 23*, 65–84.

Anson, A. R. (1995). Risk and protection during the middle school transition: The role of school climate in early adolescent development. *Disseration Abstracts International: Section B: The Sciences and Engineering, 56*(3-B), 1716.

Asch, S. E. (1955). Opinions and social pressures. *Scientific American, 193*(5), 31–35.

Ayres, L. R. (1994). Middle school advisory programs: Findings from the field. *Middle School Journal, 25*(3), 8–14.

Babad, E. (1995). The "teacher's pet" phenomenon and students' perceptions of teachers' differential behavior. *Journal of Educational Psychology, 87*(3), 361–366.

Ballou, M. B., Fetter, M. P., Litwack, K. P., & Litwack, L. (1992). *Health counseling.* Kent, OH: American School Health Association.

Benne, K. D., & Sheats, P. (1948). Functional roles of group members. *Journal of Social Issues, 4*(2), 41–49.

Bennis, W., & Shepard, H. (1956). A theory of group development. *Human Relations, 9*, 415–457.

Bergmann, S., & Baxter, J. (1983). Building a guidance program and advisory concept for early adolescents. *NASSP Bulletin, 67*(463), 49–55.

Berman-Rossi, T. (1993). The tasks and skills of social workers across stages of group development. *Social Work with Groups, 16*(112), 69–80.

Bosworth, K. (1995). Caring for others and being cared for: Students talk about caring in school. *Phi Delta Kappan, 76*(9), 686–693.

Bosworth, K., Espelage, D. L., & Simon, T. R. (1999). Factors associated with bullying behavior in middle school students. *Journal of Early Adolescence, 19*(3), 341–362.

Botvin, G. J., Dusenbury, L., Baker, E., James-Ortiz, S., & Kerner, J. (1989). A skills training approach to smoking prevention among Hispanic youth. *Journal of Behavioral Medicine, 12*(3), 279–296.

Braddock, J. H., & McPartland, J. M. (1993). Education of early adolescents. In D. L. Hammond (Ed.), *Review of Research in Education, Vol. 19.* Washington, DC: American Educational Research Association.

Brandler, S., & Roman, C. P. (1991). *Group work: Skills and strategies for effective interventions.* Binghamton, New York: The Haworth Press.

Brown, D. (2001). The value of advisory sessions for urban young adolescents. *Middle School Journal, 32*(4), 14–22.

Bruce-Sanford, G. (1998). A simulation model for training in group process. *International Journal of Group Psychotherapy, 48*(3), 393–399.

Bukowski, W. M., & Sippola, L. K. (1996). Friendship and morality. In W. M. Bukowski & A. F. Newcomb (Eds.), *The company they keep: Friendship in childhood and adolescence* (pp. 238–261). Cambridge: Cambridge University Press.

Burkhardt, R. M. (1999). Advisory: Advocacy for every student. *Middle School Journal, 30*(3), 51–54.

Carew, D. K., Parisi-Carew, E., & Blanchard, K. H. (1986). Group development and situational leadership: A model for managing groups, *Human Training and Development Journal,* 46–50.

Carnegie Council on Adolescent Development (1989). *Turning points: Preparing American youth for the 21st century.* Washington, DC: Carnegie Council for Adolescent Development.

Cartwright, D., & Zander, A. (1968). *Group dynamics research and theory.* New York: Harper & Row.

Casey, D., Roberts, P., & Salaman, G. (1992). Facilitating learning in groups. *Leadership and Organization Development Journal, 13*(4), 8–13.

Cohen, E. G. (1994). *Designing groupwork: Strategies for the heterogeneous classroom* (2nd ed.). New York: Teachers College Press.

Cole, C. (1992). *Nurturing a teacher advisory program.* Columbus, OH: National Middle School Association.

Cole, C. (1994). Teachers' attitudes before beginning a teacher advisory program. *Middle School Journal, 25*(5), 3–7.

Compas, B. E., Davis, G. E., & Forsythe, C. J. (1985). Characteristics of life events during adolescence. *American Journal of Community Psychology, 13*(6), 677–691.

Compas, B. E. (1993). Promoting positive mental health during adolescence. In S. G. Millstein, A. C. Petersen, E. O. Nightingale, (Eds.), *Promoting the health of adolescents: New Directions for the 21st Century* (pp. 159–179). New York: Oxford University Press.

Connell, D. B., Turner, R. R., & Mason, E. F. (1985). Summary of findings of the school health education evaluation: Health promotion effectiveness, implementation, and costs. *Journal of School Health, 55* (8), 316–332.

Corey, M. S., & Corey, G. (1997). *Groups: Process and Practice* (5th ed.). Pacific Grove, CA: Brooks/Cole Publishers.

Corey, G. Corey, M. S., Callanan, P., & Russell, J. J. (1992). *Group techniques* (2nd ed.). Pacific Grove, CA: Brooks/Cole Publishers.

Cushman, K. (1990). Are advisory groups "essential"? What they do, how they work. *Horace, 7*(1), 4–11.

Devencenzi, J., & Pendergast. S. (1999). *Belonging: Self and social discovery for children and adolescents. A guide for group facilitators*. San Luis Obispo, CA: Sovereignty Press.

Dore, M. M., Zlupko, L. N., & Kaufmann, E. (1999). "Friends in need": Designing and implementing a psychoeducational group for school children from drug-involved families. *Social Work, 44*(2), 179–190.

Dreikurs, R. (1972). *Coping with children's misbehavior.* New York: Hawthorn Books.

Dreikurs, R., Grunwald, B. B., & Pepper, F. C. (1971). *Maintaining sanity in the classroom: Illustrated teaching techniques.* New York: Harper & Row.

Dunphy, D. C. (1990). Peer group socialization. In Rolf E. Muus (Ed.). *Adolescent Behavior and Society* (4th ed., pp. 171–183). McGraw Hill College Division.

Eccles, J. S., & Midgley, C. (1989). Stage/environment fit: Developmentally appropriate classrooms for early adolescents. In R. Ames & C. Ames (Eds.), *Research on Motivation in Education* (Vol. 3, pp. 139–181). New York: Academic Press.

Eccles, J. S., Wigfield, A., Midgley, C., Reuman, D., MacIver, D., & Feldlaufer, H. (1993). Negative effects of traditional middle schools on students' motivation. *The Elementary School Journal, 93*(5), 553–569.

Eisenberg, N. (1986). *Altruistic emotion, cognition, and behavior.* Hillsdale, NJ: Lawrence Erlbaum.

Eisenberg, N., & Fabes, R. A. (1998). Prosocial development. In W. Damon (Series Ed.) and N. Eisenberg (Vol. Ed.), *Handbook of child psychology (Vol. 3): Social, emotional and personality development* (5th ed., pp. 701–778). New York: John Wiley.

Elias, M. J., & Branden-Muller, L. R. (1994). Social and life skills development during the middle school years: An emerging perspective. *Middle School Journal, 25*(3), 3–7.

Elias, M. J., Gara, M., Ubriaco, M., Rothbaum, P. A., Clabby, J. F., & Schuyler, T. (1986). Impact of a preventive social problem solving intervention on children's coping with middle-school stressors. *American Journal of Community Psychology, 14*(3), 259–275.

Espe, L. (1993). The effectiveness of teacher advisors in a junior high. *The Canadian School Executive, 12*(7), 15–19.

Fabes, R. A., Carlo, G., Kupanoff, K., & Laible, D. (1999). Early adolescence and prosocial/oral behavior: The role of individual process. *Journal of Early Adolescence, 19*(1), 5–16.

Fast, J. (1999). Where were you fifth period? Five strategies for group formation in high schools in the 1990s. *Social Work in Education, 21*(2), 99–105.

Fatum, W. R., & Hoyle, J. C. (1996). Is it violence? School violence from the student perspective: Trends and interventions. *School Counselor, 44*(1), 28–35.

Fibkins, W. L. (1999). Stronger advisory programs can stem the spread of school violence. *Middle Ground, 3*(2), pp. 41–43.

Forsyth, D. R. (1998). *Group dynamics* (3rd ed.). Belmont, CA: Wadsworth.

Galassi, J. P., & Gulledge, S. Z. (1997). The middle school counselor and teacher-advisor programs. *Professional School Counseling, 1*(2), 55–61.

Galassi, J. P., Gulledge, S.Z., & Cox, N. D. (1998). *Advisory: Definitions; descriptions; decisions; directions.* Columbus, OH: National Middle School Association.

Galassi, J. P., Thornton, B., Sheffield, A., Bryan, M., & Oliver, J. (1998). Reaching agreement on advisory goals using a card sorting and a goal ranking approach: A professional development school inquiry. *Research in Middle Level Education, 22*(1), 1–15.

Garland, J., Jones, H., & Kolodney, R. (1965). A model for stages of development in social work groups. In S. Bernstein (Ed.). *Explorations in Group Work: Essays in Theory and Practice*. Boston: Boston University School of Social Work.

George, P. S. (1999). A middle school—if you can keep it: Part II. *Midpoints Occasional Papers*, Fall 1999, pp. 1–11. Westerville, OH: National Middle School Association.

George, P., & Oldaker, L. (1985). Evidence for the middle school. Columbus, OH: National Middle School Association, 1985.

Gibson, R. L., & Mitchell, M. H. (1999). *Introduction to counseling and guidance* (5th ed.). Upper Saddle River, NJ: Merrill.

Gill, J., & Read J. E. (1990). The "experts" comment on adviser-advisee programs. *Middle School Journal, 21*(3), 31–33.

Gitterman, A., & Shulman, L. (1994). *Mutual aid groups and the life cycle.* (2nd ed.). New York: Columbia University Press.

Gladding, S. T. (2000). *Counseling: A comprehensive profession* (4th ed.). Upper Saddle River, NJ: Prentice-Hall.

Goguen, C. (2000). *The effects of community violence on children and adolescents: A National Center for PTSD fact sheet. www.ncptsd.org.*

Goldberg, M. F. (1998). *How to design an advisory system for a secondary school.* Alexandria, VA: Association for Supervision and Curriculum Development.

Gordon, T. (1976). *Parent effectiveness training in action.* New York: Wyden Books.

Graham, J. E., Updegraff, K. A., Tomascik, C. A., & McHale, S. M. (1997). Someone who cares: Evaluation of school advisor programs in two community settings. *Applied Developmental Science, 1*(3), 28–42.

Greenberg, J. S. (1995). Health education: *Learner-centered instructional strategies* (3rd ed.). Madison, WI: Brown and Benchmark.

Gumaer, J. (1986). Working in groups with middle graders. *The School Counselor, 33*, 230–238.

Hagborg, W. J. (1993). Middle-school student satisfaction with group counseling: An initial study. *The Journal for Specialists in Group Work, 18*(2), 80–85.

Hamblen, J. (2000). *PTSD in children and adolescents: A National Center for PTSD fact sheet. www.ncptsd.org.*

Halebsky, M. (1991). *Group therapy for adolescents: A practical list of group ideas.* Arvada, CO: Personal and Professional Growth Organization.

Hamburg, D. O. (1993). The opportunities of early adolescence. In R. Takanishi, (Ed.), *Adolescence in the 1990s: Risks and opportunities* (pp. 8–13). New York: Teachers College Press.

Hare, A. P., Blumberg, H. H., Davies, M. F., & Kent, M. V. (1995). *Small group research: A handbook.* Norwood, NJ: Ablex Publishing.

Hawkins, J. D., Catalano, R. F., & Miller, J. Y. (1992). Risk and protective factors for alcohol and other drug problems in adolescence and early adulthood. Implications for substance abuse prevention. *Psychological Bulletin, 118*(1), 64–105.

Henderson, P., & LaForge, J. (1989). The role of the middle school counselor in teacher-advisor programs. *The School Counselor, 36*(5), 348–351.

Hereford, N. (1999). Positive school climate: Creating a place where people want to be. *Middle Ground, 3*(2), 10–16.

Hoffman, M. L. (1991). Empathy, social cognition, and moral action. In W. M. Kurtines & J. L. Gewirtz (Eds.), *Handbook of moral behavior and development (Vol. 1): Theory* (pp. 275–301). Hilsdale, NJ: Lawrence Erlbaum.

Horne, A. (1993). Declining resources, opportunities for groups. The *Journal for Specialists in Group Work, 18*(1), 162–163.

Houck, J. W. (1992). A preservice to service collaboration model for school counselors and classroom teachers. *Counseling and Human Development, 25*(3), 1–14.

Hoy, W. K., & Hannum, J. W. Middle school climate: An empirical assessment of organizational health and student achievement. *Educational Administration Quarterly, 33*(3), 290–312.

Hudson, P. E., Doyle, E., & Venezia, J. F. (1991). A comparison of two group methods of teaching communication skills to high school students. *The Journal for Specialists in Group Work, 16*(4), 255–263.

Hunt, G., Wiseman, D., & Bowden, S. (1998). *The middle level teacher's handbook.* Springfield, IL: Charles C. Thomas Publisher.

Huston, A. C., & Alvarez, M. M. (1990). The socialization context of gender role development in early adolescence. In R. Montemayor & G. R. Adams (Eds.), *From childhood to adolescence* (pp. 156–179). Newbury Park, CA: Sage Publications.

Irwin, D. (1992). *Special Issues in Group Work.* New York: The Institute for Child Mental Health.

Jacobs, E. E., Masson, R. L., Harvill, R. L. (1998). *Group counseling: Strategies and skills* (3rd ed.). Pacific Grove, CA: Brooks/Cole Publishing.

James, M. (1986). *Adviser-advisee programs: Why, what and how.* Columbus, OH: National Middle School Association.

Jarrell, A. (2000, April 2). The face of teenage sex grows younger. *New York Times,* Section 9, 7–8.

Jenkins, J. (2000). Banishing anonymity: Advisement and advocacy in high schools. *Presentation to the National Association of Secondary School Principals.* San Antonia, TX: February 4–8,2000.

Jessor, R., Donovan, J. E., & Costa, F. M. (1991). *Beyond adolescence: Problem behaviors and young adult development.* New York: Cambridge University Press.

Johnson, D. W., & Johnson, F. P. (2000). *Joining together: Group theory and group skills (7th ed.).* Boston: Allyn & Bacon.

Kellam, S. G., & Brown, H. (1982). *Social adaptational and psychological antecedents of adolescent psychopathology ten years later.* Paper presented at a research workshop on prevention aspects of suicide and affective disorders among adolescents and young males, Harvard School of Public Health and Harvard School of Medicine, Boston.

Kern, C. (1999). Professional school counselors: Inservice providers who can change the school environment. *NASSP Bulletin, 83*(603), 10–18.

Khalsa, S. S. (1996). *Group exercises for enhancing social skills and self-esteem.* Sarasota, FL: Professional Resource Press.

Killin, T. E., & Williams, R. L. (1995, April). Making a difference in school climate, counseling services, and student success. *NASSP Bulletin,* 44–50.

King, K. A. (1999). Fifteen prevalent myths concerning adolescent suicide. *Journal of School Health, 69*(4), 159–161.

Kirby, L. D., & Fraser, .W. (1997). Risk and resilience in childhood. In M. W. Fraser (Ed.). *Risk and Resilience in Childhood: An Ecological Perspective* (pp. 10–33). Washington, DC: NASW Press.

Kohlberg, L. (1969). Stage and sequence: The cognitive-developmental approach to socialization. In D. A. Goslin (Ed.), *Handbook of socialization theory and research* (pp. 347–480). Chicago, IL: RandMcNally.

Kohn, A. (1997). How not to teach values: A critical look at character education. *Phi Delta Kappan, 78,* 428–439.

Kottler, J. A. (2001). *Learning group leadership: An experiential approach.* Needham Heights, MA: Allyn & Bacon.

Kottler, J. A., & Kottler, E. (2000). *Counseling skills for teachers.* Thousand Oaks, CA: Corwin Press.

Kronholm, K., & Jespersen, D. (1987). Homeroom/advisement program brings middle level adolescents, teachers closer. *NASSP Bulletin, 71*(498), 113–116.

Kuperminc, G. P, Leadbeater, B. J., Emmons, C., & Blatt, S. J. (1997). Perceived school climate and difficulties in the social adjustment of middle school students. *Applied Developmental Science, 1*(2), 76–88.

Latham, V. M. (1987). Task type and group motivation: Implications for a behavioral approach to leadership in small groups. Small Group Behavior, *18*(1), 56–71.

Lipsitz, J. (1984). *Successful schools for young adolescents*. New Brunswick, NJ: Transaction Books.

Luft, J. (1970). *Group processes: An introduction to group dynamics. 2nd ed.* Palo Alto, CA: National Press Books.

MacIver, D., & Epstein, J. (1993). Middle grades research: Not yet mature, but no longer a child. *Elementary School Journal, 93*(5), 519–533.

Malekoff, A. (1997). *Group work with adolescents: Principles and practice.* New York: The Guilford Press.

Marcus, G., Gross, S., & Seefeldt, C. (1991). Black and white students' perceptions of teacher treatment. *Journal of Educational Research, 84*(6), 363–367.

Margolin, S. (2001). Interventions for non-aggressive peer-rejected children and adolescents: A review of the literature. *Children and Schools, 23*(3), 143–159.

McEwin, C. K., Dickinson, T. S., & Jenkins, D. M. (1996). *America's middle schools: Practices and progress, a 25 year perspective.* Columbus, OH: National Middle School Association.

Mertens. S. B., Flowers, N., Mulhall, P. F. (1998). *The middle start initiative, phase I: A longitudinal analysis of Michigan middle-grades schools.* Urbana-Champaign, IL: The Center for Prevention Research and Development at the University of Illinois.

Mills, Helene (1985). A participative program for developing an advisor-advisee program. *Middle School Journal, 16*(6), 6–7.

Morganett, R. S. (1990). Skills for living: Group counseling activities for young adolescents (Vol. 1). Champaign, IL: Research Press.

Myrick, R. D., Highland, M., & Highland, B. (1986). Preparing teachers to be advisers. *Middle School Journal, 17*, 15–16.

National Middle School Association. (1997). *Portraits in change: Celebrating the month of the young adolescent. "Stop Sign" Case Curriculum Video.* TCI and Time Warner Cable.

National Middle School Association. (1982). *This we believe.* Columbus OH: National Middle School Association.

Nelson, M. D. (1999). Middle school improvement initiatives: An exploratory study. *NASSP Bulletin, 83* (610), 106–116.

Nightingale, E. O., & Wolverton, L. (1993). Adolescent rolelessness in modern society. In R. Takanishi (Ed.), *Adolescence in the 1990s: Risks and Opportunity* (pp. 14–28). New York: Teachers College Press.

O'Neil, M. (1997, March/April). Making time for caring. *Schools in the Middle,* pp. 23–26.

Paulson, S. E., Rothisberg, B. A., & Marchant, G. J. (1998). Teachers' perceptions of the importance of an adolescent development knowledge base for instructional practice. *Research in Middle Level Education Quarterly, 22*(1), 25–38.

Peterson, J. S. (1995). *Talk with teens about feelings, family, relationships, and the future: Fifty guided discussions for school and counseling groups.* Minneapolis, MN: Free Spirit Publishing.

Phelan, P., Davidson, A. L., & Cao, H. T. (1992). Speaking up: Students' perspectives on school. *Phi Delta Kappan, 73,* 695–704.

Phillips, T. H., & Phillips, P. (1992). Structured groups for high school students: A case study of one district's program. *The School Counselor, 39,* 391–393.

Piaget, J. (1977). *The science of education and pschology of the child.* New York: Penguin Books.

Pierce, C. (1994). Importance of classroom climate for at-risk learners. *Journal of Educational Research, 88*(1), 37–42.

Price, G. E., & Dinas, P. (1995). Group work with clients experiencing grieving: Moving from theory to practice. *Journal for Specialists in Group Work, 20*(3), 159-168.

Pryor, C. B., Sarri, R. C., Bombyk, M., & Nikolovska, L. (1999). Urban youth's views of violence in their communities: Implications for schools. *Social Work in Education, 21*(2), 72–88.

Putbrese, L. (1989). Advisory programs at the middle level—the students' response. *NASSP Bulletin, 73*(514), 111–115.

Reed, D. G., McMillan, J. H., & McBee, R. H. (1995). Defying the odds: Middle schoolers in high risk circumstances who succeed. *Middle School Journal, 27*(1), 3–10.

Roeser, R. W., Eccles, J. S., & Sameroff, A. J. (1998). Academic and emotional functioning in early adolescence: Longitudinal relations, patterns, and prediction by experience in middle school. *Development and Psychopathology, 10,* 321–352.

Roeser, R. W., Eccles, J. S., & Sameroff, A. J. (2000). School as a context of early adolescents' academic and social-emotional degvelopment: A summary of research findings. *Elementary School Journal, 100*(5), 443–471.

Rose-McLernon, D. H. (1994). *A descriptive study of "family groups" in New York City secondary schools.* Unpublished thesis. New York: The School of Education, The City College, The City University of NY.

Rubenstein, J. L., Heeren, T., Housman, D., Rubin, C., & Stechler, G. (1989). Suicidal behavior in "normal" adolescents: Risk and protective factors. *American Journal of Orthopsychiatry, 59*(1), 59–71.

Scales, P. C. (1999). Care and challenge: The sources of student success. *Middle Ground, 3*(2), pp. 21–23.

Scales, P.C., & McEwin, C. K. (1994). *Growing pains: The making of Americas' middle school teachers.* Columbus, OH: National Middle School Association.

Schoenlein, J. (2001). Making a huge high school feel smaller. *Educational Leadership, 58*(6), 28–30.

Schonert-Reichl, K. A. (1999). Relations of peer acceptance, friendship adjustment, and social behavior to moral reasoning during early adolescence. *Journal of Early Adolescence, 19*(2), 249–280.

Shockley, R., Schumacher, R., & Smith, D. (1984). Teacher advisory programs—strategies for successful implementation. *NASSP Bulletin, 68*, September, 69–74.

Simpson, G., & Boriack, C. (1994). Chronic absenteeism: A simple success story. *The Journal of the Texas Middle School Association, 2*(2), 10–14.

Singh, S., & Darroch, J. E. (1999). Trends in sexual activity among adolescent American women: 1982–1995. *Family Planning Perspectives, 31*(5), 211–219.

Slavin, R. E. (1994). School and classroom organization in beginning reading: Class size, aides, and instructional grouping. In R. E. Slavin, N. L. Karweit, & B. A. Wasik (Eds.), *Preventing early school failure: Research, policy, and practice* (pp. 122–142). Boston: Allyn & Bacon.

Spink, K. S., & Carron, A. V. (1994). Group cohesion effects in exercise classes. *Small Group Research, 25*(1), 26–43.

Stevenson, C. (1998). *Teaching ten to fourteen year olds (2nd ed.).* New York: Longman.

Strahan, D. (1986). *Guided thinking: A research-based approach to effective middle grades instruction.* NMSA Research summary No. 12. www.nmse.org..

Takanishi, R. (1993). Changing views of adolescence in contemporary society. In R. Takanishi (Ed.), *Adolescence in the 1990s: Risk and opportunity* (pp. 1–7). New York: Teachers College Press.

Tamminen, A., Gum, M., Smaby, M., & Peterson, T. (1976). Teacher advisors: Where there's a skill there's a way. *Personnel and Guidance Journal, 55*(1), 39–42.

Tarter, C. J., Sabo, D., & Hoy, W. K. (1995). Middle school climate, faculty trust, and effectiveness: A path analysis. *Journal of Research and Development in Education, 29*(1), 41–49.

Tatcher, D. C. (1986). Promoting learning through games and simulations. *Simulation and Gaming, 21*, 262–273.

Thompson, R. A. (1986). Developing a peer group facilitation program on the secondary school level. *Small Group Behavior, 71*(1), 105–112.

Totten, S., & Nielson, W. (1994). Middle level students' perceptions of their advisor/advisee program: A preliminary study. *Current Issues in Middle Level Education, 3*(2), 9–33.

Trubowitz, S. (1994, Winter). The quest for the good advisor-advisee program. *Middle Ground*, pp. 3–5.

Tuckman, B. (1965). Developmental sequence in small groups. *Psychological Bulletin, 63*, 384–399.

Van Hoose, J. (1991). The ultimate goal: A/A across the day. *Midpoints, 2*(1), 1–7.

Van Hoose, J. & Strahan, D. (1986). *Young adolescent development and school practices: Promoting harmony.* Columbus, OH: National Middle School Association.

Vars, G. F. (1989, January). Getting closer to middle level students: Options for teacher-adviser guidance programs, p. 6. *Schools in the middle: Areport on trends and practices.* Reston, VA: National Association of Secondary School Principles.

Wallis, C. (1999, July 5). The kids are alright. *Time*, pp. 56–58.

Weissberg, R. P. (1990). Support for school-based scoial competence promotion. *American Psychologist, 45*, 986-987.

Weist, M. D. (1997). Expanded school mental health services: A national movement in progress. In T. H. Ollendick and R. J. Prinz (Eds.) *Advances in Clinical Child Psychology*, Vol. 19, pp. 321–351. New York: Plenum Press.

Wentzel, K. R. (1997). Student motivation in middle school: The role of perceived pedagogical caring. *Journal of Educational Psychology, 89*(3), 411–419.

Whealin, J. (2000). *Child sexual abuse:* A National Center for PTSD fact sheet. www.ncptsd.org.

White, G. P., & Greenwood, S. C. (1991). Study skills and the middle level adviser/advisee program. *NASSP Bulletin, 75*(537), 88–95.

Wilson, C. (1998). The real meaning of middle school advisory programs. *Contemporary Education, 69*(2), 100–103.

Worchel, S. (1994). You can go home again: Returning group research to the group context with an eye on developmental issues. *Small Group Research, 25*(2), 205–223.

Young, M. E. (1998). *Learning the art of helping: Building blocks and techniques.* Upper Saddle River, NJ: Merrill.

Zander, A. (1982). *Making groups effective.* San Francisco: Jossey-Bass.

Ziegler, S., & Mulhall, L. (1994). Establishing and evaluating a successful advisory program in a middle school. *Middle School Journal, 25*(4), 42–46.

Index

~~~~~~~~~

282   *Student Advisories in Grades 5-12: A Facilitator's Guide*

About the Author

photo by Amber Kayo

Susan MacLaury is a social worker and health educator. Currently an Associate Professor of health education at Kean University in Union, New Jersey, she has trained several hundred school staff to be advisors in ten middle schools and high schools in New York and New Jersey. She has also developed a graduate course in advisory group facilitation for prospective teacher-advisors. Susan believes very strongly that students need, and deserve, a "safe place" in which they can feel free to express themselves honestly. She is committed to helping teachers and related school staff to refine their listening and facilitational skills to afford students this opportunity.

Susan has been a presenter on the topic of advisories at numerous state, regional and national conferences and has published on this topic in professional journals. Married with two children, a dog and two cats, she lives in Montclair, New Jersey.